REDEFINING EUROPE

REDEFINING EUROPE

New Patterns of Conflict and Cooperation

Edited by
Hugh Miall

PINTER
PUBLISHERS
London and New York

THE ROYAL INSTITUTE OF
INTERNATIONAL AFFAIRS

Distributed in the United States and Canada by St Martin's Press

Pinter Publishers Ltd.
25 Floral Street, London WC2E 9DS, United Kingdom

First published in 1994

Distributed exclusively in the USA and Canada by St Martin's Press, Inc., Room 400, 175 Fifth Avenue, New York, NY10010, USA

British Library Cataloguing in Publication Data

A CIP catalogue record for this book is available from the British Library

ISBN 1 85567 257 X (hb)
    1 85567 258 8 (pb)

Library of Congress Cataloging-in-Publication Data

Redefining Europe : new patterns of conflict and cooperation / edited
    by Hugh Miall.
        p.   cm.
    Includes bibliographical references and index.
    ISBN 1-85567-257-X. – ISBN 1-85567-258-8 (pbk.)
    1. Europe–Politics and government–1989–   I. Miall, Hugh.
II. Royal Institute of International Affairs.
D2009.R43   1994
940.55'9–dc20   94–15091
                                                                      CIP

Typeset by Mayhew Typesetting, Rhayader, Powys
Printed and bound in Great Britain by Biddles Ltd, Guildford and King's Lynn

Contents

Contributors

Hussein Agha	Middle East Research and Information Consultants, London, and Associate Fellow, Middle East Programme, Royal Institute of International Affairs
Dr Judy Batt	Centre for Russian and East European Studies, University of Birmingham
Dr Vincent Cable	Director, International Economics Programme, Royal Institute of International Affairs
Dr Andrei Georgiev	Centre for the Study of Democracy, Sofia
Professor Emil Kirchner	Centre for European Studies, University of Essex
Dr George Kolankiewicz	ESRC East-West Coordinator, Department of Sociology, University of Essex
Professor Robert Keohane	Stanfield Professor of International Peace, Harvard University
Dr Hugh Miall	Research Fellow, European Programme, Royal Institute of International Affairs
Professor James Mayall	Department of International Relations, London School of Economics
George Schöpflin	University of London
Professor Gordon Smith	The European Institute, London School of Economics
Haruhisa Takeuchi	Japanese Foreign Ministry and Royal Institute of International Affairs

Professor Trevor Taylor	University of Staffordshire and Royal Institute of International Affairs
Dr Emil Tzenkov	Centre for the Study of Democracy, Sofia
Dr Peter van Ham	Western European Union Institute for Security Studies, Paris
Professor Helen Wallace	Sussex European Institute, University of Sussex
Dr Andrei Zagorski	Vice Rector, Moscow State Institute of International Relations

Acknowledgments

This volume has been prepared in the course of a project on the post-Cold War European order, following an earlier project on 'Changing Paradigms of European Order'. The National Institute for Research Advancement in Tokyo funded both projects and we gratefully acknowledge their generous support.

We particularly thank the members of the steering group who have guided this project, and acknowledge with many thanks the comments and insights of those who participated in study groups and at the conference which was held to discuss the draft chapters in October 1993. I would like to acknowledge the comments of the outside discussants at the conference: David Begg, Colin Crouch, Chris Cviic, Geoffrey Edwards, Soledad Garcia, Adrian Hyde-Price, Charlie Jeffrey, Neil Malcolm and Rein Mullerson. I am also grateful for the insights of Anna Michalski, Thomas Oatley, Jack Spence, William Wallace and Stephen Woolcock. Last but not least, I thank the contributors to this book.

The Chatham House librarians, as always, provided invaluable assistance. We gratefully acknowledge the work of Margaret May and Hannah Doe in the Publications Department and of the editors at Pinter. Rami Tzabar ably coordinated the administration of the project and the pre-publication production work. I am grateful to Susie Symes for her direction and editorial suggestions and for keeping the whole project on time.

February 1994   Hugh Miall

Introduction
Hugh Miall

Europe is being redefined. It no longer means western Europe alone, but a wider Europe. West and east European societies are closely linked and the impact they have on each other is growing.

The wider Europe is not as easy or comfortable a place to live in as western Europe. It does not have uniformly high standards of living and social welfare, nor can one be complacent about its security. Economic conditions are more diverse than in western Europe, and pluralistic democracies have to work together with societies that have endured 50 years of totalitarian communist regimes.

Nevertheless, the wider Europe is the one in which we have to live. This is most obvious in the case of Germany, which has to unify the two former systems in one country. But other countries in Europe are also forced to adjust to the tectonic upheavals which have followed the Cold War. In western Europe domestic politics have sometimes been recast (as in Italy), relationships between west European states are being redefined, and the roles of the European institutions are being reappraised. In central and eastern Europe the need for readjustment has been even more acute. Societies have had to adapt to the withdrawal of secure employment and state welfare and accustom themselves to new entrepreneurial economies, new political systems and new distributions of wealth, influence and status. States have had to define new domestic and foreign policies, often starting from a position of weakness and sometimes of contested legitimacy. What will be the character of this wider Europe? Where will its boundaries lie? Can its political, social and economic differences be contained within common institutions? Will the European Union grow into the organizing framework for the wider Europe, and will it be able to redefine itself to cope with the pressures of enlargement? Will the societies of central and eastern Europe emerge from the post-communist transition ready to join the Union, or do they risk a long period of being left out in the cold, or worse, being derailed by economic failure and authoritarianism? How will the unstable economic and political dynamics in the former Soviet Union impact on the wider Europe? Are external shocks and crises likely to deepen European disorder? Or will it be possible to navigate through this period of turbulence and find a basis for promoting cooperation in the wider Europe and inhibiting the crystallization of new patterns of conflict?

To provide a framework to address these questions, this book is organized into three parts. The first surveys the main political developments in western Europe, east central Europe, the Balkans and Russia and the CIS. The second examines the longer-term political, economic, social, security and institutional trends which are shaping the prospects for the wider Europe: the authors have deliberately attempted to span western and eastern Europe in addressing their themes. The third deals with the implications of change in the wider Europe for other parts of the world. Newly emerging relationships between states inside and outside Europe are themselves one of the factors redefining Europe. The opening chapter introduces these themes and explores the implications of the changing post-Cold War order for conflict and cooperation in Europe as a whole.

In Part I, *Helen Wallace* surveys western Europe and the EU. The malaise that has gathered around the European project is more deep-rooted than the difficulties which arose after Maastricht, she argues; its sources of dynamism were already weakening. Enlargement can engender a fresh dynamism, but the EU also needs to find a new modernization agenda if it is to build new constituencies of support within and across European countries. *Judy Batt* analyses the impact of the communist legacy on the political transformation in the countries of east central Europe. On one side of the coin, she finds a 'virtuous circle' of radical change, democratization and western integration; on the other, a 'vicious circle' of failed change, demagoguery and exclusion from the West. She charts the course of the Visegrad countries between these two paths. *Andrei Georgiev and Emil Tzenkov* address the Balkans. They discuss the break-up not only of Cold War patterns but of the post-1918 order, and assess the implications of the war in the former Yugoslavia for the politics of the region. *Andrei Zagorski* deals with Russia and the CIS. He discusses whether Russia is part of Europe and what the relationship between Russia and Europe should be. He argues that expectations for reform should not be too high, but that nevertheless there is a strong case for the West remaining engaged in Russia's reforms and for consulting Russia in decisions over Europe's future.

Part II deals with themes and trends which cross western and eastern Europe. *Vincent Cable* explores the prospects for a single economic space in the wider Europe. He discusses economic trends in the European economies and uses scenarios to develop the case for a more flexible and open form of economic integration than Europe has seen hitherto. *Gordon Smith* analyses the contrasts between the political cultures in western and eastern Europe. He highlights what a long way there is to go from the 'destructured' political societies which emerged from communism to polities which are pluralist civil societies in more than form. In an analysis which adds weight to this argument, *George Schöpflin* looks at the forces which explain the rise of support for anti-democratic forces in eastern Europe. He argues that people in the 'traditional' segment of these societies who were never fully reconciled to the communist version of urban industrial society feel threatened now by the western version and are prepared to offer their support to populist leaders. Turning to sociological themes, *George Kolankiewicz* examines the rise of an underclass in both western and eastern Europe. He argues that this development is undermining the cohesion of European societies, and argues for 'social Europe' policies to redress them.

The next two chapters deal with international relations. *Trevor Taylor* analyses security issues in Europe. He discusses the basis of the security community in western Europe, and argues that it can only be extended eastward relatively slowly. He also investigates whether collective security can be made to work. *Peter van Ham* discusses whether the European institutional complex was only a by-product of the Cold War which cannot be expected to survive, or whether it provides a sufficiently robust framework through which states can pursue their interests in the new environment. His conclusion is that the benefits of cooperation are so important that states are unlikely to allow the institutions to break up, but that the challenges of enlargement are almost as severe as those of creating new institutions. The final chapter in this part deals with Germany, which is singled out because this one country and its external relations encapsulate some of the key questions about the wider Europe. *Emil Kirchner* argues that Germany will maintain its place at the centre of a dense group of European institutions, but that there will be strong pressures for Germany to pursue more narrowly defined national interests within the EU.

Part III assesses the implications of changes in the wider Europe for other parts of the world. *Robert Keohane* examines the implications for the international system generally. What matters, he argues, is how states redefine their interests in the light of the sudden transformation of international politics. The key to stability in Europe will be how Russian leaders define Russia's interests, and whether Russia can build, with Western help, an institutional infrastructure to promote social order, economic development and gradual democratization. *Hussein Agha* surveys the post-Cold War relationship between Europe and the Middle East, and offers a Middle Eastern perspective on bilateral relations, EU-Arab relations and relations between post-Christian Europe and political Islam. *Haruhisa Takeuchi* analyses the implications of changes in Europe since the Cold War for the Asia-Pacific region, and specifically Japan.

In the concluding chapter, *James Mayall* and I argue that a new European order can be built only gradually, by opening societies to democratic scrutiny, strengthening international institutions across Europe, and developing transnational links at all levels. Europe faces a number of difficult challenges, but there is little alternative but to engage with them: out of this process of engagement and adjustment there may develop a more open and cooperative European order.

1

Wider Europe, Fortress Europe, Fragmented Europe?

Hugh Miall

What is to be the basis for order in post-Cold War Europe? Four years after the fall of the Berlin Wall, the answer to this question is still unclear. The visions of a 'return to Europe', a Europe 'free and whole', and a 'European peace order' have not been fulfilled, and yet the need for a framework to assimilate the societies of western and eastern Europe still appears pressing – the more so as order breaks down, with tragic results, in parts of south-eastern and eastern Europe.

Any viable framework must be based on present realities and sensitive to existing trends. In thinking about a new order, therefore, it is necessary to analyse these trends, and most of the chapters in this book are devoted to this task. Any new order will grow out of old conditions and find its constituent elements in the past, even if it recasts them in surprising new patterns. It must also look forward to the new possibilities created by turbulent change.

After a transformation in the structure of international relations as profound as that of 1989–91, however, it is not always easy to identify solid ground or to be sure of the direction of trends. In 1990–91, many analysts perceived a process of growing integration in western Europe and growing disintegration in eastern Europe.[1] In 1993–94, this direction no longer seems assured. The drive towards political and economic integration in western Europe met powerful setbacks, while in central and eastern Europe a range of responses emerged to the challenges of the transition from communism. In the CIS, Russia began to reassert its influence over the newly independent states, despite the weakness of central power in Russia and its erratic process of economic and political reform.

The bipolar order of Cold War Europe has given way not to a single system of democratic market states, but rather to a new

1

regionalization. It is possible to identify four broad regions which have similar constellations of political and economic patterns (though each region is also diverse): western Europe, east central Europe, the Balkans and the European states of the former Soviet Union. It is an open question whether the very different polities and societies in these regions can be brought together into an effective common political framework. They are all affected by the powerful influence of transnational market forces, which are reshaping societies in both their external and internal relationships. They are also, to a lesser or greater extent, suffering a crisis of identity. This manifests itself both in a widespread if elusive European consciousness and in a strengthening of national identity.

The order in Europe is of course intimately related to the wider international order of which it forms a part. The disappearance of one superpower and the partial withdrawal of the other leaves Europeans collectively in greater charge of their own affairs, although it remains uncertain whether they will be able to coordinate their actions or speak with a single voice on the world stage. The central relationships of the world economic system, between the United States, Europe and Japan, appear unstable, despite the successful completion of the Uruguay Round. Europe is not the only area of the world where states are affected both by greater openness to global economic change, and by a tendency towards inward-looking politics on the national scale.

In western Europe, after a long period of significant if fitful steps toward economic and political integration, the cohesiveness of the west European community of states has been put into question. The unification of Germany and the geopolitical changes which followed upset the old balances within the EC, and at the same time modified the driving force behind German commitment to further integration. In central and eastern Europe, following the revolutionary changes of 1989–91, a partial transformation has taken place. Multi-party market systems have been established, but important remnants of the communist legacy survive: namely weak states and institutions, polarized political systems and high personal insecurity. Links between the two Europes have grown, yet western Europe remains partly closed to eastern Europe, and eastern Europe is deeply disillusioned with western Europe. On the other hand, the very diverse states in this region accept a common set of international norms, and have agreed to open their security systems and human rights performance to international scrutiny; and in the western part of the continent, a remarkable 'security community' persists, in which war between states is incredible; these societies are also relatively prosperous and stable. On the global scale, the march of economic liberalization and globalization proceeds, but leading states are withdrawing from leadership, international institutions look weak, and states find it difficult to coordinate their actions in global common interests.

These long-term trends are related to changes in the structure of international society in Europe. States remain crucial actors and interstate relations play the dominant role in the international system, but states have been obliged to coordinate their actions at an international level in order to operate effectively in a more inter-dependent world. They also have to respond to powerful domestic pressures. Domestic events are more and more affected by international forces, while international events cannot be analysed in isolation from domestic developments. The end of the Cold War certainly cannot be explained in isolation from domestic events.[2]

Subsequent chapters explore the nature of the post-Cold War order in Europe in particular regions, analyse key themes and explore the extra-European implications of European change. This chapter con-centrates on the question: how are changes in the European order, in the sense of the arrangement of states, societies and international institutions, affecting the patterns of cooperation and conflict within and between European societies?

The following sections set out three factors which influence these patterns: the structure of the state system; the nature and extent of interdependence across societies; and the pattern of state–society relationships. All these have changed following the end of the Cold War.

The new state system in Europe

There have been many efforts to construct theories which relate the structure of the state system to patterns of cooperation and conflict. According to realist thinking, a system of sovereign states with separate interests is likely to generate conflicts as interests clash, even in the absence of ideological sources of conflict. The more states there are in the system, the greater the potential for disputes. Some theorists argue that a multipolar system is more likely to be associated with violent conflict than a bipolar one.[3] Mearsheimer, in a well-known article,[4] argued that the transition from bipolarity to multipolarity in post-Cold War Europe is in itself likely to be a source of conflict. Another body of theory argues that major shifts in the structure and distribution of power in the international system tend to be accompanied by wars and conflicts.[5]

However, besides the number of states in the system and the distribution of power, the character of the international society is also important. A 'raw' anarchy, in which states pay little attention to one another's interests, is likely to be more prone to violent conflict than a more mature anarchy.[6] In these conditions security dilemmas appear between states which regard one another as threats. Where international society is relatively well developed, with norms and institutions which regulate government action and an effective system of multilateral diplomacy, conflicts of interest are more likely to be managed through bargaining and consensus.[7]

States sometimes manage to sustain cooperation for long periods; and this is possible even in the absence of a harmony of interests.[8] Theorists have explored conditions which sustain cooperation when a mixture of common and conflicting interests obtains. Cooperation is more likely if the actors take a long-term view of their interests, if they are aware of the reciprocal consequences of defection, if linkage across issues is possible, and if they operate in a climate of transparency and open information. Regimes and international institutions can support cooperation by institutionalizing coordinated behaviour, by shaping expectations, and by establishing rules and rewarding compliance with them. Strong regimes may so succeed in embedding cooperation that they affect their members' perception of their own national interests and create overriding common interests; in principle this can ultimately lead to the formation of federations or new actors. Integration is a method of institutionalizing cooperation which can powerfully reinforce expectations of compliance and offer incentives for striking successful bargains and agreeing policies.[9] Regimes are likely to be sustained when governments perceive that the public goods they create exceed the costs of the concessions to national interests that are necessary to preserve them.

The new state system in Europe is not uniform in these respects; indeed, it is arguable that the evolution of the state and of inter-state relations is at different stages in different parts of Europe. Western Europe has a set of mature states which have maintained intact a rich pattern of common institutions and regimes, some cooperative and some integrative. The states in central and eastern Europe now constitute a new state system, but with important differences between, for example, the Visegrad group, the former Soviet republics and the states in the Balkans (which themselves break down into states of different ages and character). Almost the entire group of states is linked by membership of the CSCE and, in most but not all cases, by cooperation or association agreements with the EU.

Interdependence

The interests of states are conditioned by a network of links between their societies and economies. States have always been inter-dependent, but the extension of globalization since the 1970s has led to substantial development of the networks of links that join them together. These take the form of trade, investment, and capital flows, cross-national corporations, large-scale movements of people, dense patterns of rail, road, sea and air traffic, and a vigorous sharing of information, news, and ideas.[10] West European states especially became subject to similar social movements, economic shocks, and even political developments.

Western and eastern Europe, however, developed very different patterns during the Cold War period, and these have been slow to converge. Transnational flows in eastern Europe were both less dense than western Europe and more controlled. Economic links developed mainly on the basis of a radial pattern in which the Soviet Union was the hub. Subsidised Soviet energy and raw material supplies were exchanged for industrial and agricultural products. The basis for this system has now collapsed.

High levels of interdependence between societies do not of themselves determine either cooperation or conflict, but they increase the stakes of relationships. Sometimes they may foster a sense of common interests, at other times they may lead to a sense of vulner-ability and threat. What matters is how, and whether, the inter-dependence is managed.

Western European societies have very high levels of interdepen-dence, created by their trading links, cross-border investment and common institutions. Together with the sense of community that has developed out of shared cultural and political values and similar postwar development, these links have created both an economic community and a security community (in Karl Deutsch's sense of a group of societies that have lost the fear of fighting one another). This community of 'informally integrated' societies is wider than the EC and includes non-EC members, such as the Nordic states, Austria and Switzerland.[11] The benefits of participation in this community are very clear to both insiders and outsiders, even if membership of the EC itself is still controversial among the publics of west European states.

In fact, a very large set of institutions manage interdependence in this region. This includes not only the EC, EFTA and many functional international institutions, but also national governments, multinational corporations, and sub-national groups. What characterizes the region is the emergence of a multi-level international society in which international institutions, states and sub-national organizations all play important roles in managing cross-national transactions. It is costly for governments to abandon habits of cooperation when countries are densely linked, even if interests pull in different directions.

Western Europe is also part of a wider network of interdependent relationships within the OECD area as a whole. The links with eastern Europe are important and are growing more so, but they are much more significant for the east Europeans than for west Europeans. East central European societies, therefore, look likely to repeat their historical experience and again to become dependent on western Europe.

Within eastern Europe, the level of cross-national transactions is much lower. Comecon never achieved any significant degree of real economic integration, and most of the states of this region see their future in finding markets in western Europe.

The collapse of Comecon trade in 1990–91 affected the whole region. Subsequent political developments have tended to further reduce rather than increase the level of economic interdependence. This is most clear in the states which have broken up. The Czech and Slovak republics suffered economically from their divorce – especially Slovakia – and the two introduced separate currencies, although they maintained a customs union. Shedding the perceived burden of the Slovak economy was clearly a motive for Klaus in pursuing the divorce. The Yugoslav breakup was much more damaging economically, since it was accompanied by war; Slovenia was the only republic not to be economically devastated. In the former Soviet Union, a steep decline in inter-republican trade occurred, as difficulties arose in servicing payments and inter-enterprise debt; the different pace of reforms in Russia and other republics, and disagreements over monetary policy, added to the difficulties. There is probably both scope and value in rebuilding this inter-regional trade, but up to 1992 it was still in decline.[12] Economic differences have certainly soured relations between, for example, the Ukraine and Russia, and between the Baltic States and Russia. Yet economic weakness in the newly independent republics, including Ukraine and Belarus, led to the ascendance of factions arguing for economic reintegration with the East (i.e. with Russia) in late 1993.[13] Belarus, for example, proposed an East European Economic Community.

When interdependence is poorly managed, it can be a source of conflict. For example, the Baltic ports are potentially an important trade outlet for Russia, and the Baltic states get over 90 per cent of their oil from Russia. Transit rights are crucial for Russia to supply the isolated Kaliningrad enclave. These factors can make for cooperation or conflict, depending in part on whether international institutions moderate state interests, and in part on how domestic politics shape national strategies.

Governance and domestic state–society relations

Karl Deutsch has argued that in order for societies to form a pluralistic security community, it is necessary for their political elites to share a basic level of political values and to be mutually responsive to one another.[14] Differences over how to organize society lay at the heart of the Cold War and in the post-Cold War Europe different patterns of governance are again coming to influence patterns of conflict and cooperation. They no longer take an ideological form. But post-Cold War Europe has a considerable diversity of patterns of governance. This includes mature democracies with well-established party systems, newly democratic post-communist societies which have undergone a rapid transformation, but in which party systems and civil societies are still being consolidated, and former communist governments which now emphasize a democratic or a nationalist message, but which have not undergone a substantial change of personnel. How far will these differences inhibit the development of a common political framework? How compatible do societies have to be in order to sustain a cooperative order and to permit the widening of the existing security community?

The issues of governance and relationships between state and society are especially crucial for European order because the main threats to security are now from internal sources. In much of the post-communist world, there has been a crisis of legitimacy for the new states, which are facing the difficulties of operating in a transformed environment with limited financial resources and political capital. Parties have yet to develop deep roots in society and much of political debate is concentrated among a limited elite. Highly charged and polarized politics, volatile swings from one direction to another and sharp challenges to government authority are to be expected; and

in some of the republics of the former Soviet Union these have
generated armed conflicts.

Added to this is perhaps the most important challenge to the
European order: the place of national minorities in central and east
European states. West European states, even with their mostly rather
homogeneous national composition and civic political traditions,
experience difficulties in relations between minority and majority
communities. In eastern Europe, where many states now have
minorities composing 20 per cent to 30 per cent of the population,
and where different national communities are often poorly integrated,
the problem is severe. The main political project in eastern Europe
since 1989 has been the construction of new or newly independent
states, and the position of national minorities within these states has
become an acutely important issue. Given the prevailing climate of
nationalism, demands for secession, or new states, or for 'greater'
states bringing together dispersed groups, have been powerful. The
problem combines with the dubious legitimacy of new state
boundaries and opens the issue of redrawing frontiers – hitherto
taboo within the norms of the European international society. Strong
national identities and weak states combine with economic insecurity
to make a dangerous cocktail, nowhere more evident than in the
Balkans.[15]

Issues of identity and state legitimacy are also important in western
Europe, although here different currents are in play. On the one hand,
there is evidence, especially among the educated elites, of the
development of a European identity, which is held in tandem with a
national identity. At the level of mass politics, however, a combination of factors, including reaction against the movement towards
European Union, fears of immigration, reactions against recession
and unease created by more open economies, has fuelled a growth in
west European nationalism.

This nationalism, however, is different in kind from that of east
European nationalism – and from the nationalism which was such a
powerful factor in nineteenth-century Europe. Then nationalism was
associated with a wave of modernization, reflected in the growth of
industrial working classes and the rise of large cities. In post-communist societies, nationalism was used to mobilize support, often by
former communists whose version of modernization had failed, and
from people for whom western-style modernization represented a
threat.[16] The new west European nationalism is better interpreted as a
defensive reaction to rapid and bewildering change accompanying
the present wave of modernization associated with globalization.

These contrasts highlight the differences in social development and historical experience between European states. Societies and states are at different stages and perhaps on different paths of historical evolution. There is no prospect of east European societies rapidly adjusting to west European patterns. Does this mean that it is impossible to develop a common European order? Or is the developing pattern of transnational, intergovernmental, economic and institutional links capable of creating cooperation and limiting conflict across these divides?

Patterns of cooperation and conflict at the end of the Cold War

The Cold War system polarized patterns of cooperation and conflict around the East-West conflict. While the self-sustaining military and ideological deadlock persisted, it was difficult to generate realistic proposals for changing European order. The defining characteristic of the Cold War system was the dominance of the superpowers and the priority given to military/security issues over other issue areas. Separate subsystems developed in western and eastern Europe (although neither of them were ever comprehensive) with NATO and the Warsaw Pact, Comecon and the EC playing partly symmetrical roles. In both halves of Europe, the Cold War formation overlaid earlier conflicts. East European resistance to the Soviet Union and domestic opposition to the communist regimes largely replaced earlier conflicts between and within states in the region. In western Europe the creation of new cooperative institutions accompanied a genuine reconciliation of earlier conflicts (a phase completed by the 1960s).

The Cold War pattern began to weaken in the 1970s with the fading of US hegemony and the development of detente. But it was not until the mid-1980s that it began to break up. The Soviet leadership, spurred on by economic difficulties, initiated the decisive steps. At this stage Gorbachev's vision of a Common European Home was an important contribution to the shaping of European order, since it provided a framework within which Soviet foreign policy could become reconciled to the loss of the east European buffer and to German unification.

One of the most remarkable features of the restructuring of international relations which followed the end of the Cold War was its cooperative and peaceful character – at first. The unification of

Germany, the dismantling of the Warsaw Treaty Organization and the withdrawal of Soviet forces from former East Germany were carried out by negotiated agreements. The restructuring was achieved in such a way that none of the parties had an immediate interest in undoing it, and compared favourably with previous major international settlements.[17] It was the prelude for far-reaching aspirations to a common international society in Europe, based on CSCE norms, as set out in the Charter of Paris, and hinted at in German proposals for a European peace order. These developments reached their high-point with the institutionalization of the CSCE.

While the military aspects of the disengagement were consolidated through the completion of the CFE Treaty, signed in November 1990, the broader question of the political form that the European order would take remained to be tackled. The immediate impulse was to consolidate the one remaining 'sub-order', by integrating the unified Germany into the EC and NATO. The European Commission and the Federal Government rushed through arrangements for the accession of the five new Länder into the EC, and NATO membership was effectively extended, subject to conditions about the exclusion of nuclear weapons and non-German troops.

The larger question was how unified Germany would fit into the EC's political order. President Mitterrand and Chancellor Kohl agreed that it was necessary to strengthen the EC, both to accommodate a unified Germany and to respond to developments in eastern Europe. The member states dusted off old plans for a (west) European political union, which was now prepared in great haste, in tandem with the proposals for Economic and Monetary Union that had been prepared to follow up the creation of the Single Market. The resulting structure did not immediately alter the nature of the west European polity: the nation-states remained in charge, and the main extensions to cooperation and integration lay in the future. Nevertheless, public debate over the treaty gave the impression that a major step from national to supranational governance was taking place; and the decision in principle taken at Maastricht in December 1991, to move towards a common currency (with British and Danish derogations), a common foreign policy and possibly an ultimate defence identity, signified both a step towards political integration and an attempt to strengthen the system of west European cooperation.

This was still an effort to consolidate only western Europe, albeit a western Europe which accounted for over 80 per cent of the GNP of Europe up to the borders of the former Soviet Union. It coincided with new interest in joining the Community on the part of governments of the EFTA countries, which flowed from their desire to participate in the benefits of the Single Market and their dissatisfaction with the European Economic Area as a half-way house. The simultaneous steps towards a political Union and an EFTAn enlargement promised to bring almost all the states of western Europe into a common institutional group, based on a common west European identity, to manage their economic interdependence. Far from destroying cooperation in western Europe, then, the immediate effects of the end of the Cold War appeared to be to consolidate it.

In central and eastern Europe, meanwhile, the dismantling of the quasi-integration imposed by the Soviet system proceeded apace. From 1989 to 1991, new democratic governments consolidated themselves in Czechoslovakia, Poland, Hungary and Bulgaria; postcommunist or nationalist-communist governments of various complexions operated in Romania, Albania and most of Yugoslavia; while Gorbachev faced rising nationalist challenges and rapid economic deterioration in the Soviet Union. The collapse of Comecon trade reduced links between the countries of the former Eastern Europe, while economic output plunged. Instead, increased economic links were established with western countries; plans for market reform based on western models, using western advisers, came into force; and as marketization proceeded, societies in east central Europe, Bulgaria and Romania became interdependent with western Europe. Meanwhile institutional bonds with western Europe were made, through the Council of Europe and the EC. However, the difficulty of accomplishing a radical political and economic transformation, while also carrying sufficient public support, was to make the prospective move to EU membership a long haul.

The Soviet coup-attempt in August 1991 marked a critical turning point in the development of post-Cold War Europe. Up until that point the possibility of a return to cold war and to a new form of bipolarity in Europe could not be excluded. Afterwards, it became clear that even the residual possibility of a Soviet military threat to the West had disappeared. The end of the Soviet multinational system saw the beginning of a large new state system, with a number of unpropitious features. Excluding the Baltic States, the non-Russian states had no recent experience of self-government, little basis for a national economy, a heterogeneous mixture of nationalities, and not even a widely shared national tradition – in Ukraine, for example, about half the citizens spoke no Ukrainian. The state system as a whole had many undefined and contested borders and enormous military forces that needed to be shared. In the short term, the dissolution of the Union was remarkably peaceable. As time went on, however, ethnic conflicts and power struggles broke out in and between a number of the new states, especially in the Caucasus and on the southern periphery. Russia gradually asserted itself in a new 'post-imperial' role, yet central authority in Russia itself was compromised by the prolonged constitutional struggle between president and parliament, and by the growth of regionalism in the Russian Federation. After swinging toward the West in foreign policy in 1991–92, Russian foreign policy in 1992–93 emphasized Russia's national interests in the 'near abroad'. A number of factors suggested a more difficult relationship with the West – namely, the rise of military influence after the storming of parliament, the defeat of the radical economic reformers, and the strong showing of Zhirinovsky in the December 1993 elections. The undefined position of east central Europe and the western CIS states left open the possibility of the consolidation of new rivalries and *'cordons sanitaires'*, on the one hand, and of overlapping frameworks for regional and international cooperation, on the other. Developments in the Baltic States would be a litmus test of how these patterns would unfold.

In the Balkans, meanwhile, the gradual collapse of the Yugoslav federal system in 1991 and the rise of nationalist leaders plunged the successor states into war. The end of the Cold War and the post-Yugoslav war raised acute questions about the viability of the borders and states in the region. The CSCE and the EC showed themselves powerless to halt or settle the conflicts. Indeed, the EC's maladroit interventions probably made them worse. The Europe agreements between the EU and Bulgaria and Romania were a stabilizing influence, but the war contributed to the diplomatic tensions and fears in the region making it extremely difficult to establish a multilateral framework for regional security. Not surprisingly, the actors in the region sought salvation in NATO enlargement, but NATO members made it clear that this was not on offer in the short term.

While the Community's reputation was damaged by the Yugoslav war, it also had to face growing internal problems. In June 1992 the Danish population narrowly voted to reject the ratification of the Treaty of European Union. Although the treaty was ultimately ratified, the bruising public debate in west European countries undermined the public consensus for integration, and virtually paralysed the Community for a year; it also provided the opportunity for the markets to destroy the narrow-band ERM. These blows to progress towards monetary and political union left the Community without a sense of direction. They coincided with deep economic recession in western Europe and declining public support in the EFTAn countries for pursuing their applications for membership. Following the public reactions to the Maastricht debate, national leaders hardened their positions on several issues, which in the case of the largest countries in the Community, and the only net contributors (France, Britain and Germany), were already tending to diverge. Jacques Delors, president of the Commission, expressed fears that the Community might break up within 15 years if the European Community became no more than a minimal free trade zone.[18] But there seemed no immediate prospect of achieving a strengthened EC of the Twelve. A more immediate possibility was that the trend within the Community to different 'circles' of cooperation and integration, with countries choosing which to opt into, might be accentuated, with a relatively narrow core group pursuing the original integrationist goals.

Prospects for the European order

The immediate developments in the post-Cold War period, then, were the attempts to consolidate cooperation in western Europe and to undo old regimes in central and eastern Europe. By late 1993, these had led to the anti-integrationist reaction in western Europe and to the formation of a new state system in which nationalism was the most powerful force in eastern Europe. These developments, together with the GATT accord, suggested that the 'fortress Europe' scenario was unlikely to occur. However the risks of moving towards a 'fragmented Europe' seemed quite severe. This would be a Europe in which bilateral interstate relations would again play the most important role.

Nevertheless, a 'wider Europe', based on the network of cooperation, association and 'Europe' agreements and eventual enlargement of the EU remained a feasible possibility. It was favoured by Germany, now the most influential and economically central state in the Community, as well as by Britain and Denmark. (France, Spain and Portugal did not regard the prospect of an east European enlargement with favour but had not explicitly rejected it.)

In order to moderate the risk of anarchy in the European state system and sustain cooperation, it is desirable to strengthen the basis for the European international society; the EU, together with the Council of Europe and the CSCE, are important vehicles for this. It is also necessary to promote and manage interdependence between western and east European societies, across a range of policy areas. Achieving economic development in eastern Europe is very much in the long-term common interest of all Europeans, on both economic and security grounds.

The end of the Cold War does not necessarily undermine, but certainly recasts, the basis for cooperation in Europe. A revitalized transnational approach to the wider Europe may require a more thorough re-examination of the purposes, interests, costs and benefits of cooperation between states, societies and international institutions in Europe than has taken place so far.

Notes

1. Alexander Bessmyrtnykh, 'Integration and Disintegration in Modern Europe', *Vestnik*, Moscow, March 1992; David Arter, *The Politics of European Integration in the Twentieth Century*, Dartmouth, 1993.
2. Hugh Miall, *Shaping the New Europe*, London: RIIA/Pinter, 1993, Chapter 2.
3. K. Waltz, *Theory of International Politics*, Reading, PA: Addison-Wesley, 1975; K.W. Deutsch and J.D. Singer, 'Multipolar power systems and international stability', *World politics*, 16: 390–406.
4. John Mearsheimer, 'Back to the Future: Instability in Europe after the Cold War', *International Security*, vol. 12, no. 1, Summer 1990.
5. F.H. Hinsley, *Power and the Pursuit of Peace*, Cambridge University Press, 1979; C.F. Doran, 'Power Cycle Theory of Systems Structure and Stability', in M.I. Midlarsky (ed.), *Handbook of War Studies*, Unwin Hyman, 1989.
6. Barry Buzan *et al.*, *The European Security Order Recast*, London: Pinter, 1990.
7. Hedley Bull, *The Anarchical Society: A Study of Order in World Politics*, London: Macmillan, 1977; James N. Rosenau and Ernst-Otto Czempiel (eds), *Governance without Government: Order and Change in World Politics*, Cambridge University Press, 1992.
8. Robert Axelrod, *The Evolution of Cooperation*, New York, Basic Books, 1984; Kenneth Oye (ed.), *Cooperation under Anarchy*, Princeton University Press, 1986; A.J.R. Groom and Paul Taylor, (eds), *Frameworks for International Cooperation*, London: Pinter, 1990; Stephen D. Krasner (ed.) *International Regimes*, Ithaca and London: Cornell University Press, 1983; Robert Keohane and Joseph Nye, *Power and Interdependence*, London: Harper Collins, 2nd edn, 1989.
9. Alan Milward, 'Interdependence or integration', in A. Milward (ed.), *The Frontiers of National Sovereignty*, Routledge: London and New York: Routledge, 1993, pp. 16–20.

10. William Wallace, *The Dynamics of European Integration*, London: Royal Institute of International Affairs/Pinter, 1990.
11. William Wallace, 'Introduction' in W. Wallace (ed.), *The Dynamics of European Integration*, pp. 8–12.
12. For data on the CSFR, for example, see Jan Svejnar, 'Czech and Slovak Federal Republic: a solid foundation', in Richard Portes (ed.), *Economic transformation in Central Europe*, London: Centre for Economic Policy Research, 1993.
13. 'Weak Ukraine plays into Russian hands', *Financial Times*, 17.9.93.
14. Karl W. Deutsch *et al.*, *Political Community and the North Atlantic Area: International Organization in the Light of Historical Experience*, Princeton, NJ: Princeton University Press, 1957.
15. See Hugh Miall (ed.), *Minority Rights in Europe: The Scope for a Transnational Regime*, London: RIIA/Pinter, 1994. Of course, historical conditions vary across the region. Russians, for example, have a relatively weak sense of nationhood and are accustomed to strong states. Russian minorities, such as those in Estonia, have sometimes indicated that they do not object to living in other states so long as they are given equal civic rights.
16. George Schöpflin, *Politics in Eastern Europe*, Oxford: Blackwell, 1993, Chapter 10.
17. K. Holsti, *Peace and war: armed conflicts and international order, 1648–1989*, Cambridge: Cambridge University Press, 1991, pp. 340–43.
18. 'Delors fears EC breakup', *Financial Times*, 18.10.93.

Part I
Europe after the Cold War

2

The EC and Western Europe after Maastricht

Helen Wallace

This chapter addresses the question of how the EC, its member states and other west Europeans have responded to the huge changes that have occurred across the continent since 1989 and examines some of the consequences for the future. It is tempting to see Maastricht as the villain of the piece – a poorly thought out treaty on which the whistle was blown by public and parliamentary opinion in many corners of the EC. If only Community decision-makers had been more circumspect. . . . Or perhaps the real problem lies in the economic cycle which has blown the EMU project out of the water and even seriously damaged the EMS. . . . Or maybe the long drive towards (west) European integration was bound to reach an insurmountable hurdle at the point at which the proposal emerged to enter the realms of real high politics. . . . Or perhaps the war in Bosnia has revealed that actually west European governments (and/or their publics) always had a narrow vision of Europe which did not extend to regarding the problems of the Balkans as their problem, whether in Bosnia or in the neighbouring ex-Yugoslav republics or in the adjacent countries that have also suffered the political and economic ricochets of the Yugoslav war.

There are grains, even quite large grains, of truth or plausibility in each of these explanations for the profound malaise that has settled around what the French call the 'European project'. Yet this chapter argues that 'Maastricht' is more a symptom than a cause and that the debate about what we now have to call the European Union would benefit from a more considered reflection of the longer-term changes in Europe that bear down on the processes of European integration and disintegration.

The ending of the Cold War was universally recognized as a stimulant of turbulence in central and eastern Europe. Indeed, this turbulence was initially greeted there and in western Europe as constructive, in that it would provide the dynamic impulses for the transition to liberal democracy and market economy. The prevailing assumption in 1989/90 was that a calm western Europe, its own political and economic habits well embedded, would provide the hub and spoke mechanisms that would link the countries of central and eastern Europe to mainstream Europe. Yet, and hindsight is always a useful asset, it turned out that the end of the Cold War was a catalyst of turbulence in western Europe as well. Once the certainties of the past 40 years had been swept away, it began to become evident that certain parts of the stabilizing framework of both EC integration and of some individual EC member states had also been weakened.

The links are clear in the cases of Germany and Italy. The unification of Germany was in some crucial respects handled remarkably successfully both within Germany and by the international community. Indeed, the EC showed remarkable speed and adroitness in absorbing the new Länder. There were fears, sometimes explicitly stated and almost everywhere *sotto voce* implied, that the larger Germany would be disturbingly overbearing and much less amenable to the constraints of its EC partners. Such fears have, so far at least, seemed to be confounded. On the contrary, Germany has in some respects been weakened by its own enlargement, understandably distracted by its own problems of internal adjustment and less willing or able to bear the weight of its position at the core of Europe. Already the initial impulses that produced the Maastricht process thus represented a mistaken diagnosis and therefore hardly surprisingly failed to produce remedies for the long-run adjustment needs of Germany. Indeed, to rest so much of the argument on the speedy construction of an economic and monetary union that depended crucially on German economic robustness was a risky choice, irrespective of the objective or subjective cases for and against a single west European currency.

In Italy, the postwar political system had been fashioned by the stubborn persistence of a communist party with a freely delivered and substantial electoral base and the countervailing bastions of Christian democracy. As we now know more clearly, the distortions of politics and corruption of public power and patronage that went with this were actually undermining the Italian political system. Once the threat of external communism faded and with it the opportunity to attack the credentials of the Italian Communist Party, the shield that had protected the rest of the Italian political class also fell away. This, and the cumulative resentments that the Lega Nord has exploited, have combined to create turmoil in the Italian polity, a turmoil that has been limited more by the resilience of Italian civil society and the continuing if reduced strength of the Italian economy than by the external props of the past.

In most west European countries the permissive consensus that supported European cooperation had been sustained by the East/ West divide. Its erosion has been evident in alliance countries and the declining pertinence of neutrality to the modern condition of the continent has also weakened the political cement of the neutral countries. Finland, Spain, Portugal, Ireland and Greece seem to be exceptions in retaining public support for European solidarity, quite probably because their core public policy concerns remain closely linked to the survival of a vigorous European framework. The weakening of public confidence has coincided with, and been exacerbated by, the period of efforts symbolized by Maastricht to raise the political threshold of European political integration.

It has become common over the past year for the economic cycle to be blamed for the decline in the credibility of the EC, and certainly the linkage between the two is supported by public opinion evidence, in both member and applicant countries. Indeed, the impact is not limited to the EC but also palpably erodes support for national-level politicians, with only the qualification that the EC is so often cited as the scapegoat. The promise of the single market has quickly become a contested factor within countries and in those regions and sections of society that have been most exposed to the recession, again with exceptions so far in the EC's cohesion countries where the EC has retained higher public standing.

Rather less attention has been given by commentators to the political cycle, except to the extent that it is driven by the economic cycle. However, it is also important to note that there have been several significant shifts in the politics of west European countries. With the exceptions of Spain and Portugal, which are led by cohorts of post-authoritarian reconstructors, the political leadership cohorts have almost entirely lost the generation engaged in both postwar (i.e. Second World War) reconstruction and the building of the European welfare state. Instead the dominant generation is now drawn from those who grew up with the East-West division and the welfare state as 'normality' and givens, thus belonging to what some called the end of ideology era. They are perhaps better characterized as a political generation not defined by the specificities of ideological debate which marked the immediate postwar political class.

To be cynical, one might argue that the consequence has been to produce political leaders who stand out for their dullness. At the very least one should note the real difficulties which some political parties have had in establishing an attractive and credible leadership – the British Labour Party and the German SPD both exemplify the problems of leadership renewal. The point here is not nostalgia for the past but rather to note the absence of politicians with the experience of severe struggles tied either to the shadows of the past or to the shadows of the future. In particular what seems to have disappeared from the debate are both the sense of historical shifts to be achieved and of 'Europe' as an important element of stabilization and reconstruction.

Instead what has emerged in different variants is the 'new politics' of radicalism, sometimes the neo-liberal version, sometimes a new populism, sometimes with xenophobic connotations, sometimes with a regionalist (i.e. sub-state) focus, sometimes with a particular issue focus, such as that of the Greens. Interestingly some became attached to the European project, but most did not. The neo-liberal shift was a powerful factor in underpinning the EC agenda of the mid-1980s onwards, as advocacy of marketization and deregulation became attached to the 1992 programme. But this version of trans-European agreement, perhaps of deconstruction rather than reconstruction, also became decoupled from the social contract that had been such an important feature of the postwar period.

With this issue we may have come to the nub of the explanation about the simultaneous decline in public support for both the Single Market and European integration from 1990 onwards, i.e. pre-Maastricht. Alan Milward sets out a controversial and perhaps overstated case that the EC process was tied not to supranationalism but to the restoration of the individual states of western Europe.[1] He perhaps makes too sharp a distinction between intentions and effects, in that the postwar political generation did include some who sincerely sought to link European integration and domestic reconstruction as symbiotic and mutually dependent. They also belonged to a period of belief in institution-building at both domestic and international levels. Both dimensions contributed to the process of redefinition of the west European state as the welfare state. The huge investment, both political and economic, in reinforcing the powers of the state was striking, albeit in western Europe, unlike in eastern Europe, it was in a benevolent form. What was important was the extent to which this gave the citizen several real stakes in the success not just of the state but of any public authorities that produced public goods and individual benefits, whether through European or national policies. The European dimension to this was not trivial, in that it was a component of a process of transformation and modernization which included the strengthening of public authority and gave it a cosmopolitan character.

Here we should add a point about European security and the NATO framework, noticing in passing that in the public mind the connection between NATO and the EC as related ventures was quite strong. The pattern of west European defence cooperation that emerged in the 1950s depended on a strong state participation to deliver recurrent support for collective defence. It also required, or at least induced, a strong state involvement in the economy to produce the defence equipment that Alliance policy demanded, maintaining a version of the patterns that had emerged in the Second World War. Also it should be recalled that neutral west European countries mostly had strong and relatively expensive defence policies.

Both of these elements of state reinforcement have begun to fall away. In the defence case the end of the Cold War is leading to a retrenchment of states' commitments, to efforts to reduce costs (partly by eroding some of the economic base built up for the defence industry over 50 years) and to declining public acceptance of defence engagements – all these in an area of crucial importance for the definition of public authority. It remains to be seen whether the Gulf war marked the end of an era, but the reluctance to engage in Bosnia may signal more than a dislike of intervention in a particularly complicated conflict. In parallel, in the political economy there has been a sharp turn away from the over-extension of the state to efforts to retract the state from the economy and the welfare system. Citizens and private agents are instead being pressed to be more self-reliant and to expect and to receive less support from the state, in what looks to be not just a tailing off of publicly provided goods, but rather a real reduction in what are defined as public responsibilities.

What, then, have been the implications for the EC? Whatever the causal connections the design of the EC was attached to the process of transformation of the west European states. The investment in institution-building and consensus mechanisms was at the centre of the project. It was dominated by the same kind of 'public policy engineers' who were prominent in reconstruction within states. It clearly linked memories of the shadows of a less safe and less prosperous past to aspirations that the future could be made better by active public governance. It gave citizens, or at least some citizens, a very direct stake in the success of the EC. Some would say the stake was too great in the case of the agricultural sector but the political salience of the stake is not to be underestimated. Thus the EC, like the welfare state, was about modernization through accretions of public power at both European and national levels. The EC was also a vehicle of stabilization of the economy, vis-à-vis external competition and intra-European beggar-my-neighbour policies, and of politics, vis-à-vis both external aggressors and internal conflicts and chauvinisms.

By the late 1970s and early 1980s the change of context was palpable. The interaction of the global competitiveness debate with the mounting costs of social welfare was calling into question the basic assumptions of the previous decades. The loss of belief in Keynesianism and in various versions of the social market was a key change. Detente, with its dulling of the security threat and the ensuing period of heightened tension, had been met by the emergence of a significant and vocal peace movement well before 1989. At the very least this made the conventional wisdoms of west European defence policies begin to look a little stale. New and different issues were beginning to emerge in the political debate which did not easily attach to the EC project, although of course there were European dimensions to the peace, green and women's movements; these were, however, often defined in terms that made the EC seem part of the problem and not part of the solution. This fluidity in turn broke some of the tightness of the links between domestic politics and European collaboration. The regionalization of politics in several west European countries also meant that traditional central governments no longer commanded so much of the political ground and were therefore also less able to deliver cohesive support for transnational collaboration. It is more important to identify this mass of emergent factors as contributing to the sense of drift in the EC than to accept the common but simplistic language of Eurosclerosis.

Into this shifting kaleidoscope came the debate which led to the Single European Act as the intended vehicle of renewal of the EC project. In some respects it was strikingly successful in combining the language of the old European agenda with part of the new agenda of west European politics. It was greatly aided by the arrival of new member states, notably Portugal and Spain, which became whole-hearted advocates of the EC as their vehicle of political and economic modernization. It linked the EC firmly to the emergent neo-liberal reformulation of the need to alter the relationship between public authorities and the market. EC integrationists hoped that the removal of national powers over the economy, as the deregulation programme bit, would nonetheless endow the EC with new regulatory authority and legitimacy and that the EC would ride on the success of this version of west European modernization.

This worked, but only up to a point. The SEA and its surrounding policy commitments captured wide public credibility and helped some individual governments to shift their domestic policies in a direction that, left to their own devices, might have been less easy. But the very narrowness of the SEA agenda was also a signal of the limits of the cross-country consensus that had been established. In particular a disjunction was made between the market-related agenda and the social contract which had been such an important part of the previous era, except for the cohesion countries, the governments of which had insisted on the availability of measures to cushion, and visibly cushion, the industrial adjustment process. Of course, throughout the SEA debate the social dimension hovered as an element to be considered and of course some of those involved, notably Jacques Delors, argued hard for the inclusion of social measures, social conditionality and social confidence-building measures. But here there was no consensus, not only because of the policies of the UK government, but because of the changing contours of the discussion elsewhere in the EC and the rising costs of government debt. It is also true that in the drafting of the Spaak Report a similar debate had taken place in which Pierre Uri and others lost the argument for introducing a strong social dimension into the Treaty of Rome. The difference, however, was that in the 1950s and 1960s the social side of the bargain was delivered by individual countries.

The Maastricht debate thus arrived on the scene when not only had the Cold War ended and Germany been united, but structural changes were already at work in western Europe and the SEA had strongly reinforced only a limited version of EC solidarity. To make things even more complicated the issues of EC reform could not easily be confined to the preoccupations of the Twelve since it was clear that a lengthening queue of other European countries were actual or potential applicants for membership. In these circumstances it is perhaps not surprising that the negotiators should have found it so hard to get their heads round their agenda. Without a reformulation of their mental maps of the new Europe or a redefinition of the structural changes affecting western as well as eastern Europe a clear sense of direction was hardly likely to be achieved. The result was that Maastricht's content reflected more a restatement of the old EC agenda than the definition of a new agenda.

Three features of Maastricht deserve emphasis in this context: EMU, CFSP and the infamous social chapter. First, the unification of

Germany within a clear Community context was a stunning success, yet only a partial success. The whole EMU project, conceived before the collapse of the Berlin Wall, always depended on Germany and the Deutschmark for its realization. It was always a controversial project within and between countries, as earlier variants of the debate had shown. Unlike the Single Market, it could not command and be made to ride on only the pliant consensus of policy engineers and entrepreneurs. And it always depended on the performance of the real economy, which cannot be moulded by words on a piece of paper, even in the form of a solemn and 'binding' treaty. The Germans turned out to be too overwhelmed by the consequences of unification to generate either the economic weight or the political support to sustain EMU; the controversies persisted; and the real economy took a different path of recession and divergence.

Secondly, the drive for a common foreign and security policy was made precisely at the point in European history where its rationale could not be established. A CFSP in relation to whom or what? The absence of clear and agreed threats left a vacuum as to goals and removed any real urgency from the endeavour, quite unlike the context in which western Europe's collective defence policy was formulated in the late 1940s and 1950s – and even then agreement had not been easily achieved. The need for greater European self-reliance in the 1990s was not a trivial aim, yet the continued, if reduced, US engagement in Europe took the sharpness out of the argument, which was in any case only lightly stated by those who were afraid of precipitating US withdrawal. The case for locking latent German aspirations into a reinforced collective framework certainly motivated some politicians in other European countries, yet the very introversion of a Germany preoccupied with its internal adjustments dulled the edge of this argument too. Moreover the fragmented and diffuse character of the other tasks mooted for collective action did not, perhaps could not, stimulate a strong sense of shared purpose or clearly defined 'common interests'. One of the most obvious candidates for priority attention – namely the stabilization of the continent – did not find its way into the Maastricht text. The EC was simultaneously engaged in devising the Europe Association formula for central and eastern Europe. But by confining this in the language of trade and aid measures and by gagging on the issue of eastern enlargement, the Maastricht treaty drafters resisted the linkage to EC reform and regeneration.

Thirdly, the social chapter had to bear too much of the weight of the case for giving EC citizens a stake in the next stage of building EC cooperation. Jacques Delors and his supporters had conceived the social chapter originally as a cushion for the adjustments to the Single Market and subsequently to EMU, as well as a means to reinforce the link between the EC and the citizen. But by 1991 the debate across the EC on social issues was already moving away from the measures envisaged under the social chapter. All EC governments were struggling with the question of how to handle their social welfare programmes. Unemployment began not only to rise, but to emerge as being as much structural as cyclical. The social chapter began to appear as more irrelevant than dangerous, though in the absence of agreement on an alternative it was left awkwardly in the protocol to the Maastricht treaty. Maybe a different and more positively formulated version of the 'citizenship' chapter of Maastricht could have compensated for this, but as eventually reduced it barely scratched the surface of what would have been required. Maybe a different version of social cohesion could have been induced by a more explicit collective commitment to an EC migration policy, but this would have been to embrace an inflammatory and volatile policy arena that might have produced quite different and xenophobic results. The more recent debate on growth, competitiveness and employment around the new Commission White Paper of December 1993 perhaps marks the redefinition of the EC agenda in this domain.

Perhaps even more notably lacking in the Maastricht process, however, was an underlying common value set. Its absence from the much more narrowly focused SEA mattered less. But if Maastricht was intended, at least by some, to ratchet up the process of political integration it had a missing component. Instead the debate became locked into the familiar controversy between supranationalism and intergovernmentalism. Yet if integration depends on a belief that it can provide a vehicle for a collective improvement of welfare, broadly defined, and for stronger collective capabilities, a more potent mix of shared values and agreed substantive rewards needed to be defined. In particular the case for strengthening the exercise of shared public powers and the provision of shared public goods had limited credibility in a period of deconstruction of the state and erosion of public goods and publicly provided welfare.

In other words, to echo the experiences of the early years of the EC, the 'reconstruction', 'modernization' and 'stabilization' elements were missing; or at least they were limited to a minority in the EC in terms of position within the political spectrum and to a minority of member states, namely the cohesion countries. Meanwhile the countries that could identify with the EC as a modernization and reconstruction project, both EFTAns and central and east Europeans, were on the outside and not on the inside, thus prevented from injecting dynamics into the EC debate. Their influence was even more reduced by the bilateralism of their relationships with the EC. A multilateral format for their relationships with the EC might have provided some different impulses.

The questions which follow are then less about Maastricht and more about whether this analysis reveals an absolute threshold to the inherited model of European integration or rather that what is missing is its reformulation for a very different Europe. Is the British government correct in arguing that the only plausible version is a looser, more flexible and less constraining version? Or would an upturn in the European economy, while maybe only a partial palliative, nonetheless make possible a renewed spurt for political integration? Of course the answers to such questions depend partly on value judgments and preferences, but then that was always true of the experiment in integration. The famous Monnet memorandum of May 1950, which bears constant rereading, argued that the task of the enlightened political engineer was not to be overwhelmed by adverse 'givens', but to be prepared to change the givens in order to progress.

Part of the Monnet argument in 1950 rested on the view that to leave things as they were was an unsafe option, since it was more likely to produce a deterioration than an improvement. In the current context it would therefore seem pertinent to reflect on the costs and benefits of a looser and more fragmented Europe, as well as on the costs and benefits of a reinforced 'solidarity' Europe – not to be confused with a 'centralized' Europe. In so doing one should bear two points in mind. First, we have no reason to suppose that the current state of the EC is a stable state or that it has reached a sustainable equilibrium point. Secondly, the notion that Europe could ever have acquired a highly structured and centralized form has always been contestable and, for this author at least, is a distorting straw figure. No model of integration has a chance of working unless it is supple, but equally integration depends on investments in building and sustaining solidarity. It is hardly surprising, for instance, that in a period where the talk is of loosening integration in favour of more intergovernmentalism, the French should have felt less constrained by collective solidarities in the Uruguay Round. The incentive structure to toe the line has been severely weakened in the past year or so.

To draw lessons from previous experience a renewal of the integration process would require several elements:

- overarching goals linked to positively stated values;
- institutional reinvestment;
- clear and pertinent policies for the participating states;
- a modernization agenda backed by 'reconstructors';
- a stabilization agenda for the continent;
- a stake for citizens in the process; and
- preservation of the parity-based multilateralism of the EC.

This last point matters because of the need to harness the energies of all members, including the smaller members for whom the stakes are higher and the alternatives limited. It takes us directly to the issue of enlargement and partnership with other Europeans. The first phase of building the EC depended on an exclusiveness of the Six vis-à-vis other Europeans. Early enlargement experiences produced mixed results for the EC in terms of its internal dynamics. Yet the most recent accessions showed that enlargement linked to reconstruction could be a source of dynamic impulses. It would seem very important for the supporters of further integration to ensure that would-be members of the EC retain a belief that EC membership would aid their political and economic renewal, which is immediately relevant to the content of the current enlargement negotiations and to the development of the Europe Agreements. It also follows that further enlargement and multilateral partnerships with other Europeans may be crucial ingredients for the future.

Note

1. Alan Milward, *The European Rescue of the Nation-state*, London: Routledge, 1992.

3

The Political Transformation of East Central Europe

Judy Batt

East Central Europe's place in Europe in historical context

External and internal vulnerability

A constant theme in the politics of east central Europe in the twentieth century has been the close linkage between domestic developments and the external environment. This arises from what is often referred to as the region's 'geopolitical predicament', which is one of vulnerability to external pressures and endemic challenge to the internal integrity of the state. The states of east central Europe are relatively small, and sandwiched between the much larger, more powerful and traditionally expansionist Germany and Russia. They lack obvious natural frontiers, and their current frontiers, having been drawn and redrawn within living memory, lack the psychological solidity of time-honoured historical frontiers. Moreover, there has been a mismatch between political and ethnic frontiers, which has led to the region being divided against itself and has weakened its capacity to resist domination by its stronger neighbours.

The permeability of the region, and centuries of incorporation within the sprawling multi-ethnic Russian, Prussian and Habsburg empires, led to successive waves of migration across and within the region. The result, in demographic terms, was that the population was not settled in compact ethnic territories but was rather mixed up in a complex ethnic patchwork. Although national self-determination was ostensibly the *raison d'être* of the states which emerged after the collapse of the empires in the First World War, their borders were not (and could not be) defined according to this principle: Poland and Czechoslovakia were multi-ethnic states, while about three million Hungarians were left outside the borders of the much-reduced

Hungarian state. Ethnic diversity posed a challenge to internal political integration and state legitimation, and gave rise to irredentism on the part of Germans and Hungarians. The mutual antagonism and mistrust which resulted in interstate relations was exploited to devastating effect by Hitler. The culmination was the dismemberment of Czechoslovakia in 1938–9, and the repartition of Poland between Germany and Russia. The legacy of this was a set of lasting resentments not only against the external aggressors, but also against those within the region who had secured temporary gains: the Czechs bitterly resented the separate Slovak Republic set up under Nazi protection in 1939, and also the Polish seizure of Těšín; and the Hungarians' wartime territorial gains in Slovakia, Transylvania and Bacska (Vojvodina) confirmed their neighbours' worst suspicions about their national character.

The Second World War and its aftermath brought about greater ethnic homogeneity within these states: the Jewish communities were decimated by genocide and emigration; the German minorities were expelled in retribution for their disloyalty; and Poland was shifted 200 miles westward, leaving the sizeable Byelorussian minority behind in Soviet-controlled territory. But substantial ethnic problems remained, notably the Hungarian minority question and Czech-Slovak relations, but these were effectively suppressed for the four decades of communist rule, only to re-emerge after 1989 as a concomitant of the process of democratization. As President Havel recently observed,

> It is astonishing to discover how, after decades of falsified history and ideological manipulation, nothing has been forgotten. Nations are now remembering their ancient achievements and their ancient suffering, their ancient statehood and their former borders, their traditional animosities and affinities – in short, they are suddenly recalling a history that, until recently, had been carefully concealed or misrepresented.[1]

Economic backwardness

A second theme in the politics of east central Europe is the problem of relative economic backwardness:

> By virtually every relevant statistical index, East Central Europe was less productive, less literate, and less healthy than West

Central and Western Europe. A potentially rich region with poor
people, its interwar censuses record not so much a distribution of
wealth as a maldistribution of poverty.[2]

The exceptions here were the Czech Lands (Bohemia and Moravia),
which comprised the most industrialized part of the region, successfully integrated into the wider European economy on the basis of
liberal, open economic policies. By contrast, the other economies were
heavily dependent on low-productivity peasant agriculture and
locked in what Joseph Rothschild describes as 'a vicious cycle of rural
undercapitalization, underproductivity, underconsumption, under-
employment, overpopulation, and pervasive misery'.[3]

Economic backwardness shaped internal politics by accentuating
the idea (already present in the prevailing nationalist ideological
context) that the state should play an active, interventionist role,
initiating programmes for industrialization and modernization,
substituting for the lack of such initiative from society itself, and
protecting domestic producers and 'infant industries' against foreign
competition.[4] Economic backwardness also contributed to the
region's external vulnerability: in the interwar period, Germany
became the major market for agricultural exports, and a pattern of
economic dependence was set up which underpinned Germany's
growing political stranglehold over the region. After the Second
World War, the communists were able to win some credibility by
advocating the 'Soviet model' of nationalization and state planning as
the solution to the problem of economic backwardness. The adoption
of this 'model' entailed a peculiar pattern of industrialization which
bound the economies of the region to the Soviet Union, on which they
depended for supplies of cheap fuel and industrial raw materials. The
collapse of the Soviet system in turn now leaves the uncompetitive
and debt-burdened east central European economies exposed to the
full force of the world market, raising the spectre of a 'new
dependency' on the West, and on Germany in particular.

East, West or Centre?

These two interlocking themes of political and economic vulnerability
have shaped east central Europe's understanding of its place in the
wider Europe. A basic question which has preoccupied and divided
the region's intelligentsia is whether east central Europe's destiny is
with the western 'mainstream', or whether it should follow a 'Third

Road', neither communist nor capitalist, appropriate to its special position between East and West. The latter concept was developed furthest by Hungary's populist intellectuals in the interwar period, who, idealizing the peasantry as the truest embodiment of the virtues of the Magyar race, propounded an anti-industrial, anti-urban vision of a 'Garden Hungary' of agricultural smallholders as a humane alternative to 'greedy' capitalism and the arid supranationalism of Marxism. The anti-western overtones of this idea were frequently accompanied by undertones of anti-semitism. An alternative vision was that of the Hungarian 'urbanists', many of whom were Marxist radicals who saw Hungary's destiny with the rest of Europe, driven by the inexorable laws of history towards socialism.[5]

A variant of 'Third Road' thinking reappears in the idea of east central Europe's role as a 'bridge' between East and West. For example, President Beneš advocated such a role for Czechoslovakia immediately after the Second World War. His aim was to preserve Czechoslovakia's independence and democratic traditions, while building up a 'special relationship' with the Soviet Union which had liberated the country after its betrayal by the West at Munich. Moreover, many Czechs at the time were disillusioned with capitalism in the wake of the 1930s slump, admired the achievements of the Soviet Union, but sought a social-democratic middle way for their country.[6] The 'bridge' idea resurfaced within the ruling communist parties of Hungary and the GDR in the early 1980s at the time of breakdown in US-Soviet relations in the wake of Afghanistan and the Polish Solidarity crisis. Both parties had, in rather different ways, become dependent on the preservation of East-West detente in Europe: the Kádár regime in Hungary depended on continued access to hard currency, borrowing to satisfy popular consumerist expectations, and Honecker had seized the opportunities offered by West Germany's *Ostpolitik* to shore up his fragile domestic legitimacy. By advocating a special role as a 'bridge', both regimes were resisting pressures from Moscow to cut ties with the West which had become essential to their survival.[7]

Echoes of 'Third Road' ideas could be detected in the debate on 'central Europe' conducted by east central European opposition intellectuals in the 1980s, but the general drift of the argument tended in a quite different direction. The purpose of defining a specific 'central European' identity was to overcome the internal divisions within the region which had, in the past, allowed it to be dominated by first Germany then Russia. But all the definitions encountered the problem of defining a coherent geographical and historical entity: the 'central Europe' which the east central European intellectuals had in mind was not the same as the earlier concept of *Mitteleuropa*, which implied German cultural and political hegemony;[8] nor could it be a revival of the former Habsburg Empire, because twentieth-century history had so changed the face of those territories with the establishment of separate nation-states, the expulsion of the Germans and the destruction of Jewish communities. Moreover, the Poles felt they did not belong in a 'central Europe' so defined.[9]

The focus of the definition, then, was on values rather than geography: 'central Europe' was a *Weltanschauung*, not a *Staatsangehörigkeit*, as the Hungarian György Konrád put it. The values were those which had evolved within the democratic opposition to communist rule after 1968, and the effort to define them was part of a deliberate strategy of building links and common platforms among the various national opposition movements of the region. The common themes were a moralistic aversion to politics and power *per se* (in Konrád's term: 'antipolitics'); the need to focus on building 'civil society' as the key to change, rather than waiting for 'reform from above' from within the communist party;[10] the advocacy of non-violence, because violence had been the source of degeneration of all previous revolutions into totalitarian dictatorship;[11] and a qualified support for and collaboration with western peace movements against 'Great Power' politics perpetuating the division of Europe, as long as it was understood that 'peace' also depended on each state respecting human rights in its internal affairs.[12]

The unresolved question was to what extent these values were distinctively central European, or merely a restatement of essentially western values. For the Hungarian writers such as Konrád and Agnes Heller, 'central Europe' did represent a middle way between western individualism and eastern collectivism.[13] Echoes of the neutralism of the western peace movements could be detected in Václav Havel's general moralistic aversion to 'technological civilization' whether in its western variant of commercialism and consumerism or its Soviet variant of repressive 'automatism'.[14] But for Milan Kundera, the 'tragedy of central Europe' was that it was 'culturally in the West and politically in the East'.[15] Central Europe had been 'kidnapped' by Russia, which represented 'an *other* civilization' which threatened to smother the essentially western identity of central Europe. Writing in the autumn of 1989 as events in east central Europe unfolded with astonishing speed, Jaques Rupnik declared that the idea of 'central Europe' had been 'one of the major intellectual developments of the 1980s and [would] no doubt be a vital ingredient in the reshaping of the political map of Europe in the post-Yalta era.'[16] But in fact the choice for the region very rapidly turned out to be the stark one of either East or West, and not some middle way between. The basic problem with the idea of central Europe as a 'bridge' was that bridges got walked over. Moreover, as Krishan Kumar perceptively noted, 'when faced with the practical task of state-building, the idea of a separate central European identity proves too ghostly, too insubstantial, to provide the essential building blocks.'[17] The values which east central Europe's intellectuals sought to realize in the post-communist political reconstruction – democracy, tolerance, diversity, human rights – all pointed to the adoption of a competitive, pluralist parliamentary model of politics essentially no different from that found in the West. And the long and unhappy experience of partial economic reform or 'market socialism' in the region pointed equally unambiguously to the unviability of a middle way between socialism and capitalism: 'The Third Way leads to the Third World', as Czechoslovakia's unabashedly neoliberal Finance Minister (now Czech Prime Minister) Václav Klaus put it. When east central Europe's intellectuals promised their compatriots a 'return to Europe' after 1989, there was no doubt that this meant the West.

The 'return to Europe'

The slogan of the 'return to Europe' nicely captures the inextricable linkage of the internal and external dimensions of the post-communist transformation of east central Europe. The task internally is to reconstruct politics on the basis of open, democratic principles and the rule of law, and to reconstruct the economy on the basis of the market and the predominance of private property. Internal transformation is intended to meet the people's demands both for a politics that is representative of and fully accountable to the nation, and for an economy that satisfies their material aspirations for consumption and welfare. But at the same time, the internal transformation also serves to demonstrate allegiance to 'European' values, and as such represents a claim to be rightfully included as a full member of European institutions, above all the European Community and NATO. In turn, external recognition and support from western governments and west European institutions for the new governments of east central Europe and for their policy programmes enhances their credibility and legitimacy at home. Thus ideally, a self-reinforcing 'virtuous circle' should emerge, allowing radical change to be implemented within the framework of internal and external stability.

However, all these linked processes could also form up into a vicious circle: democracy creates opportunities for nationalist demagogues and 'macroeconomic populists'[18] protesting against economic liberalization; if governments give in to such temptations in order to retain popular support, they will lose the confidence of western governments and western investors, and their access to European institutions will be delayed; perceived western indifference and/or western pressures on governments to reverse undesirable policies can convert the existing, and quite understandable, hypersensitivity of east central Europeans on the question of national sovereignty into anti-westernism and xenophobia, thus strengthening the hand of nationalists, proponents of a 'Third Way', and economic protectionists.

Competition between 'virtuous' and 'vicious' paths of development can be seen in each of the three dimensions of the 'return to Europe': namely democratization, economic transformation and international reintegration.

Democratization in post-communist society

The use of the term 'totalitarianism' to describe the workings of communist systems was hotly disputed among western political scientists, many of whom argued convincingly that it ignored the conflictual nature of the decision-making process and the existence of bureaucratic lobbies and interests. But the term gained a new lease of life in the writings of east central European dissidents – notably Václav Havel – whose perspective focused on the peculiarly destructive impact of communist rule on society and individual psychology. In the post-communist period, this aspect of communist rule has emerged as one of its most significant and intractable legacies: establishing democracy in post-communist societies is proving to be a rather more complex and problematic process than was the case in the post-authoritarian societies of southern Europe, precisely because of the much more profound and far-reaching – that is, 'totalitarian' – nature of the communist system. The extent of state power, in particular over the economy, meant that society was far more dependent on the state for its shape and structure and, with the collapse of the communist state, has disintegrated into a rather homogeneous and amorphous mass. Social interests are in a state of flux and regrouping as the command economy is dismantled and each individual strives as best he or she can to find a new role and new means of securing a livelihood in the uncertain conditions of the transition.

From a political point of view, society is thus an unknown quantity both to itself and to the new political entrepreneurs trying to identify political constituencies in the competition for votes. In this social context, an obvious political strategy was to build broad-based 'umbrella movements' uniting as many people as possible behind a very general programme against communism, for democracy and for the market. The basic choice which presented itself at first was simple: *either* communism, *or* democracy and the market; full political pluralism with competing alternative parties seemed premature when there seemed to be a basic consensus on the fundamental tasks of the transition period, and the primary need at first was to mobilize general social support behind the new governments. But in fact, the umbrella movements – Civic Forum in the Czech Republic, Public Against Violence in Slovakia, and Solidarity in Poland – very rapidly broke up, and the situation has become one of a multiplicity of parties which themselves frequently splinter, producing a form of pluralism which at times seems to display pathological features of centrifugalism and fragmentation. As a consequence, governments in Poland, Slovakia and Hungary are based on weak and unstable coalitions with unpredictable and unreliable parliamentary backing.

Two types of argument, which are not mutually exclusive, have been put forward to explain this pattern of development. Firstly, George Schöpflin has argued that where interests are in a state of dissolution and reformation, the politics of interests, characterized by pragmatic calculation, bargaining and compromise, cannot operate, and instead we find the predominance of values, which are inherently non-negotiable and absolute.[19] In the east central European context, value-based politics means unavoidably the politics of nationalism.

The leading role of intellectuals in transitional politics is also a factor promoting the primacy of value-based politics, and the background of many politically active intellectuals in the embattled anti-communist underground opposition can also be adduced to explain the unwillingness to compromise which is a striking feature of post-communist politics.[20] While Poland's foremost opposition intellectual, Adam Michnik, has been a consistent proponent of the need for compromise in politics, the ferocious and unfair attacks on his position as a form of 'pink' defense of entrenched *nomenklatura* privilege point to a wider tendency in post-communist societies to see compromise as a 'dirty' business.[21] The demand for a radical break with the past is understandable, but it can develop into a pattern of politics which is intolerant and vengeful, and which uses the same methods as the communists. Thus we see how far the political culture of the society is still shaped by the experience of communist rule.

Another way of explaining the problem has been put forward by András Körösényi. He argues that the emergence of an 'adversarial "Lager" mentality' among the divided new political elites has little to do with the existence of deep value cleavages or 'segmentation' within society itself, but on the contrary is a product of the homogeneity of post-communist society, which means that there is an unusually open 'political market'.[22] In order to attract votes, political leaders accentuate differences between themselves to the point where they portray their opponents as 'enemies', and strive to build up and consolidate their position by creating their own separate network of civil institutions as well as fostering links with existing or emerging societies, interest groups, churches, etc. In this context, cooperation or merger with other political parties is risky, threatening the position they have achieved, rather than consolidating their hold on power.

The problem is compounded by the institutional framework inherited from the communist period. Poland, Hungary and Czechoslovakia all took over the constitutions which had been drawn up in the communist period. Partial amendments were made, but the elaboration of wholly new constitutions has been blocked by the fragmentation and polarization of politics which has intervened in the meanwhile. These constitutions were not designed to work in practice, since real power resided with the communist apparatus, and their shortcomings as frameworks for conciliating divergent positions and managing conflict have become apparent. A common feature has been the relative strength of parliament, unusually strong constraints on the power of the executive, and poorly developed mechanisms for resolving deadlock.

Poland's parliaments between 1989 and 1993 provide an unhappy spectacle, as Louisa Vinton reports:

> . . . [T]he opposition's strength (its combined forces outnumbered the government coalition, even at the best of times) and its simultaneous fragmentation into warring camps that could provide

no alternative worked to promote gratuitous obstructionism. . . . Increasingly, the Sejm became a soapbox for opposition to everything the government proposed; parties would even oppose intiatives that matched their declared platforms. This forced the government to maintain a state of constant mobilization, lest vital legislation fail through the 'accidental' absence of one deputy or another.[23]

Perhaps the most disastrous example of these problems is that of Czechoslovakia, where they culminated in the breakup of the state. What is significant is the apparent lack of popular support in Slovakia for the establishment of a separate state; but this is what they got. What appears to have happened is the emergence of an opportunist political entrepreneur, the Slovak Vladimír Mečiar, who broke away from Public Against Violence with a programme appealing to genuine Slovak aspirations for self-government and well-founded Slovak anxieties about the impact of the radical neoliberal economic policies of the federal government in Prague. At the same time, the Czechoslovak federal constitution contained the provision that major pieces of legislation covering both constitutional reform and most economic policy win the support of two-thirds of all elected deputies in both chambers, including in each of the two sections of the Chamber of Nationalities voting separately. This gave effective veto-power to the small number of Slovak nationalist deputies in the Slovak section over both the economic transformation, and over any proposals for constitutional reform. Moreover, the president found that he lacked the formal powers either to dissolve the assembly or to call a referendum in order to break the deadlock.

The combination of looming paralysis, and growing Czech mistrust of Mečiar as the leader of the Slovak delegation at the extra-parliamentary talks held to resolve the constitutional crisis, eventually persuaded the Czechs that their own best interests would be better served by cutting the link with Slovakia. This happened after the June 1992 election brought to power in the Czech Republic Václav Klaus, leader of a party which stood above all for rapid economic trans-formation, and in the Slovak Republic, returned Mečiar with convincing popular support both for a programme promising slower pace of economic change and an ambiguous form of 'sovereignty' for Slovakia, which the Czechs read as a cynical attempt to preserve the economic benefits of federal subsidies without the political commitment necessary to make a common state work to mutual benefit.

Economic transformation in 'uncertain democracies'[24]

The strains and stresses of the economic transition have contributed their share to the tribulations of the democratic transition. Part of the problem derives from the insistence of economic experts and their western advisers that, in Mrs Thatcher's memorable phrase, 'There Is No Alternative'. This insistence was not just an accidental product of the prevailing international fashion among economists for neo-liberalism, but was deeply rooted in the long and unhappy experience with gradual and partial market-type reforms within the framework of communist rule. Both Hungary and Poland had flirted for decades with variants, more or less inconsistently applied, of 'market socialism' – a form of 'Third Way' which sought to derive the benefits of the market while preserving state-ownership of most productive assets, a modified variant of central planning, and extensive state intervention in the form of wage controls, subsidies, monopoly control of foreign trade, etc. In practice, this led to an even worse outcome than preserving the traditional Soviet-type system intact, as happened in Czechoslovakia. A major indicator of failure was the accumulation of massive hard-currency debt, a particularly bitter legacy for economies now desperately in need of capital to finance adjustment and restructuring. Hence Václav Klaus's dictum, 'The Third Way leads to the Third World'.

If there is no alternative, however, there is no room for politics, which is all about free choice between competing alternatives. The radical consistency and rapidity with which enthusiastic reformers such as Klaus and the Polish Finance Minister Leszek Balcerowicz went about implementing the 'Big Bang' was bound, however, to provoke a political reaction. In a peculiar way, the radical neo-liberals appeared to be resurrecting an old, familiar pattern of 'revolution from above', in which intellectuals take up the reins of state power in order to enforce a blueprint for the wholesale transformation of society, ostensibly in the best interests of society but in practice at enormous social cost. Klaus was accused of using 'Bolshevik methods' to implement capitalism; but in fact, he has been remarkably successful in winning fairly wide political support for his programme in the Czech Republic. The price of his radicalism was, however, the alienation of the Slovaks, who found in Mečiar's electoral promises what looked like a more reassuring alternative of 'gradualism'. The optimism of the Czechs about their economic prospects is due not only to Klaus's personal effectiveness as a politician, but also to the Czech context: unlike Poland and Hungary, the Czechs are not suffering from 'reform fatigue' after decades of failed reform experiments, and they may indeed be prey to illusions about the possibility of a 'soft landing' in their specific, in some respects more favourable, circumstances. But for the moment the economic transition is proceeding relatively well as far as they are concerned, thus contributing to stable politics. In Poland and Slovakia, however, and (to a somewhat lesser extent) Hungary, economic difficulties are provoking a backlash and creating the conditions for a nationalist and/or ex-communist revival.

Symptomatic of the politics of the 'Big Bang' in Poland was the closure of the Gdańsk shipyard, the cradle of Solidarity, the most effective opposition movement ever to emerge under communist rule. The bedrock of Solidarity's support was in the large state enterprises produced by the communist industrialization drive, and the alienation of the workers from the communist regime which created them was to be the regime's downfall. But now, in the post-communist period, Poland's workers were alienated from the new liberal government as a result of its policies; many of them voted for the ex-communist Democratic Left Alliance which was returned to power in the elections of September 1993. Another key social source of Poland's strong anti-communist tradition were the farmers, who had put up a uniquely successful resistance to collectivization in the late-1940s and early-1950s; but in 1990 and after this group rapidly signalled its opposition to the new government in mass protests against the agricultural pricing policy, and in September 1993, gave its votes to the Peasant Party, a former ally of the communists under the old regime. Former communist parties now look set to strengthen their electoral position, as soon as the opportunity presents itself, in both Slovakia and Hungary. The difficult question is what this development will mean for the economic transition.

Both the Hungarian Socialist Party and the Party of the Democratic Left in Slovakia have undergone significant internal reforms, which have weakened, if not wholly displaced, the traditionalists of the era of Soviet domination, and brought to leading positions well-educated, sophisticated technocrats, presenting themselves credibly as competent, experienced and professional alternatives to the existing governing teams whose political amateurism is at times painfully obvious. Some doubts can be entertained as to whether the Polish Democratic Left Alliance has undergone as thorough a self-transformation. All three parties now profess commitment to continuing the economic transformation, including privatization, but with some modifications to soften its social impact. However it is, to say the least, debatable whether, when in power, they will be able to find the resources to finance their promises on wages, pensions, welfare payments and continued support for large state enterprises in trouble.

At this point, they will encounter the potent external constraints posed by debt and dependence on the international financial institutions and western governments; the temptation then could be to join forces with anti-western nationalists, who have also been vocal critics of liberal economic policies, and especially of the close links between the new governments and foreign advisers from the international financial institutions and western governments. The latter are accused by nationalists of inflicting immeasurable damage on the vital national economic interests of weak and defenceless east central European countries, by imposing conditions and policies which would be quite unacceptable in their own countries. Sometimes it is suggested that this is part of a deliberate international (for which read 'Jewish') conspiracy to destroy national integrity and independence. A vivid example of this was the essay by the Hungarian populist István Csúrka, who described Hungary's political elite as a 'gang of parachutists' who always managed to land on their feet, preserving their privileges and power through all changes of regime by serving the interests of foreign powers. The liberal President Göncz was alleged to be in the service of 'Paris, New York and Tel Aviv'.[25]

Privatization, particularly sale of state assets to foreigners, offers ample scope for nationalist rhetoric. While the main problem associated with foreign investment has in fact been too little of it, rather than too much, for nationalists, foreign investment raises the spectre of a 'new hegemony', substituting German for Russian control. The sale of state assets to foreigners becomes acutely controversial where it is likely to lead to rationalization and slimming down the labour force, and all such sales are open to challenge where there is a lack of objective information on the real economic value of the firm, and where there is a wide discrepancy between the public's perception of the prestige and strategic significance of a well-known national enterprise, and western capitalists' hard-nosed calculations of its viability and prospects.

Reintegration into a Europe in flux

The internal dynamics of the politics of democratization and economic transformation have external repercussions: political polarization, weak governments, the rise of nationalism, the resurgence of support for the communists, the progress of economic transformation all affect relations between the east central Europeans themselves, as well as their relations with the wider Europe.

Firstly, let us consider the disappointing record of initiatives to increase cooperation among the east central Europeans themselves. On 15 February 1991, the presidents and prime ministers of Hungary, Poland and Czechoslovakia met at Visegrad and pledged to work together closely to speed up their full reintegration into Europe. As President Havel put it, 'Our best chance of shortening the road and catching up with western Europe is for us to assist one another along the way.'[26] At the time, commentators noted that the summit was the fulfilment of the idea of 'central Europe', and the fruit of previous cooperative links forged among the participants when they had still been underground opposition activists. The case for cooperation seemed overwhelming: as the Summit Declaration noted, 'The similarity of the situation which arose in the course of the last decades compels the three states to work for the achievement of essentially similar goals.'[27] A subsequent further development was an agreement in December 1992 to set up a Free Trade Zone among the Visegrad signatories.[28] Both developments were warmly welcomed by western governments and the European Community because they offered evidence of a new capacity for mature, cooperative behaviour in international affairs, which would have to be demonstrated before full membership in European institutions, chiefly the EC, could be considered. Moreover, it now became possible to deal with the states of the region as a group, rather than separately, which would greatly relieve the overburdened EC Troika and the Commission.

In practice, however, Jaques Rupnik's prediction of the key role of the concept of 'central Europe' has been at best only partially realized: competition has been at least as apparent as cooperation among the Visegrad Four.[29] Cooperation only really developed a life of its own in the face of a clear common external threat, which occurred at the time of the Soviet coup in August 1991 (just as the clearest definition of 'central Europe' in the 1980s debate had been the negative one, of being not Soviet and not Russian). Although in general terms there could be agreement that cooperation was a good thing, when it came to specifics, divergent interests and priorities and historical factors intervened. The very sameness of the economic legacy of communism in each state was argued to be a reason why little could be gained from increasing mutual trade, since each would be seeking to export similar low-quality products which could not be sold for Deutschmarks. Until full convertibility of their currencies is achieved, barriers to economic cooperation will remain. Meanwhile, the demands of economic restructuring and modernization seem to dictate that each country accord top priority to trade with the West.

A major disruptive factor in Visegrad integration was the breakup of Czechoslovakia. Although the 'divorce' was handled quite well, nevertheless it can hardly be counted as a success in terms of enhanced regional cooperation. The plan to maintain a common currency rapidly collapsed, with damaging results for Czech-Slovak trade, and thus for growth and economic stability in both states. The erection of border controls and customs posts was also a painful psychological shock. A further ramification of the split was heightened Slovak-Hungarian antagonism over the Hungarian minority issue, which became unfortunately entangled with the conflicting interests of the two states in the controversial Danube Dam project. The Visegrad framework proved insufficiently robust to secure a resolution of the latter conflict, and the EC found it necessary to take the initiative and mediate between the two. Since the split, Czech prime minister Václav Klaus has displayed a markedly dismissive attitude to the whole Visegrad enterprise which has soured relations with both Poland and Hungary, although in fact there is some understanding in both countries of his argument that Visegrad cooperation may become a 'parking lot' to which the EC can conveniently consign the east central Europeans while it focuses on more pressing priorities; and all three share a reluctance to allow the pace of integration with the EC to be set by the weakest and slowest developer in their group, which is the inherent danger in the EC treating them as a group.

Relations with the EC have proved a disappointment to the east central Europeans, who may have entertained unrealistic expectations about achieving early full membership, not perhaps being fully aware of the implications of the *acquis communautaire* and the distance between their own economic level and that required for full participation.[30] But the self-interest of existing EC member states was an equally important factor conditioning the EC's cautious approach, which has been criticized with justification for its meanness.[31] The Association Agreements which set out the basic framework for the east central Europeans' economic relations with the EC were attacked (most notably by former EBRD President Jacques Attali) for closing markets rather than opening them, raising tariffs and tightening quotas. The latter charges are not accurate, but nevertheless, the trade liberalization measures did not go far or fast enough. A basic source of friction was that those goods in which the east central Europeans had comparative advantage were precisely the most sensitive in the internal political economy of the EC and its member states: steel, agricultural products and textiles. On the other hand, the fears were exaggerated: the exports of the Visegrad Four account for barely 3 per cent of EC imports. But the EC is by contrast by far the largest market for each of the Visegrad countries' exports, and restrictions on trade with the EC were clearly holding up the pace of their economic transformations. By mid-1993, the EC had built up a substantial trade surplus with the Associates, which argued strongly for further liberalization of trade.

A deeper source of contention, however, was the issue of membership itself. While the Association Agreements had included a reference to the ambition of each state to join, there had been no commitment on the EC's part to eventual membership. This was psychologically offensive to east central Europeans, and politically damaging to their governments, who appeared to have allowed the EC to dictate the economic and political terms of the relationship (including 'political conditionality' clauses in the revised separate Czech and Slovak Agreements negotiated in 1992), without extracting any firm commitment in return. This supplied ammunition to nationalist demagogues: the 'Europe' to which the liberals had been promising to return their countries turned out not only to be an exclusive club for the rich, but one driven by the national interests of its members.

Fortunately, the Association Agreements provide a framework for continual EC-east central European consultations and renegotiation of the terms of the trade provisions. A major improvement in the situation was reached at the June 1993 Copenhagen Summit, at which, for the first time, the EC committed itself to an understanding of the purpose of the Association Agreements as the framework for preparing the Associates for eventual full membership when they are ready. No specific time deadline or precise criteria of 'readiness' were defined, and, although this can be interpreted as another manifestation of EC member states' foot-dragging, it can also be argued that precise targets are as likely to delay accession as to accelerate it. The Copenhagen summit also offered further trade liberalization, and although many commentators would argue these still did not go far enough, the flexibility of the Association Agreements and their openness to further renegotiation in future was thereby demonstrated.

The experience with the EC has been a salutary one for the foreign policy thinking of the east central European states. Their rather starry-eyed vision of a benign and conflict-free 'Europe' has given way to a harder-headed understanding of what the 'return to Europe' will involve: above all, that they approach it as consolidated nation-states able to assert their interests and hold their own in competition with others. This in turn requires that they press on at home with the tasks of building democracy and transforming the economy.

Notes

1. Václav Havel, 'The Post-Communist Nightmare', *New York Review of Books*, 27 May 1993, p. 9.
2. J. Rothschild, *East Central Europe between the Two World Wars*, Seattle and London: University of Washington Press, 1974, pp. 14–15.
3. Rothschild, p. 15.
4. See D. Chirot, 'Ideology, Reality and Competing Models of Development Between the Two World Wars', *East European Politics and Societies*, vol.3, no. 3, Autumn 1989, pp. 378–411.
5. On these competing currents of thought, see B. Kovrig, *Communism in Hungary*, Stanford CA: Hoover Institution Press, 1979, pp. 123–7.
6. See M. Myant, *Socialism and Democracy in Czechoslovakia 1945–48*, Cambridge: Cambridge University Press, 1981; and J. Bloomfield, *Passive Revolution*, London: Allison and Busby, 1979.
7. See R. Asmus, 'The Dialectics of Detente and Discord: the Moscow-East Berlin-Bonn Triangle', *Orbis*, vol. 28, no. 1, Winter 1985, pp. 743–74; R. Tokes, 'Hungarian Reform Imperatives', *Problems of Communism*, vol. XXXIII, no. 5, September–October 1984, pp. 1–23; M. Szűrős, 'Interaction of the National and the International in Hungarian Policy', *New Hungarian Quarterly*, vol. XXV, no. 93, Spring 1984, pp. 8–18.
8. See T. Garton Ash, 'Mitteleuropa?' *Daedalus*, vol. 119, no. 1, Winter 1990, pp. 1–21.
9. See J. Rupnik, 'Central Europe or Mitteleuropa?' *Daedalus*, vol. 119, no. 1, Winter 1990, pp. 249–78.
10. See Adam Michnik's seminal essay, 'A New Evolutionism' in *Letters from Prison and Other Essays*, Berkeley, Los Angeles and London: University of California Press, 1985, pp. 135–48.
11. See A. Michnik, 'Towards a New Democratic Compromise', *East European Reporter*, vol. 3, no. 2, March 1988, pp. 24–9.
12. See T. Garton Ash, 'Does Central Europe Exist?' *New York Review of Books*, 9 October 1986, pp. 45–52.
13. Quoted by K. Kumar, 'The 1989 Revolutions and the Idea of Europe', *Political Studies*, vol. XL (1992), p. 447.
14. See V. Havel, 'The Power of the Powerless' in V. Havel *et al.*, *The Power of the Powerless*, London: Hutchinson, 1985, pp. 23–96.
15. M. Kundera, 'The Tragedy of Central Europe', *New York Review of Books*, 26 April 1984, pp. 33–8.

16. Rupnik, p. 250.
17. Kumar, p. 451.
18. The term is defined more precisely by Rudiger Dornbusch and Sebastian Edwards in their study of the Latin American case; see 'Macroeconomic Populism', *Journal of Development Economics*, vol. 32, 1990, pp. 247–77.
19. See G. Schöpflin, 'Post-Communism: constructing new democracies in Central Europe', *International Affairs*, vol. 67, no. 2, April 1991, pp. 235–50.
20. A useful discussion of the ambiguous attitude of intellectuals to democratic politics is provided by András Körösényi, 'Intellectuals and democracy: the Political Thinking of the Intellectuals', unpublished paper.
21. See Timothy Garton Ash's account of the views of one of Michnik's critics in 'Eastern Europe: Après le Déluge, Nous', *New York Review of Books*, 16 August 1990, p. 52.
22. A. Körösényi, 'The Divided Republic: the Distribution of Power in Hungary 1990–92', unpublished paper delivered at the Minda de Gunzburg Center for European Studies, Harvard University, March 1993.
23. L. Vinton, 'Poland: Governing without Parliament', *Radio Free Europe/ Radio Liberty Research Report*, vol. 2, no. 26, 25 June 1993, pp. 8–9.
24. The term 'uncertain democracies' is taken from the conclusion of G. O'Donnell and P. Schmitter (eds), *Transitions from Authoritarian Rule*, Baltimore and London: Johns Hopkins University Press, 1986.
25. Quoted in Judith Pataki, 'István Csúrka's tract: Summary and Reactions', *Radio Free Europe/Radio Liberty Research Report*, vol. 1, no 40, 9 October 1992, pp. 17–18.
26. Quoted by Jan de Weydenthal, 'The Visegrad Summit', *Radio Free Europe Report on Eastern Europe*, vol. 2, no. 9, 1 March 1991, p. 28.
27. See text of the Summit Declaration, *Radio Free Europe Report on Eastern Europe*, vol. 2, no. 9, 1 March 1991, pp. 31–2.
28. See K. Okolicsanyi, 'The Visegrad Triangle's Free Trade Zone', *Radio Free Europe/Radio Liberty Research Report*, vol. 2, no. 3, 15 January 1993, pp. 19–22.
29. See Rudolf Tokes, 'From Visegrad to Krakow: Cooperation, Competition and Coexistence in Central Europe', *Problems of Communism*, vol. XL, no. 6, Nov–Dec 1991, pp. 100–14.
30. For a full economic analysis of the implications for the EC and for the east central Europeans of accession, see the Centre for Economic Policy Research, 'Is Bigger Better? The Economics of EC Enlargement', London: CEPR, *Monitoring European Integration*, no. 3, 1992.
31. See for example, *The Times* editorial of 5 January 1993. A fuller critical analysis is Heinz Kramer, 'The European Community's response to the "New Eastern Europe"', *Journal of Common Market Studies*, vol. 31, no. 2, June 1993, pp. 213–44.

4

The Troubled Balkans

Andrei Georgiev and Emil Tzenkov

Introduction

The profound and all-encompassing crisis of the post-communist Balkan societies, coinciding with the dissolution of Yugoslavia, has become a crucial test of the territorial integrity and national cohesion of both the existing Balkan states and the new ex-Yugoslav successor states. Age-old enmities have revived and a combination of state revanchism and ethnic anarchy threatens to plunge the whole region 'back into history'.

The Balkan states are relatively recent formations, created out of the fragments of supranational empires in the late nineteenth and early twentieth centuries. The European great powers, for whom the Balkans were traditionally an arena of conflict, negotiated and imposed the frontiers between them. Nevertheless, with the exception of Yugoslavia, a fairly viable formula had been found – mainly at the expense of Bulgaria – for nation-states in which the national majorities had a comfortable margin over the local minorities.

During the Cold War, the Balkan sub-system was subordinated to the East-West confrontation. The inclusion of Bulgaria and Romania into COMECON, and the integration of Greece and to a lesser extent Turkey into western institutions created the necessary conditions for the relative economic stability of these countries and the region as a whole. Even so, the Cold War did not entirely override national differences. Yugoslavia and Albania managed to escape the blocs altogether – Yugoslavia by following a non-aligned foreign policy, Albania by its self-imposed Stalinist isolation. Romania resisted Soviet domination, without breaking out of the Warsaw pact. In the South, NATO membership did not prevent Greece and Turkey from pursuing their disputes over Cyprus and the Aegean Sea. Internally, states on both sides of the Iron Curtain subordinated the interests of ethnic minorities to the majority nation. Paradoxically, it was

Yugoslavia which represented a relatively civilized example of power distribution, based on the recognition of the cultural identity of different nationalities.

The crumbling of communism in the Balkans

The Balkan 1989

The crumbling of the Marxist authoritarian regimes followed the general logic of the 'communist domino'. However, in the Balkans this process reflected national peculiarities in the different countries.

In Romania, the bloody clashes between Ceauşescu's supporters and the opposition culminated in the killing of the dictator. In Bulgaria, the ruling communist party's attempt to reform itself by getting rid of Todor Zhivkov was overshadowed by the Bulgarian variant of the 'velvet revolution'. A somewhat similar development took place in Albania from 1990 to 1992, although the political confrontation there took more extreme forms and the former communists were evicted from power more resolutely. In Yugoslavia, the end of Tito's communism was tantamount to the dissolution of the federation he had created; the process of ethnic polarization there prevented the emergence of a civil society and of democratic state structures.

Transitional political formations, struggling for control over the newly created institutions, filled the political vacuum caused by the collapse of communism. The main antagonists became the crypto-communist or post-communist parties on the one hand (the National Salvation Front in Romania, the Bulgarian Socialist Party, the Albanian Socialist Party), and the anti-communist organizations (the Democratic Convention in Romania, the Union of Democratic Forces in Bulgaria, the Democratic Party in Albania) on the other.

The demolition of the centralized party-state and its institutions permitted the foundation of pluralistic political systems and consti-tutional frameworks for democratic rule. For the first time after the Second World War these countries began to enjoy some of the fundamental rights of civilized societies including liberty of expression, association and religious beliefs.

However, progress towards the emergence of a modern civil society and the stabilization of the democratic institutions was hampered by the lack of legitimacy and by what Charles Gati calls an 'environment contaminated with guilt and suspicion'.[1] Post-communist society as seen in the Balkans bears all the signs of the crisis: profound polarization, to the extent of rejecting 'the other'; lack of legitimacy of the new-found values; institutional fluidity; the rise of organized crime and violence; and the coinciding interests of the newly emerged mafia organizations and corrupt state officials.

The transition to democracy in these societies is further compli-cated by the deepening economic crisis, the main parameters of which are the paralysis of the centralized economic system, industrial recession, the slow pace of privatization, high inflation and growing unemployment.

Predictably, the transition to democracy in the post-communist Balkan countries led to a revision of the old patterns of intra-ethnic relations.

The adherence of the main political actors to universal democratic values implied curbing nationalism in both domestic and foreign policy. The new pro-western parties and coalitions prided themselves on their liberal internationalism as opposed to the old isolationism and communist nationalism. The ethnic minorities, suppressed under communist rule, were now permitted to form political parties and to participate in both the legislative and the executive branches of government. The process of political legitimization of the minorities, for example in Bulgaria, Romania and Albania, further eroded old notions about the monolithic character of the state.

However, with the re-establishment of national sovereignty, old nationalistic themes resurfaced in political discourse. The resurgence of nationalism was motivated by the need to check dangerous centrifugal tendencies, and to adjust to the Balkan 'return to history'.[2] It was also fuelled psychologically by some extreme forms of negation of national identity and by the aggressive imposition of western values and American pop-culture at the expense of local cultures and traditions.[3] Different political forces – from the former communists to the old-time fascists and nationalists – were quick to exploit the opportunities for disseminating such prejudices among the local public.

In Bucharest, the myth of 'Greater Romania'[4] has been resurrected with the prospect of rapprochement and reunification with Moldova. In Tirana, the worries of the new authorities about the fate of the Albanians in Kosovo, Sanjak and Tetovo are fuelling the idea of a 'Greater Albania'.[5] Nationalists from Serbia, Greece, Bulgaria and Russia share similar visions about redrawing Balkan frontiers to fit their geopolitical priorities.[6]

The return to nationalist themes is combined with constant attacks on the activities of the ethnic parties in all three countries. In Albania, the Greek deputies are frequently treated as a 'fifth column'. In Bulgaria, the ethnic Turkish Rights and Freedoms Movement has been criticized by almost all the other parties for wanting to 'Turkicize' the non-Turkish Muslims and for its links with Ankara. In Romania, the Hungarian Democratic Union, which denounced the 'discriminatory policies' of Bucharest towards the Magyar minority, is under constant pressure from the Romanian nationalists.[7]

In addition to these themes, some old racial prejudices are on the rise in countries such as Romania and Bulgaria, reflected in widely shared public attitudes towards the local gypsy communities. In Bulgaria, the relatively new phenomenon of xenophobia is directed at the steadily growing Arab community.[8]

As far as Yugoslavia is concerned, 1989 marked the beginning of the last stage in the erosion of Tito's federation. During his lifetime, the federal system was based on a compromise between Serb domination in the centre and autonomy in the non-Serb republics, with the army and the federal communist party imposing effective control. After Tito's death in 1980 and with the waning of his charismatic spell, ethnic cleavages began to develop. The Albanian riots in Kosovo during 1981 were the first serious test of the viability of the post-Tito Yugoslav federation.

With the growth of centrifugal tendencies, Serb nationalism gained in strength, both within the ranks of the communist party, which Slobodan Milosevic headed from 1987, and among the nascent democratic opposition. The elimination of autonomy in Kosovo and Vojvodina in February 1989 was another step from the federal system towards a Serb-dominated and repressive state.

The promulgation of the total independence of Slovenia and Croatia and their recognition by the international community marked the end of Tito's Yugoslavia.[9]

The combination of ethno-nationalist confrontation and the disintegration of the federation was a sinister omen for the transition to multi-party democracy in Serbia. The post-communist nationalists, led by Slobodan Milosevic, easily defeated the democratic opposition at the first democratic elections in 1990. The opposition leader, Vuk Draskovic, was himself divided between his loyalty to nationalistic values and liberal views. A partial success in preserving a federalist façade to serve Serb national interests was the formation of the so-called United Republic of Yugoslavia comprising Serbia and Montenegro.[10]

Even in the other post-Yugoslav states, nationalism turned out to be an impediment to democracy. Instead of improving their human rights record, these new states began to exert pressure on their minorities to comply with the interests of the majority nation. In this way the post-Yugoslav wars fuelled local ethnic nationalisms and further complicated the relations between the South Slav peoples.

The end of bipolarity in regional relations

The revolutionary democratic transformations in the former communist states in the region at first gave rise to exceptionally high expectations about their speedy reintegration into the community of civilized nations.

The normalization of relations with Europe and the United States coincided with the strengthening of pro-western sympathies among the public. With the lifting of barriers to western mass culture (and American culture, in particular), new values and standards of behaviour began to displace communist stereotypes and traditional ways of thinking.

At the regional level, the end of communism for a country like Bulgaria meant that its southern border (with Greece and Turkey) ceased to be a front-line between the blocs. Bulgaria concluded political and military agreements with Greece and Turkey, and troops on both sides of the Bulgarian-Turkish border were relocated, reducing the danger of incidents.[11]

Greece and Turkey, as members of the coalition which won the Cold War, benefited from the disappearance of the 'danger from the North' and the opening of new opportunities in the region. Ironically, their increased mutual rivalry, which developed into an open contest for regional pre-eminence, undermined the improvement in their strategic security. Nevertheless, they were beneficiaries of the new Balkan division between privileged and post-communist states. Greece became an advocate for Bulgaria and Romania in their applications for membership of the European Community. Turkey launched the Black Sea Economic Cooperation Initiative, which aimed at bringing a good number of post-communist states together in a regional zone of economic integration.[12] Greek and Turkish goods began to flow into Bulgaria and Romania on a large scale, and gradually into Macedonia and Albania too.

From the outset of their transition to democracy, the Balkan post-communist states indicated their desire to join the main Euro-Atlantic institutions: the EC, the Council of Europe and NATO. Although the Balkan states fell behind the Visegrad group, which received a warmer response, they gradually became associated with some of these organizations. Bulgaria and Romania negotiated 'Europe' agreements with the EC, Albania negotiated a trade and cooperation agreement, and all the former WTO states joined the NACC.

However, the limited character of these agreements and NATO's reluctance to provide security guarantees to the post-communist countries in the region strengthened their conviction that their stability was threatened by a new strategic vacuum in a period when a dangerous revival of nationalistic expansionism was occurring. The non-inclusion of the Balkans as a whole into a Euro-Atlantic security zone may pave the way to a new intensification of the Greek-Turkish rivalry, which may have a dangerous regional spill-over.

The Yugoslav agony

The disintegration of Yugoslavia and the revision of the Versailles system in the Balkans

The proclamation of the independence of Slovenia, Croatia, Macedonia and Bosnia-Herzegovina signalled not only the end of Tito's federation but also that of the unitary state of the South Slavs, created at the Paris Peace Conference following the First World War.

The disintegration of this state outlined the priority of the principle of self-determination over those of federalism and territorial integrity. The intra-federal frontiers, drawn more or less for administrative purposes, became international state borders. Because they did not and could not possibly coincide with the division between the different Slav nationalities, the new 'nation-state' formula was contested from the outset both by the post-Yugoslav entities and by circles in the neighbouring Balkan countries. In other words, the assertion of self-determination legitimized a process of secession, which may be described as 'an ethnic domino'; a process which in turn endangered the stability of the post-Yugoslav states.

It was, above all, the ethnic minorities which challenged the legitimacy and viability of the new 'nation-states'. In Croatia, a Serb republic of Krajina was proclaimed; in Macedonia, the Albanian minority demanded the status of a 'constituent people' and proclaimed the republic of Ilirida; in Bosnia-Herzegovina, the Serbs and Croats led a war aimed at creating 'ethnically pure' entities. The backing of 'parent nations' (Serbia, Croatia, Albania) for these demands for independence created a dangerous phenomenon of cross-border ethnic solidarity.[13] Belgrade played a crucial role in this respect, launching and organizing the Serb offensive in Bosnia-Herzegovina.

Although the neighbouring countries did not become directly involved in the internal crisis, they could not content themselves with the role of impartial observers. On the one hand, Romania and Greece offered diplomatic help for Belgrade's efforts to preserve Yugoslavia's integrity. On the other, Bulgaria and Turkey backed the post-Yugoslav states in their diplomatic struggle for recognition. The neighbouring states all perceived their interests to be at stake.

Greece was concerned that the 'ethnic domino' in the Yugoslav context could create a disturbing precedent, which could eventually endanger its own national integrity. Fears of Macedonian claims to northern Greece led the authorities in Athens to obstruct the establishment of a Macedonian state.[14]

The Romanian government was anxious to maintain good relations with Belgrade. For Bucharest, it was of paramount importance not to lose a strategic ally in its post-communist confrontation with Budapest over the fate of the Hungarian minority in Transylvania. Some Hungarian politicians even fear a restoration of the so-called 'Little Entente' between Bucharest, Belgrade and Bratislava against Hungary.[15]

Bulgaria initially shared Greek apprehensions of Skopje's potential expansionism and continued to claim that Macedonians are of Bulgarian origin and that 'Macedonia' is merely a geographical name. As the denial to Belgrade of control over the 'Macedonian card' began to be perceived as of prime importance to Bulgaria, it became the first country to recognize Macedonia along with the other post-Yugoslav states.[16] The initial ambiguity of Bulgaria's position on Macedonia ('yes' to the Macedonian state, 'no' to the Macedonian nation), betrayed Sofia's fears of the potential claims to a different ethnicity of the Bulgarians living in Pirinska Macedonia.[17]

For Skopje, the debate over the name 'Macedonia' and over the nationality of 'Macedonians' raised fears of a new partition between Greece, Serbia and possibly Albania.[18]

As far as Turkey is concerned, the Yugoslav disintegration created conditions for Ankara to play the role of protector toward the Muslim minorities in the Yugoslav area and, in the case of Bosnia-Herzegovina, to help establish a Muslim state there. The self-restrained and rather balanced Turkish attitude in the context of the Balkan crisis may be partly explained by the fact that Ankara is in the comfortable position of getting involved only when it suits its interests.

In turn, Ankara's position fuelled the Greek apprehensions about the creation of a hypothetical 'Islamic arc', linking Ankara, Tetovo, Tirana, Kosovo and Sarajevo. Athens reacted by reviving the so-called 'orthodox axis', linking Greece itself, Serbia and Romania, with Moscow taking a favourable view. Slovenia and Croatia returned to the bosom of catholicism, with the expectation of increased economic integration into central Europe completing the picture of new religious and geopolitical cleavages.

These new relationships and proto-axes, together with the dissolution of Yugoslavia, illustrated the revision of the Versailles system in the Balkans.

The war in Bosnia-Herzegovina: from 'ethnic cleansing' to 'ethnic states'

The conflict between the Bosnian Serbs, backed by the local units of the Yugoslav army, the Muslims and the Croatians of Bosnia-Herzegovina led to the widespread practice of 'ethnic cleansing', launched initially by Belgrade. Milosevic encouraged the Bosnian Serbs to reject the results of the referendum and the independence of this republic. It was the Serb community in Bosnia-Herzegovina which started the hostilities, aiming to establish their own state to be affiliated with Serbia. The Bosnian Croats had similar motivations, and proclaimed their own mini-state in Bosnia-Herzegovina. The Muslims themselves were initially encouraged to seek a revision of the Lisbon agreement – a step which turned out to be disastrous for them.[19]

'Ethnic cleansing' was a logic of civil war and its application led to a two-year conflict comparable, in atrocities committed against the civil population, to the genocide during the Second World War in this part of the world. Tens of thousands of civilians were killed and over three million refugees were displaced, thousands of them seeking refuge in European countries.[20]

The rise of ethnic nationalism and the doctrine of 'ethnic cleansing' as a state-building principle create a dangerous precedent for the

Balkans. It implies further disintegration of the post-Yugoslav states. It has pushed a religious community – that of the Bosnian Muslims – towards identifying themselves as a separate nationality,[21] with dangerous implications for other religious groups in the Balkans.[22]

The principle of 'ethnic cleansing' could be applied in Croatia, where the Republic of Serb Krajina is struggling for a reunification with its 'mother-nation'. Another 'ethnic domino' could be Kosovo, where the Albanian majority (up to 90 per cent of the inhabitants) has already declared its will to accept nothing less than independence. In the worst-case scenario, the Macedonian Albanians living in Tetovo would secede, which in turn would inevitably lead to involvement of the neighbouring Balkan countries.

Even if 'ethnic cleansing' is limited to the Bosnian conflict, it has already doomed the three main communities there to constant instability and mutual suspicion. These South Slav peoples, united in the recent past by their similar languages and culture, are divided as a result of the war by a profound abyss of hatred and painful memories. Bosnia-Herzegovina, a symbol of the federation during Tito's rule, has become the symbol of its disintegration.

Regionally, the worst direct impacts of Bosnia's conflict on the Balkan countries were economic. As a result of the UN sanctions on Serbia and Montenegro, Bulgaria and Macedonia were virtually cut off from Europe.[23] Greece, Romania and Turkey also suffered from the disruption of land transportation and communications with the West, in addition to the indirect losses caused by the war.

The war in the international context

One could speculate about whether the Balkan crisis and the post-Yugoslav war were the result mainly of intra-regional or extra-regional factors. What is clear is that the external disintegrative impulses were a by-product of the transition from bipolarity in world politics. The complexity of this transition, however, does not absolve the leading international bodies such as the EC, NATO, the UN Security Council and their permanent members. Their unsatisfactory responses to the events in former-Yugoslavia are exemplified both by their unsuccessful attempts to avoid the 'domino effect' and by their 'unintentional' actions to simultaneously stir it up. Attitudes vacillated between *realpolitik* and liberal internationalism; and differing priorities were expressed regarding the rights of minorities and those of individuals.

NATO accepted an out-of-area role (enforcing the no-fly zone, sending patrols to the Adriatic, and agreeing to send peacekeepers to police an eventual settlement). However, it was slow and ineffective in coping with the crisis in Bosnia-Herzegovina. NATO and Security Council officials referred responsibility for military action in Bosnia-Herzegovina to each other. As a whole, the world community was unable to deal with the negative effects of the sanctions on third countries and to provide them with compensation to offset the damage to their economies. Undoubtedly, the differences between the United States and Europe also influenced the process, as well as the differing attitudes of the European countries towards the Balkans, and especially of Germany, the UK and France.[24] Russia's Balkan policy is also unclear.

The ambiguity and the inconsistency of the external responses to the Yugoslav crisis were obvious during the two stages of its development: the peaceful stage, which was characterized by attempts to avoid a total Yugoslav disintegration; and the second stage, that of the creeping war and the collapse of the federation. This 'zigzag' approach may continue into the next period, when the post-Yugoslav states will seek to consolidate their positions by trading parts of the territories under their control using both diplomacy and paramilitary operations.

Indicative of the Yugoslav case has been the extremely inconsistent way in which the international community defined its attitude with regard to the two fundamental state-building principles – the ethnic principle and the political principle.[25]

The conflicting attitudes of the extra-regional powers undermine the thesis that the war in the Balkans has a growing international importance. According to this thesis, from 1991 on, the war evolved from a 'Yugoslav affair' to an 'all-European concern' to become, finally, an issue of 'world priority', which affects the interests of the United States.[26]

Undeniably, the war and the Balkan crisis are attracting a lot of diplomatic and media attention. However, the reasons for the involvement of outside powers are unclear. On the one hand, one may infer that the efforts of the international community are aimed at a regional encapsulation of the conflict, using measures and approaches which instead of quenching the fire may be adding fuel to it. On the other, one may even be tempted to suspect that the world powers are using the Balkan situation as an opportunity for testing the post-Cold War balance of power in the new competition amongst themselves.[27]

Towards a new Balkan order?

Geopolitical aspects

The crisis of the old Balkan order, the Yugoslav war and what amounts to an anarchy in regional relations all point to the need for a new type of regional stability. Until it can be achieved, however, the Balkans appear doomed to be an arena where various types of international state-political order will be revived and revised.[28]

The historical, national and religious heritage which now burdens Balkan relations will continue to put its imprint on the regional order. This will be a lengthy process of interposition, conflict and cohabitation between different geopolitical projects.

At the basic subregional level is the model of a 'great nationalistic' self-determination. The conditions of the Yugoslav disintegration and the Balkan crisis in general revived aspirations towards ethnically homogeneous states. Throughout the region political formations are mushrooming, advocating, with varying success, the thesis of *grandeur nationale*: Greater Serbia, Greater Croatia, Greater Albania, Greater Romania, Greater Bulgaria, Greater Macedonia and, last but not least, Greater Turkey.

It is obvious that if all these nationalistic projects were to be implemented simultaneously, the new 'great states' would need another continent in addition to the whole of Europe as 'building material'. Even a partial accomplishment of such 'national ideas' would imply a radical revision of state borders in the Balkans, which in accordance with historical traditions and the Yugoslav example cannot be achieved without resort to war.

A peculiar and hardly predictable element in the situation is the scenario of religious/cultural integration. In addition to the possible development of an 'Islamic arch' and an 'orthodox axis', which will depend on the internal developments in both Turkey and Russia, the concept of a further division between the western and eastern branches of Christianity is acquiring a new vitality. The permeability of the dividing line between these two spheres will depend primarily on the attitudes of the EC and, to a certain degree, also on the positions of Germany and perhaps some other central European states. A possibility some foresee is the division of post-communist states into two categories: a 'Latin group' to be associated with Europe, and a 'Byzantine group' (Russia, Ukraine, Serbia, Romania and Bulgaria) to be left to Moscow. Such suggestions are likely to fuel apprehension that the Balkans are to be left 'at the gate of Europe'.[29]

Interregional in scope and somewhat similar to the geographical outlines of the religious and cultural areas are the projects of the Black Sea Economic Cooperation and the central European initiative. The Visegrad group influences Balkan developments not only because it attracts Slovenia and Croatia into its orbit but also because of its geopolitical role. Whatever the future evolution of this initiative, it would constitute an additional obstacle between the south-eastern and western parts of Europe. The different treatment of the former members of the Warsaw Treaty undoubtedly fuels the ambitions of the Visegrad group to be viewed as more acceptable for reintegration in the western institutions and accordingly to maximize the distance from its former allies.

However, all these geopolitical schemes are likely to have less impact on the region than the processes of European integration, which will be decisive for the fate of the Balkans. Such integration would fulfil the most auspicious expectations and would present virtually the only non-confrontational prospect for the region.

At the continental level, there are now different options: united Europe, divided Europe, fragmented Europe. Each would imply corresponding configurations in the Balkans. From the point of view of the vital interests of the Balkan peoples, the most important solutions are those which open new opportunities for their inclusion into a stable European order.

Should the Balkan countries, whose aim is to be integrated in Europe, join the continental and the Euro-Atlantic structures individually or through some form of preliminary regional cooperation? Smaller countries are easier to manage and are supposed to create fewer problems when offered a suitable formula for association with the EC or NATO. On the other hand, a protracted period of integration might turn out to be difficult to endure for the isolated Balkan states, which are faced with economic crisis, national rivalries and hardships resulting from the embargo and military threats.

From this perspective the creation of a regional formation may be instrumental in stabilizing the situation and in gradually developing intra-Balkan cooperation with an emphasis on cross-border economic, social and cultural relations. Such a regional cooperation could be successful only if approved and actively supported by the EC and NATO. The consequence of failure to transform such local cooperation into European integration could be a negative regionalization: the Balkans would be isolated from beneficial outside influences, and national conflicts and cultural differences would get the upper hand.[30]

Of crucial importance, also, is the question of the rate and order of integration – whether the priority should be on integration in the economic or the defence/security fields. Understandably, influential circles in the West are stressing their preference for giving priority to widening the European Community and the Western European Union over accepting post-communist states as NATO members.[31]

Their opponents argue that economic integration is a lengthy process. Furthermore, the economies of the post-communist Balkan states are in very difficult situations. Their problems, which include the restructuring of foreign debt, the difficulty of market access and the slow inflow of foreign investment, are all too well known.[32] One could add that even the Balkan states with traditionally pro-western orientation – Greece and Turkey – face some difficulties in their economic development.

It is, therefore, a logical assumption that in the troubled aftermath of the Cold War, integration in the security field must take precedence. Despite the delicate character of this sphere, some opportunities here are easier to materialize than those in the economic field. Early integration of the post-communist Balkan states into the Euro-Atlantic military and political structures could not possibly answer all the challenges facing the Balkans, but it would provide them with greater stability and give an impetus to regional cooperation and to the shaping of the new order in the Balkans.

The premises of the new order

Freed from the restrictions of the Cold War, the Balkan countries have gained more room for manoeuvre and can employ their diplomatic skills in their own national interests.

On the whole this foreign policy 'renaissance' will have a positive impact on the formation of a new Balkan order; in this respect, however, the Balkan states must be helped by the EU, NATO and the international community. What is needed is greater participation by Balkan states in the process of discussion, consultation and in certain instances decision-taking on Balkan problems. One could hardly question the fact that the Balkan states have not been seriously consulted over the problems of the post-Yugoslav settlement, recognition of the new states, the peace negotiations, sanctions, etc. It appears to us that this is the only sound manner in which to respect the interests of these states and to guarantee their cooperation with measures taken by the world community.[33]

Otherwise, local observers may become confirmed in their perception that the Balkan states face relative geopolitical isolation, having been more closely associated with European politics during the bipolar era than they are now now. Analysts are describing this somewhat paradoxical phenomenon as the 're-Balkanization' of the Balkans.

One of the important elements in establishing a new order is the efforts of those states in the region not involved in the Yugoslav war to enhance their military security. The former Soviet allies, Romania and Bulgaria, are gradually liberating themselves from their dependence on Moscow and reorientating themselves towards the leading western countries (in the case of Bulgaria, mainly towards the United States). Of course, one should not forget the necessity of a new balancing effort towards Moscow.

In sharp contrast are the efforts of Greece and Turkey to modernize their armies in the framework of the Vienna agreements.[34] This fact is the more disturbing, if one bears in mind that in addition to their old disputes, these two countries have close ties with the warring sides in the Bosnia war. The anxiety of states like Bulgaria, which had to cut down their military arsenals under the same agreements – a quite inappropriate measure in view of the recent changes in the security situation – is only too natural. As long as any revision of these agreements is unlikely some form of regulation of the rearmament of Greece and Turkey is in the interest of Balkan security.

A new order is unthinkable without active economic cooperation in the Balkans. Here one may signal the unfolding of a process of 'positive re-Balkanization' in the economies of Romania, Bulgaria, Greece, Turkey, Albania and Macedonia. Since 1991, the mutual trade of these countries has overcome the recession during the troubled period from 1989 to 1990 and in a number of cases has even exceeded the pre-crisis peaks.[35]

This has to be qualified by the consideration that both in the period before 1989 and nowadays the mutual trade of the Balkan countries is only a negligible part of their foreign trade. A serious impediment to the development of regional economic cooperation is the fact that these countries can exchange only mediocre-quality goods. Therefore, they tend to give priority to developing their ties with more dynamic markets and sources of capital in western Europe. Nevertheless, even under these conditions the relative revival of economic exchange is a positive factor for the stabilization of regional relations.

The new regional agenda

Two approaches to the new Balkan agenda can be discerned among the countries in the region.

One is the 'wait and see' approach. Here the main argument is that stabilization in the Balkans and regional and European integration are possible only after the resolution of the post-Yugoslav crisis. Since the Balkan states cannot achieve this on their own, they have to wait for the international institutions and the leading world powers to find solutions.

The other approach is a hybrid one, combining 'wait and see' with 'relying on oneself'. Its protagonists claim that the international community was ineffective in checking the 'Lebanization' of former Yugoslavia and the probable long-term division of the Balkans into hostile axes and religious areas, related to great powers. Another claim is that the threat of the growing economic isolation of central and eastern Europe still exists. The worst-case scenario is the widening of the conflict and the redrawing of the political map of the peninsula, thus postponing a new Balkan order for the foreseeable future.

On this latter approach, the mediation and peacekeeping efforts of America, the European Community, Russia and the international institutions should be welcome, but should be complemented by a coordinated Balkan policy. Such a policy must be the result of a more positive interaction of the Balkan states and societies in the fields of economy, politics, security, and cultural/religious and ethnic relations.

The implementation of this goal requires the use of three basic tools at the state/society level, which have not yet been exhausted. These are the intensification of bilateral contacts; the revival of the all-Balkan political process and its positive experience dating from the period of 1988–90;[36] and careful progress in implementing the initiative of the Black Sea Economic Cooperation in spite of present and future obstacles.[37]

Of particular importance is the ability of the Balkan peoples to find and propose a suitable formula for amending the ethno/religious logic, which has been instrumental in the emergence of some odd and unviable entities. What is needed is a new consensus, which must signal the transition from an ethnic/religious logic (which has already fulfilled its role) towards the stabilization of state borders and of states which are capable of guaranteeing the human rights of the population regardless of their ethnic composition.

Conclusion

The prevailing and seemingly paradoxical concern of the Balkan nations is to recreate a new regional order based on the nation-state principle, while sharing the readiness to surrender some of their sovereignty to the institutions of united Europe and to be integrated into a future Euro-Atlantic security zone.

A mild form of civic nationalism based on the recognition of multi-ethnic realities is thus becoming a necessary part of their new Europeanization. However, reconciling these two trends is possible only if the post-communist countries in the region are supported by the EU and NATO in their quest for European identity and stability. If these peoples feel abandoned by Europe, nationalist isolationism and regional revanchism are likely to gain the upper hand. Therefore, a stable and democratic Balkan order could be conceived as an integral part of the process of unification of Europe.

Such an order should be based on a civilized approach by the countries in the region to the 'national question'. This presupposes that a compromise can be reached between the civic and the ethnic elements of the state, with the accent on territorial integrity and security. What is needed is real joint exercising of national sovereignty by different ethnic groups. This is the way to prevent the minorities – ethnic and religious – striving to achieve the highest territorial status for the regions in which they live. These regions will become an ordinary geographical component of the state.

A constructive attitude by ethnic groups in asserting their common civic rights presupposes the strengthening of their sovereign states. This will be helpful in avoiding conflicts, which may be caused by maximalistic ethnic pretensions. Simultaneously, a civilized solution of the 'national question' requires that states respect the national interests of neighbouring countries as a prerequisite for the realization of their own interests. This implies mutual renunciation of territorial claims and of any intention to modify existing borders by force.

Notes

1. *Foreign Affairs*, vol. 71, no. 4, Autumn 1992, p. 67.
2. For a competent study of nationalism in the post-communist states, see *Journal of Democracy*, October 1992, pp. 17–21.
3. The seriousness of the impact of such 'self-flagellating' attitudes on the public in the post-communist countries, including Russia, had been

overlooked by western observers. In Bulgaria, for example, the extent of local 'unpatriotism' is such that the Municipality of Sofia had to impose fines on shop owners who refused to inscribe the names of their localities in Bulgarian, preferring instead to use Latin alphabet and English words.

4. The concept of 'Romistrion' has as its ultimate end the trans-historical unification of all Romanians within the boundaries of a unified national state. This embraces the claims of Romania to Bessarabia, Northern Boukovina, Banat and Southern Dobrudja, i.e. it will imply revisions of almost all of Romania's neighbouring countries' territories. See: Krassimira Naumova, *Natsionalnijat vapros, maltsinstvenite problemi i etnicheskite konflikti v Romania*, Sofia, 1993, p. 25.

5. Recently Tirana's expansionism has been encouraged by the highly publicized CIA assessment of the situation in the Balkans. With the usual American high-handedness this report validates the possibility of Albania's expanding to include Kosovo and even some parts of Macedonia. *Democratsia*, Sofia, 23 December 1993.

6. According to the leader of radical Serb nationalists Vojislav Šešelj, Macedonia has to be divided, with its eastern part going to Bulgaria. Similar views have been voiced by Mr Zhirinovsky during his bombastic visit to Bulgaria, at the end of which the leader of the extremists in the Russian Duma was declared *persona non grata* by the authorities in Sofia. See *Standart*, Sofia, 30 December 1993.

7. *Politique internationale*, no. 60, 1993, p. 132; *Duma*, Sofia, 20 September 1993.

8. However, one should not entirely put the blame for racism and xenophobia respectively on Romanian and Bulgarian majorities, ignoring such facts as the soaring crime rate among the local Gypsies and the close links between some circles of the Arab community in Bulgaria and the Middle East branches of drug and arms traffic.

9. For a Croat assessment of these events, see: *Balkan Forum*, Skopje, vol. 1, no. 4, September 1993, pp. 25–48.

10. Geopolitically the fact that Montenegro joined Serbia eliminated the danger of Belgrade being cut off from the Adriatic and therefore left without a sea outlet.

11. This step, however, was perceived to be largely symbolic and did not reduce the existing military imbalances.

12. The initiative for the Black Sea Economic Cooperation includes Albania, Armenia, Azerbaijan, Bulgaria, Georgia, Greece, Moldova, Romania, Russia, Turkey, Ukraine.

13. There is another opinion – that of solidarity ties between two identical minorities living in neighbouring states. For example, the Albanians in Macedonia are linking their future with that of Kosovo. See: *Aspekti na etnokulturnata situatsija v Bulgaria i na Balkanite*, Sofia, 1992, p. 158.

14. *Kathimerini*, Athens, 7 April 1992.

15. *Politique internationale*, no. 60, 1993, p. 135.

16. *Duma*, Sofia, 16 January 1992.

17. Opinion polls revealed recently that the Bulgarian public opposes the idea of 'Greater Bulgaria' and shares a positive attitude towards Macedonia. See *Kontinent*, Sofia, 30 December 1993.
18. *Nova Makedonija*, Skopje, 2 February 1992.
19. *Duma*, Sofia, 22 September 1993.
20. Pierre Hassner sees here a 'return to great migrations', which constitute one of the most dramatic phenomena of the current period. See: *Survival*, vol. 35, no. 2, Summer 1993, p. 52.
21. The first step towards the substitution of religious by ethnic self-identification on the part of the Bosnian Muslims was made back in 1961, when Belgrade introduced the notion of 'Muslims in the ethnic sense'. See: *Balkan Forum*, Skopje, September 1993, p. 180.
22. The impact of this phenomenon had been felt even by the Muslim Bulgarians – the so-called Pomaks (to be distinguished from the ethnic Turks and from the Gypsy Muslims in the country). The war in Bosnia and Muslim self-determination there encouraged them to raise demands for their recognition as a separate ethnic group.
23. In his speech to the General Assembly of the UN in October 1993, the Bulgarian president Zhelev evaluated the losses of his country resulting from the sanctions at about $3.5 billion until the end of 1993. See: *24 Chassa*, Sofia, 6 October 1993.
24. *Europa Archiv*, 2, 1992, pp. 37–8.
25. *Kultura*, Sofia, no. 25, 18 June 1993.
26. *Foreign Affairs*, vol. 71, no. 4, Autumn 1992, p. 98.
27. *International Herald Tribune*, 1 October 1993.
28. As was mentioned earlier the present Balkan crisis constitutes a deep revision of the Yalta and Versailles regional orders. Even the principles of sovereignty, territoriality and the European system shaped at Westphalia (1648) and further developed at Utrecht (1713) have been shaken. See: *Survival*, vol. 35, no. 2, Summer 1993, p. 57. At the same time, the religious state identity legitimized in Augsburg (1555) is experiencing a surprising revival, in addition to the syndrome according to which the national fate is sealed by the influential states, which was the basis of the 'concert' of the Great Powers in Vienna (1815).
29. A statement to this effect was recently made by the Belgian foreign minister Willi Klaas. See: *24 Chassa*, Sofia, 27 September 1993.
30. *Survival*, vol. 35, no. 2, Summer 1993, p. 57.
31. Willem van Eekelen, A speech delivered to the International Workshop 'Civilian Oversight of Security Policy', Bratislava, 13 September 1993, pp. 5–6.
32. *24 Chassa*, Sofia, 21 September 1993.
33. A good example of what should be possibly done, is the proposal of the Bulgarian president Zhelev that a conference on the sanctions and ways to compensate the losses of third countries should be held in Sofia. See: *Demokratsiaja*, Sofia, 6 October 1993.
34. *Standart*, Sofia, 5 October 1993.
35. *Balkanite pred izbor*, Sofia, 1993, pp. 104–7.

36. The multilateral political dialogue in the Balkans dates from the 1960s. It entered its active phase with the two meetings at ministerial level in Belgrade (24–26 February 1988) and in Tirana (24–25 October 1990). Both were attended by ministers from Albania, Bulgaria, Greece, Romania, Turkey and Yugoslavia. Another summit was under preparation but was postponed indefinitely because of the Yugoslav crisis.

37. Under the initiative of Turkey, the beginning of the Black Sea Economic Cooperation was set by the Declaration signed at the Istanbul Summit of presidents and prime ministers of the 11 participating states in June 1992. To date, four meetings of the BSEC foreign ministers have taken place. The initiative has importance as a forum for consultations, coordination of interests and implementation of joint projects. However, the differences of the political strategies of the participating states, the relatively low level of economic development and the common urge to seek strategic economic partners outside the region seriously hamper its speedy transformation into an 'integrational community'.

5

Russia and the CIS

Andrei Zagorski

Russia and Europe

The relationship between Russia and Europe has never been an easy one. The Cold War period was not unique in this respect, nor is the present time, when western strategic planners are still calculating worst-case scenarios on the basis of 'residual' threat (or risk) assessments, which include the possibility of Russia reversing course and entering into a new hostile relationship with the West. Current debates on Russia and Europe explicitly or implicitly recall the historical context in which Russia's place in Europe has always been somewhat ambiguous.

The historical background

As many scholars have pointed out, Russia has belonged to European civilization at least from the time of the Christian conversion.[1] Until the Mongol period (in the thirteenth to fifteenth centuries) patterns of social development in Russia were similar to those of European nations. A third class was gradually forming in cities which provided the basis for the emergence of civil society. However, the irruption of the Golden Horde arrested this development. Cities lost their autonomy and the emerging third class disappeared. As a consequence, the predominant pattern in Russia became the type of traditional society often referred to as the 'Asiatic state', one of whose characteristics was the lack of a civil society.

Attempts to develop Russia as a major European power started in the sixteenth century with Ivan IV's largely unsuccessful efforts to break through to European seas in the south and the north. Peter I's more energetic policies of Europeanization in the late seventeenth and early eighteenth centuries finally resulted in Russia's emergence as one of the major European powers. However, a retrospective analysis of Europe-oriented reform efforts in Russia reveals deep resentments against western culture deriving from the perspective 'that Western culture is deeply corruptive of the Russian character and culture, that Western Catholicism and later materialism, if allowed free rein, would pollute the springs of Russian idealism and destroy the Russian state'.[2] Historical analysis leads Neil MacFarlaine to conclude:

> . . . there appears to exist in Russian history and culture a kind of attraction/repulsion syndrome with regard to Europe, a deep sense of cultural discomfort with European influence. Russia sought to attract and take advantage of Western technology and knowledge in order to catch up the time lost under Mongol suzerainty. Many Russians were deeply attracted by Western values and culture and sought to lay Russian society open to their curative impact. Yet Russian culture displays also a sense of deep difference from the West, superiority to Western materialism, a fear of being inundated and destroyed by its cultural influences, and a frequently xenophobic reaction to the cultural threat from Europe.[3]

Russian history has witnessed periods of European orientation (mainly during times of reform) followed by periods of reaction, self-isolation and self-identification as something rather distinct from Europe. Both in the West and in Russia this ambiguous inheritance promoted the perception that Russia never truly belonged to Europe. In the West, this became explicit in Marquise Astolf de Custine's *La Russie en 1839*, which picturesquely described the superficiality of Russia's European pretensions.

Russia's geographical position and history as a major Euro-Asian power have resulted in controversial interpretations of Russia's 'historic mission' in global politics – as the bearer of a civilization with Byzantine and Greek Orthodox roots, distinct from the Roman origins of most European nations. It has again become legitimate to refer to Russia as a unique and self-sufficient civilization. Many Russian authors now imply that Russia has never been part of the European civilization and, therefore, does not belong to it. They suggest that there is no demand for Russia to 'return' to Europe.[4] Thus, the nineteenth-century debate between the 'westernizers' and 'slavophiles' has reopened. The 'Eurasianist' school has stressed not the Slav ethnicity of the Russian nation, but instead its mainly Byzantine heritage – a mixture of ethnic, cultural and confessional roots, which, as the Eurasianists state, was neither entirely European nor entirely Asian.[5]

The reopening of this debate has given way to disputes over the location of Russia among world civilizations and to diverging interpretations of Gorbachev's 'new political thinking'. Was this not merely one of the periods of reform accompanied by a stronger European orientation, inevitably to be followed by another period of self-isolation and concentration on rediscovering Russia's distinct identity and mission?

Contemporary foreign policy discourses

Current foreign policy debates in Russia, starting from early 1992, reveal various diverging discourses.[6]

The *'Atlanticist' perspective*[7] regards establishing partnership or even alliance relations with major western countries as the priority task after the end of the Cold War. Efforts in this direction were most explicit early in 1992 when Russian diplomacy sought to get the new relationship reflected in the documents signed with western countries. One of the main points common to Russian 'Atlanticists' is the aim of integrating the reforming Russian economy into world markets and ensuring Russia's involvement in major western institutions. In particular, this implied seeking Russia's admission to the Group of Seven. Focusing on developing the most beneficial environment or domestic reforms, some 'Atlanticists'[8] emphasized that if Russia did not succeed in joining the core of the world economy, it would move even further into the periphery.

The *'Eurasianist' perspective* denies the necessity of giving priority to partnership with the West. It regards 'westernizing' Russia as impossible and considers democratic and market institutions inapplicable to Russia in their western form. This perspective gives priority to consolidating the Commonwealth of Independent States (CIS) as an area of vital geopolitical interest to Russia, and puts greater emphasis on relations with the eastern states.[9] It regards it as Russia's special mission to build a bridge between the western and the eastern civilizations while remaining distinct from both. This discourse also tends to emphasize specific Russian interests as opposed to those of the West. In its extreme forms, the 'Eurasianist' perspective insists on the inherent incompatibility between the West and Russia resulting in permanent confrontation.[10]

Moderate versions of 'Eurasianism', while rejecting a western orientation for Russian politics, seek to develop a balance in relations with the West and the eastern and southern powers. They emphasize the aim of developing Russia as a regional great power in both Europe and Asia.[11]

The *'neo-anti-imperialist' perspective*[12] mainly reflects the neo-communist forces in Russia. It departs from the assumption that after the end of the Cold War and the demise of the Soviet Union the world has become unipolar, with the USA imposing its will on other nations. In the view of the neo-anti-imperialists, this US hegemony is the cause of the destabilization. The consequence drawn appears rather simple: Russia and China and other 'anti-imperialist' forces should form a coalition of countries as a counterweight to the USA. This perspective implies a restoration of global confrontation.

Although the 'Atlanticist' and the 'Eurasianist' perspectives are usually regarded as the two alternative mainstreams in Russian politics, the real state of affairs appears more complex. Opinion polls of the Russian elites conducted early in 1993[13] indicate that the 'Atlanticist' and the 'neo-anti-imperialist' discourses are the extreme positions with the 'Eurasianist' perspective representing a rather eclectic 'centrist' grey area. One-third of the Russian elite supported the statement that Russia should reassume the role of the Former Soviet Union (FSU) and oppose US hegemonic policies. Two-thirds of those polled gave priority to joining the community of western states and to absorbing western values. At the same time, however, three-quarters of those polled were prepared to support the 'Eurasianist' thesis that Russia should seek to implement its 'historic mission' of bridging the western and the eastern civilizations. That means that large parts of the Russian elite could identify with elements of both discourses at the same time.

That 'Atlanticism' and 'neo-anti-imperialism' are on the poles of elite opinion and the 'Eurasianist' perspective is in the centre is clearly revealed in the breakdown of the responses of various groups. The 'neo-anti-imperialist' perspective found the strongest support among the leaders of communist parties (56 per cent) and in the military establishment (50 per cent).[14] A majority of the same groups rejected the 'Atlanticist' thesis that Russia needs to join the community of western states (76 per cent and 66 per cent respectively).

The 'Atlanticist' perspective, on the other hand, is mainly supported by the new entrepreneurs and leaders of the non-communist parties (both 80 per cent), by artists (76 per cent), by figures from the mass media (72 per cent), and by managers of state enterprises and representatives of the executive branch (both 74 per

Table 5.1: Countries mentioned as Russian foreign policy priorities in Russian elite polls (percentage of those polled)

	July 1992	February 1993
Newly Independent States	82	44
USA	44	38
Germany	23	23
Western Europe (without Germany)	21	13
Eastern Europe	12	10
Japan	11	24
China	4	27

Source: see note 13.

cent). The majority of these groups reject the idea of restarting confrontation with the United States. It is also worth mentioning that it is the new entrepreneurs who most vigorously defend the applicability of western-type economic and social institutions to Russia, support Russia's integration into world markets, and favour developing a new relationship with western states.[15]

At the same time polls conducted in January 1993 revealed majority support for the 'Eurasianist' perspective in *all* groups of the Russian elite: leaders of the communist parties and military establishment (both 92 per cent), new entrepreneurs (82 per cent), members of the executive branch (70 per cent), leaders of non-communist parties (68 per cent), figures in the mass media (64 per cent), managers of state enterprises (60 per cent), and artists (52 per cent). The 'centrist' character of the idea of achieving a balance between a European (western) and Asian orientation, is also revealed in the ranking of the various countries (or groups of countries) within the Russian elite (see Table 5.1).

These figures point to the conclusion that the 'Eurasianist' perspective is not an alternative to the 'Atlanticist' discourse but merely an eclectic basis for an eventual 'centrist' Russian foreign policy that has been gradually taking shape since 1993. In April 1993, the Russian Security Council approved the foreign policy guidelines[16] after various drafts prepared by the foreign ministry had been discussed for about a year.[17] The final version of the guidelines produced in consultation with relevant government agencies was a compromise between the 'Atlanticist' tone of the initial draft and the mainly 'Eurasianist' criticisms that were levelled against it. On the one hand, the guidelines were oriented towards achieving partnership relations with single western countries and institutions, as well as entering the emerging political and economic space of Europe with the EC at its core. On the other hand, the guidelines indirectly addressed the western military potential as a challenge for Russia, as did the 'basic provisions of the military doctrine' approved by the Security Council on 2 November 1993. The foreign policy guidelines also focused on maintaining the integrity of the FSU and regarded attempts by other countries to interfere in the region as hostile actions.

The adoption of Russian foreign policy guidelines in April 1993 did not put an end to the debate in Moscow. Nevertheless, it marked a step toward an uneasy consensus around a 'centrist' foreign policy. It is also clear that, given the political and intellectual heterogeneity of the 'Eurasianist' perspective, any particular shape of 'centrist' policy would be determined by the balance of power between various groups in the Russian elite.

The immediate realities

While the foreign policy debate in Russia reveals intellectual disengagement from Europe at least in parts of the Russian elite, this trend is paralleled by a geographic and political disengagement from Europe as well.

Geographic disengagement

As various authors have pointed out,[18] one of the consequences of the breakup of the Soviet Union has been to increase the geographic distance between Russia and Europe, which are now separated by a number of the Newly Independent States. Russia has lost most of the FSU's direct transport links to Europe. The major trade outlets in the Baltic Sea were lost to the Baltic states – the new harbour of Tallinn, and port facilities in Riga, Ventspils and Klaipeda; the Latvian trade fleet inherited almost all of the refrigerators, as well as ships for the transportation of gas and oil of the FSU in this geographic area; and in the Black Sea, Russia lost access to all ports except Novorossiysk, whose capacity is clearly underdeveloped.

As a result, Russia finds itself in a rather unfavourable situation with respect to maintaining sea connections with Europe. Russian ships can process no more than half of the goods to be shipped. The yearly capacity of Russian ports amounts to 163 million tons while the demand amounts to 260 million tons.[19] Using the former Soviet ports, especially those in the Baltic, makes the connections with Europe rather expensive and disadvantageous. Land connections with Europe are similarly restricted and depend on relations with the western neighbours (Ukraine, Belarus, the Baltic states), with most of which Russia has political disputes.

The importance of restoring communications with Europe was recognized at an early stage. A programme developed by the Russian ministry of transportation provides for the modernization and development of the ports of Arkhangelsk, Murmansk, St Petersburg and Kaliningrad in the northern seas, and of Novorossiysk and Tuapse in the Black Sea. It also provides for the construction of a new port close to Novorossiysk on the Black Sea, and of two new ports in the Baltic Sea. The programme provides for an increase in the volume of foreign trade through Russian ports of 35 per cent by the year 2000.[20] Yet even this moderate target appears hardly realistic taking into account the huge budget deficit and the government's lack of resources.

At the same time, Russia is trying to reduce its dependence on communications via Ukraine and the Baltic states. It is exploring new sea routes for shipping oil to Europe from Novorossiysk to the Mediterranean, though this has caused tensions with Turkey, which is seeking to restrict that kind of transit through its channels.[21] With a similar intent, President Boris Yeltsin signed an agreement on the construction of a pipeline via Poland during his visit to Warsaw in August 1993.[22]

In its extreme form, the perception that Russia has been thrown out of Europe into the sixteenth century results in demands that Russia should uphold its geopolitical interests by restoring its strategic positions in the Baltic and the Black Seas, and returning to the *status quo ante* the Crimean war of the mid-nineteenth century.[23]

Political disengagement

Although maintaining connections with Europe is perceived as an important goal, developments within Russia and the FSU strengthen the trend towards a political disengagement of Russia from Europe. Three factors are most relevant in this respect, although their impact on Russia's European connections appears rather complex and contradictory. These are:

- uncertain domestic developments in Russia;
- regionalization within Russia; and
- developments within the CIS.

Uncertain domestic developments

In late 1991 and early 1992 there was a widespread expectation that, after the demise of the Soviet Union, Russia would take a lead in implementing radical economic and political reforms. The initial measures taken by the government appeared promising, although they caused greater social and political tensions. The two years of reforms have made the departure from the previous dirigiste economic system irreversible. However, expectations of a rapid and thoroughgoing market reform proved exaggerated, as did those of a democratic transformation, a radical departure from the Soviet foreign policy heritage and reshaped relations with the West.

It appeared difficult if not impossible to implement a consistent reform policy in Russia.[24] Domestic constraints postponed optimal economic decisions. Since the social costs of the reform were not only an important factor of domestic stability but also an argument of the opposition, the government was permanently forced to make concessions running contrary to the logic of the economic measures taken. Another obstacle was the lobbying of interest groups, especially the military industrial complex, resulting in continued subsidies to inefficient state enterprises as well as the failure of conversion. The burden of military expenditures contributed to the state budget deficit. This political manoeuvring left little space for real reforms.

The situation was aggravated by the power struggle within and between the new Russian elites. For a long time the power struggle between President Boris Yeltsin and the leadership of the Supreme Soviet (the former Parliament) consumed most of the energy of the elites. It was often associated with the controversy between those promoting the reforms (the president) and those opposing them and favouring a restoration of a quasi-communist rule (the parliament).

Confrontation between the president and the former Supreme Soviet, resulting in hundreds of casualties in early October 1993, revealed disagreements on various issues including foreign policy. The parliament was much more sceptical with respect to the western assistance to Russia.[25] Disagreements also arose with respect to assessing the role and importance of links to specific European institutions, for example NATO and the Council of Europe.

However, in most cases, these disagreements were not so much about substance as about the domestic power struggle. Generally, it did not appear crucial which political group exercised power in Moscow (with the exception of the extreme neo-communist or nationalist forces who rejected the idea of market reforms and rapprochement with the West). Most of the political forces in Russia would inevitably be exposed to domestic political pressures and economic constraints as well as to the necessity to continue economic reforms and to cooperate with the West. 'Centrist' politicians can be expected to avoid radicalism, and to maintain a more or less authoritarian political regime.

The real background to the controversies in Moscow was not a battle for or against reforms. It was a classic power struggle between the new elites over the exercise of power, the distribution of property, and control over the mass media and the military forces. This implies that the victory of President Boris Yeltsin over the Supreme Soviet in the dramatic confrontation of September–October 1993 did not radically change the pattern of Russian politics, either domestically or abroad. Nor does it imply an end to political controversy in Russia since new axes of political struggle have appeared to replace the old ones. It is most likely that this struggle will be conducted in the context of a more authoritarian regime than before and in a situation of greater uncertainty over Russia's democratic prospects. These conclusions were largely confirmed by the parliamentary elections of 12 December 1993. Their outcome – no clear majority in the parliament, and surprising success for the 'national-patriotic' forces – proved both that the extreme parties could not win the election and that the dissolution of the former parliament had not removed political obstacles to radical reforms.

Concentration on domestic issues is likely to continue to prevail, adding to the estrangement of Russia from European politics.

Regionalization of Russia

The role of national formations or regions inside Russia became increasingly evident by 1991 when some 'subjects' of the Federation began to claim sovereign status (like Tatarstan) or even independence (like Chechnya). All through 1992 and 1993 the trend towards greater regional economic autonomy intensified. Even ethnically Russian regions began claiming greater political autonomy and, in 1993, started adopting their own 'constitutions'.

The political crisis in Moscow in September–October 1993 strengthened regionalism still more. This could be seen not only in the renewed bargaining with the 'central' authority over the distribution of competences but also in the establishment of a new 'party of regions' in October 1993, headed by Sergey Shakhray. The new Constitution adopted by a referendum on 12 December 1993 as well as the make-up of the new parliament provide the subjects of the Russian Federation as well as the regions, at least implicitly, with a rather greater leverage in Russian politics.

Most of the alarmist warnings[26] concerning the eventual disintegration of Russia appear, however, to be exaggerated. Though a proliferation of the secessionist syndrome in some peripheral regions of Russia cannot be excluded, this is unlikely to lead toward a complete dissolution of Russia. Instead, greater regionalization of Russia appears a more likely prospect.

One of the eventual consequences could be an even deeper and more prolonged concentration of Russia on itself, with the issue of territorial integrity and domestic consolidation taking the utmost political priority. This would imply the need to reconcile the diverging interests of regions which not only have different ethnic, national, cultural or religious backgrounds but also different geographic orientations.

Some Russian experts expect the 'genuine Russia' (or its 'European core', as Vladimir Korovkin puts it) to have a greater European orientation, as a result of a 'confederalization' of Russia.[27] Though the consequences of regionalization remain uncertain, this prospect of a 'purer' European Russia as a result of fragmentation seems both unlikely and unwelcome, in view of its implications for the 'European core' of Russia itself, and the rest of Europe. The disappearance of a 'big Russia' would make it an irrelevant element in European politics with uncertain prospects for economic and political revival; and, although the nightmare of the breakup of a nuclear superpower would focus the attention of other nations on the resulting proliferation problems, the splintering of Russia into a dozen loosely connected regions would trigger unpredictable and unmanageable turbulence in the whole post-Soviet Euro-Asian space.

Maintaining the integrity of the FSU

Consolidating the CIS appears to have become one of the major preoccupations of Russian foreign policy. The foreign policy guidelines of April 1993 explicitly gave priority to this objective. The former Soviet Union is regarded as an area of vital interest to Russia where the influence of 'third countries' would not be welcome. 'Reintegrating' the Newly Independent States, in particular under the umbrella of the CIS, is considered a prime objective.

In 1992, developments within the CIS revealed the strength of the centrifugal trends. Most of the European republics of the FSU demonstrated a European orientation and appeared reluctant to support any institutionalization of the CIS.[28] The Commonwealth was losing members (of the 11 initial members Azerbaijan and Moldova refused to ratify the basic agreements on the CIS). Russia established closer cooperation with the Central Asian states (except for Turkmenistan) as well as with Armenia. This pointed to the development of a kind of Russian-Central Asian military-political alliance supported by bilateral agreements on mutual assistance.[29] A stronger Asian orientation of Russian politics appeared to be developing as a result, as some Russian experts had foreseen.[30]

In this period, Russia was pursuing a moderate policy toward the CIS. Without explicitly pressing its partners, it was:

- keeping the CIS framework ready as an instrument for the eventual reintegration of the FSU, while avoiding *faits accomplis* that might prejudice this purpose; and
- promoting the development of the CIS at 'different speeds' in order to strengthen CIS institutions with the membership of even a few of the former republics, which could be expected to be joined later by others.

Developments in 1993, however, gave rise to expectations that, owing to the economic pressures, most of the former Soviet republics would come together within a stronger CIS, and Russian policy became noticeably firmer. In January 1993 the Charter of the CIS was approved by seven CIS states to enter into force one year later. Although three states (Ukraine, Moldova and Turkmenistan) rejected the idea of an institutionalized Commonwealth laid down in the Charter, in September 1993 Azerbaijan, under Geydar Aliev's rule, rejoined the CIS. Ukraine became more cooperative both in bilateral negotiations with Russia and within the collective CIS framework after having entered a severe economic and financial crisis. Belarus joined the CIS military command and the Collective Security Treaty. Georgia applied for CIS membership in October 1993 with the application being formally approved by the CIS summit meeting in December 1993.

This new trend within the Commonwealth reveals rather controversial developments in the post-Soviet space. Although the initial 'dissidents' within the CIS (especially Azerbaijan, Ukraine, Moldova and Turkmenistan) have certainly not given up their intention to consolidate their independence and decouple themselves from Russia, their economic and military dependence forces them to agree at least to a *modus vivendi* within the CIS. At the same time, developments in Europe may leave no other alternative especially for Ukraine. The failure of the idea of establishing a Europe-wide collective security framework on the basis of the CSCE has been paralleled by the emerging extension of the NATO collective defence system to several central European states. This trend certainly diminishes the relevance of subregional frameworks through which the Ukrainian leadership was seeking to get access to European institutions. The failure of the collective security project for Europe thus helps Russia to consolidate the post-Soviet space as a sphere of influence. Whatever trend prevails in the medium to long term, Russia's concentration on the CIS certainly implies relative political disengagement from Europe.

Reintegration or isolation?

The uneasy and ambiguous relationship between Russia and Europe creates uncertainties for policy-making and hinders the elaboration of optimal strategies on both sides. Although a general intention not to isolate Russia from various European frameworks can be recognized in the West, developments in Russia are provoking increasing scepticism. This ranges from disorientation 'because of the lack of pro-European rhetoric by the Yeltsin government and its seemingly less cooperative style' and because of the difficulty of coming to terms with 'the reborn Russia and an unaccountable or even strange elite',[31] to extreme visions along Samuel Huntington's lines of the forthcoming clash of civilizations.

The rationale of Russian integration in European structures

It seems premature to draw conclusions about the future of Russian-European relations since various options remain open, and the direction developments take will depend on the actions of both sides. However, it appears that the Russo-European relationship is entering a decisive stage, and some forthcoming decisions may bring about irreversible change. In particular, the prospect of NATO's extension to Central Europe and the reluctance of western countries to play a more active role in conflict resolution in the FSU, tacitly giving that role to Russia, might consolidate the FSU as an area of Russian influence. This may strengthen not only 'centrist' but also nationalist trends in Russian politics, thus increasing the uneasiness in the relations between Moscow and Europe. This development could also leave little space for European republics of the FSU to develop alternative strategies strengthening their independent and sovereign status.

In order to develop a realistic medium- to long-term policy, it is crucial to recognize the causes of the increasing scepticism and disappointment in the West. In particular, one could mention the following aspects:

- much of the scepticism in the West results from disappointment due to the lack of expected progress of both economic and political reforms in Russia. This disappointment has led to even greater irritation after the Russian elections of December 1993. Still, real progress should not be measured against over-expectations. It should be assumed that the most likely pattern in Russian politics would be gradual reforms, an evolution rather than a revolution;
- the West is not in a position to shape developments in Russia, which are mainly determined by internal dynamics. 'Most of the inputs will have to be generated from inside. Consequently, western policy can only influence at the margin';[32] and
- western support for Russian reforms cannot be regarded as ineffective since it has helped to sustain at least the verbal commitment of the Russian leaders to economic and democratic reforms. However, western policy can not be considered efficient as it has focused so much on individual leaders and did not pay sufficient attention to promoting sustainable social institutions which would lower the dependence of Russian reforms on the personal composition of the Russian government.[33]

In view of these points, one could think of developing at least a mid-term strategy of binding Russia into the network of European institutions. The most important rationale for this is that, whatever direction developments in Russia take, it will remain a major European nation – either as an uneasy great power 're-emerging' on the European scene after a period of self-absorption, or as a cooperative partner, 'compatible' with the European civilization. Even if the latter scenario does not materialize fully, it is worth developing a cautious strategy of involving Russia into the network of European institutions. Although hesitations in this respect are understandable, it should be recognized that granting a status in European institutions is not only a result of 'satisfactory' political development but also an important instrument to influence developments. Involving Russia in European institutions and playing a more active role in conflict management in the FSU would give additional impetus to democratic, market and Europe-oriented policies in Russia.

The task of developing a special mode of affiliation with the 'greater' Europe emerging from the west of the continent is explicitly laid down in the Russian foreign policy guidelines approved in April 1993. Furthermore, there are symptoms of increasing acknowledgment of the importance of relations with Europe. After critical discussions, the issue of developing Russo-European relations has been given a higher priority than relations with the USA in the final text of the guidelines. This was a change from what had been suggested in the foreign ministry's strategic paper submitted late in 1992. The main issue, however, remains the elaboration of a mutually accepted strategy of gradually involving Russia in existing European institutions.[34]

Principal criteria for Russian involvement in Europe

Although approaches on the issue diverge in Russia itself, it is commonly acknowledged as a vital interest that there be a place for Russia in the emerging European order, whatever it looks like. The issue is not only that it would be dangerous if Russia felt isolated, but also that the links of Russia to Europe and to the European institutions should be strengthened and institutionalized in order to generate additional incentives for a European orientation.

The process of elaborating options for institutionalizing Russo-European relations should ensure for Russia the role of an equal partner in shaping pan-European developments. Certainly, this should not imply a *droit de regard* over European developments, but merely a partnership in decision-making (or pre-decision-making) in institutions where Russia cannot or will not be fully integrated. At the same time, various forms of participation in or affiliation with European institutions can be envisaged.

Foreign Minister Andrei Kozyrev elaborated Russian foreign policy objectives with respect to Europe in a speech made at Chatham House in London, on 27 October 1993.[35] He suggested that Russia and its partners in the West should raise the level of their relations from a dialogue and selective cooperation to the joint development of a strategy for transforming the post-communist Europe into an area of cooperating democratic states.

Kozyrev made suggestions for joint actions in six specific areas, namely:

- increasing peace-keeping and peace-enforcement capability while reforming existing international instruments and combining their resources;
- establishing a strict hierarchy of political responsibility for peace-making and peace enforcement with the UN and the CSCE mandating the NACC, NATO, WEU and the CIS;
- assisting Russia in peace-keeping and peace enforcement in the FSU, in particular establishing a voluntary fund for that purpose, and cooperation with NATO in peace-keeping;
- developing the CSCE as a real regional organization capable of maintaining regional security and stability;
- preventing the emergence of a new nuclear power in Europe; and
- speeding up negotiations between the EC and Russia to remove limitations on Russian exports, admit Russia to western markets, and replace COCOM by another body reflecting changes in post-communist Europe.

For the time being, the CSCE remains the only European institution in which Russia is a fully-fledged participant. This explains much of the attention paid in Moscow to strengthening its institutions and structures. However, owing to the increasing scepticism with regard to the CSCE's capacity to manage various conflicts especially in the former Yugoslavia and in the FSU, and owing to the tendencies to depart from the consensus rule, the relevance of the CSCE for Russia can not be taken for granted in the future. It is necessary to seek additional ways to foster Russian participation in European developments.

Another European institution which Russia could join as a full member in the foreseeable future is the Council of Europe. Council of

Europe membership is regarded in Russia as an important 'badge of respectability', and the recent reluctance of the Council of Europe to admit Russia after the elections of December 1993 has caused much frustration in Moscow. However, despite its undoubted relevance in assisting and protecting democratic developments in the member states, the Council of Europe can be regarded as only a necessary but not a sufficient instrument for involving Russia in European developments as it does not cover several crucial areas of cooperation such as economic integration and security.

As for the EC and NATO, it is doubtful whether one should develop a strategy for the gradual integration of Russia into these bodies. Some Russian experts argue for this, but it seems unnecessary. It is crucial, though, to institutionalize political dialogue and cooperation with both institutions to enable Moscow to articulate its interests at a pre-decision-making stage. With the EC, the issue will be solved within the partnership agreement, which will provide a framework for regular high-level contacts similar to those established in the EC's relations with the USA since 1990. It remains to be seen whether this framework will be built up as a tool for genuine political dialogue.

Shaping relations with NATO appears a more difficult problem. Taking current developments into account, especially the possible enlargement of NATO to some central European states, the relevance of the North Atlantic Cooperation Council (NACC) could diminish in the foreseeable future. This raises the issue of establishing a new framework for direct political and military-political dialogue and cooperation between Russia and NATO.

The 'partnership for peace' concept approved by the NATO summit in Brussels on 10–11 January 1994 became an important tool for implementing this option, provided that both sides take it seriously. While developing cooperation and joint training, greater attention could be paid to joint training specifically for peace-keeping and peace-enforcement operations. This might gradually overcome the reluctance of Russian officials to be engaged in peace-keeping in the FSU together with other European institutions.

These suggestions for cooperation with European structures appear compatible with various scenarios of Russian re-emergence in Europe – both pessimistic and optimistic. Without prejudicing European developments, these solutions, if implemented seriously, would leave the door to Europe open for Russia and would provide some modest means of influencing Russian developments in a more optimistic direction.

Notes

1. See: Daniil Proektor, 'Mezhdu kholodnoy voynoy i budushchim' (Between the Cold War and the Future), *Nezavisimaya Gazeta*, Moscow, 28 May 1993.
2. S. Neil MacFarlaine, 'Russia and European Security', in Hans-Georg Ehrhart, Anna Kreikemeyer and Andrei Zagorski (eds), *The Former Soviet Union and European Security: Between Integration and Disintegration*, Baden-Baden, 1993, p. 25.
3. S. Neil MacFarlaine, 'Russia and European Security', p. 26.
4. See for example an early article by Elgiz Pozdnyakov, 'The Soviet Union: The Problem of Coming Back to European Civilization', *Paradigms*, 1991, Vol. 5, no. 1/2, pp. 45–6 or Boris Kapustin, 'Evropeyskaya i rossiyskaya tsivilizatsiya: proizoydet li ikh vstrecha?' (The European and the Russian Civilization: will their meeting take place?), *MEiMO*, Moscow, 1992, no. 4, pp. 43–50.
5. On this see, for example, Assen Ignatow, 'Der "Eurasismus" und die Suche nach einer neuen russischen Kulturidentität. Die Neubelebung des "Evrazijstvo"-Mythos', *Berichte des Bundesinstituts für ostwissenschaftliche und internationale Studien*, Köln, 1992, no. 15. Among the recent publications of the early Eurasianist texts see: Puti Evrazii (Roads of Eurasia), Moscow, 1992.
6. For more on this see Andrei Zagorski and Michael Lucas, 'Rossiya pered evropeyskim vyzovom' (The European Challenge for Russia), Moscow, 1993, pp. 41–74; Andrei Zagorski, 'Russlands Beziehungen zum "fernen" und "nahen" Ausland'. *Berichte des Bundesinstituts für ostwissenschaftliche und internationale Studien*, Köln, 1992, no. 46, pp. 18–23.
7. Both the 'Atlanticist' and the 'Eurasianist' perspectives obtained these labels in domestic discussions in Russia. Although these labels are not wholly adequate in our opinion, we use them since they have become common both in the Russian and in the western literature.
8. *After the Disintegration of the Soviet Union: Russia in a New World*, Report of the Centre of International Studies of MGIMO, Moscow, 1992.
9. For modern writings on this see, e.g.: *Mezhdunarodnaya Zhizn*, Moscow, 1992, no. 3–4, pp. 87–91, 107–110; Sergei Stankevich, 'Derzhava v poiskakh sebya' (The Great Power in Search of its Identity), *Nezavisimaya Gazeta*, Moscow, 28 March 1992; Natalya Narochnitskaya, 'The World Needs Russia as Russia', *Mezhdunarodnaya Zhizn*, Moscow, 1993, no. 8, pp. 143–6; Elgiz Pozdnyzkov, 'Russia is a Great Power', *Mezhdunarodnaya Zhizn*, Moscow, 1993, no. 1, pp. 7–17; Elgiz Pozdnyzkov, 'Russia Today and Tomorrow', *Mezhdunarodnaya Zhizn*, Moscow, 1993, no. 2, pp. 23–33; Konstantin Pleshakov, 'Russia's Mission. The Third Epoch', *Mezhdunarodnaya Zhizn*, Moscow, 1993, no. 1, pp. 21–30.
10. See, for example, Alexander Prokudin, 'Ne bogataya, no sil'naya' (Not rich but strong), *Dyen*, Moscow, 22–28 November 1992.

11. On this see, for example: Heinz Timmermann, 'Europapolitische Konzeptionen in Russland und ihre Vereinbarkeit mit dem europäischen Integrationsprozess', *Stand und Perspektiven des Deutsch-Russischen Verhältnisses*. Workshop 28–30.06.1993, Bonn, 1993, p. 77.

12. For more on this discourse see Andrei Zagorski and Michael Lucas, 'Rossiya pered evropeyskim vyzovom', pp. 71–4.

13. Here I refer to the polls conducted in 1993 by the public opinion service 'Vox Populi' (Professor Boris Grushin) at the request of the Moscow State Institute of International Relations (MGIMO). The findings of the series of polls conducted throughout 1993 are forthcoming in a special pamphlet to be printed by MGIMO in 1994.

14. Here and further in this article I refer to the polls conducted before the dissolution of the Russian parliament in September 1993 and the ban of the communist parties. Recent changes in the political scene in Moscow certainly would have produced changes to be revealed in the polls of late 1993.

15. See, for example, the statement of Khakamada, Secretary General, Party of Economic Freedom at the meeting of the Council on Russian Foreign Policy later in 1992 in *Mezhdunarodnaya Zhizn*, Moscow, 1993, no. 2, p. 10.

16. For a semi-official summary of the paper, see Vladislav Chernov, 'Natsionalnye Interesy Rossii i ugrosy dlya eye besobasnosty' (National Interests of Russia and its Security Challenges) in *Nezavisimaya Gazeta*, Moscow, 29 April 1993. Large parts of the paper are also reproduced in the article of the then secretary of the Security Council Evgeny Shaposhnikov 'O kontseptsii besopasnosti Rossii' (On Russia's Security Conception), *Mezhdunarodnaya Zhizn*, 1993, no. 9, pp. 5–15.

17. The draft officially submitted to the Security Council by the Russian Foreign Ministry was published in a special issue of *Diplomatichesky Vestnik* (The Diplomatic Herald), Moscow, in January 1993.

18. On this see, for example, Vladimir Razuvayev, 'Russia and the Post-Soviet Geopolitical Area', *Mezhdunarodnaya Zhizn*, Moscow, 1993, no. 6, pp. 126–34.

19. *Rossiyskiye Vesti*, Moscow, 10 September 1993.

20. Ibid.

21. See: *Nezavisimaya Gazeta*, Moscow, 25 May, 14 and 26 August 1993.

22. *Nezavisimaya Gazeta*, Moscow, 27 August 1993.

23. See: Natalya Narochnitskaya, 'Russia is Neither East Nor West. The World Needs it Precisely As Russia and it Should Stay that Way', *Mezhdunarodnaya Zhizn*, Moscow, 1993, no. 9, pp. 46–7.

24. See, for example, Andrei Zagorski, 'Strategic Dilemmas of Russian Reform Policies', forthcoming in the proceedings of the 1993 NATO Economics Colloquium.

25. See the statement of Ruslan Khasbulatov in *Rossiyskaya Gazeta*, Moscow, 22 May 1993.

26. See, for example: Alexandre Salmin, 'Disintegratiya Rossii?' (Desintegration of Russia?), *Nezavisimaya Gazeta*, Moscow, 10 December 1992.

27. Vladimir Korovkin, 'The CIS and European Interests of Russia', Hans-Georg Ehrhart, Anna Kreikemeyer and Andrei Zagorski (eds), *The Former Soviet Union and European Security*, pp. 52–3.
28. The most explicit case is Ukraine. See: 'Pro osnovni napryami zovnishn'oy politiki Ukraini' (On the guidelines of the foreign policy of Ukraine), *Golos Ukraini*, Kiev, 24 lipnya 1993. See also: Mikhail V. Kirsenko, 'Security-Political Aspects of the Relations with the EC from the Ukrainian Point of View', Hans-Georg Ehrhart, Anna Kreikemeyer and Andrei Zagorski (eds), *The Former Soviet Union and European Security*, pp. 73–81. On Belarusian orientation see, e.g., Vyzcheslav E. Paznyak, 'Security Aspects of Belarus's Policies Towards the CIS and Western Europe', in Hans-Georg Ehrhart, Anna Kreikemeyer and Andrei Zagorski (eds), *The Former Soviet Union and European Security*, pp. 91–100.
29. For more on this see: *Commonwealth of Independent States: Developments and Prospects*, Report of the Centre of International Studies of MGIMO, Moscow, 1992; Andrei V. Zagorski, 'Major Developments and Evolutions of the Commonwealth of Independent States', in Hans-Georg Ehrhart, Anna Kreikemeyer, and Andrei V. Zagorski (eds), *The Former Soviet Union and European Security*, pp. 144–52; Andrei Zagorski, 'The Commonwealth One Year Later', *Mezhdunarodnaya Zhizn*, 1993, no. 2, pp. 47–56.
30. See, for example: Dmitry Matsenov, 'Interesy i bezopasnost' Rossii v postsovetskuyu epokhu' (Russian Interests and Security in the Post-Soviet Era), *MEiMO*, Moscow, 1992, no. 4, p. 27.
31. Barbara Lippert, 'Questions and Scenarios on EC-CIS/Republics Relations', in Hans-Georg Ehrhart, Anna Kreikemeyer and Andrei Zagorski (eds), *The Former Soviet Union and European Security*, p. 131.
32. Hans-Georg Ehrhart, Anna Kreikemeyer, and Andrei V. Zagorski, 'Challenge and Choice', Hans-Georg Ehrhart, Anna Kreikemeyer, and Andrei Zagorski (eds), *The Former Soviet Union and European Security*, p. 269.
33. See, for example: Andrei Zagorski, 'Strategic Dilemmas of Russian Reform Policies'.
34. On various scenarios see, for example, Andrei Zagorski, Michael Lucas, Rossiya pered evropeyskim vyzovom, pp. 77–107; Andrei Zagorski, 'Russlands nationale Interessen und die Zukunft der europäischen Sicherheitsstrukturen', *Stand und Perspektiven des Deutsch-Russischen Verhältnisses*, S. 41–5.
35. For the text of the statement 'Let Europe Arise', see *Segodnya*, Moscow, 4 November 1993.

Part II

Prospects for the Wider Europe

6

Key Trends in the European Economy and Future Scenarios

Vincent Cable

Introduction

European economies, west and east, are in a state of uncertainty and flux. The experiment in transformation in the east is far from complete. Some of the key elements on the economic agenda of the European Community are subject to unresolved debate, such as: the next stage of monetary integration and economic policy coordination; the extent and pace of enlargement; appropriate policy responses to rising unemployment; and trade policy towards eastern Europe (and, despite the successful conclusion of the Uruguay Round, the rest of the world). This chapter cannot do justice to the many nuances of the economic policy debate covering such a wide field, but tries to sketch out the key economic trends.

With Europe subject to such major uncertainties, there is value in a scenario approach which explores the implications of some radically different, but plausible, archetypes of Europe's future. Three such are explored: 'fragmented Europe' – a serious loss of commitment to the integration process in the West and growing numbers of economic disputes among EU members and with eastern Europe; 'fortress Europe' – an accelerated move towards a more inward-looking but tightly integrated western Europe, in the face of perceived external threats; and 'wider Europe' – the emergence of a clearer and more positive strategy than at present for integrating the economies of western and eastern Europe.

Trends and driving forces

Deepening west European integration

West European economies are becoming more tightly integrated. Two sets of data show the influence of the integration process on trade flows. First, in 1957 when the Treaty of Rome was signed, 37 per cent of EU-12 exports were intra-EU; in 1970 the share had risen to 53 per cent; it remained virtually unchanged until 1985 but, since then, has risen to 60 per cent in 1991. Second, intra-EU trade has grown by 4.2 per cent per annum as opposed to 2.1 per cent for GDP growth and 1.1 per cent for exports outside the region (since 1980).

What these trends do not tell us is whether the growth of regional trade was generated by the Common Market (as opposed to liberalization in general and income growth) and whether intra-EU trade was generated by freer trade within the EU as opposed to discrimination against other partners (trade creation versus trade diversion). As to the first question, the evidence is mixed.[1] Regression analysis of UK-EU flows after 1973 does pick up an 'integration effect'.[2] On the other hand, the degree of integration now achieved is not greatly different from what would be predicted from mere proximity;[3] and the share of intra-regional trade in total EU trade is similar to what it was in 1870 before three European wars disrupted what could be called 'natural integration' between neighbours.[4] Overall, the EU has achieved economically what it set out to achieve politically: to bury the legacy of war. Moreover, it has restored the importance of neighbourly trade even in the face of improved global communications which make such trade less obviously advantageous. As to the second question, trade diversion, recent analysis confirms that the Community has been trade-creating in the industrial sector but trade-diverting in agriculture.[5]

The above trends are being modified by two Community policies: trade creation through the deepening of internal liberalization under the 1992 Single Market Programme and trade diversion through external trade policy tightening. The Single Market should have the effect of generating substantial trade creation with benefits (from scale and dynamic effects as well as static efficiency) that are variously estimated at 0.5 per cent of GDP, 6 per cent of GDP, and 1 per cent of GDP per annum.[6] Since the process is protracted, however, it will be a long time before we can assess its full significance both on trade flows and on incomes. There are also significant omissions from liberalization (e.g. telecoms and energy); long transitions – for aviation and customs free transport; difficulties in implementing changes like duty free shopping; continuing state aids; and continued restrictions on open public procurement which accounts for 15 per cent of EU GDP.

On the external front, there has been protectionist sabre-rattling and there are sectors (textiles) and countries (eastern Europe) where clearly identifiable barriers have been raised. But there is also evidence of growing market penetration by manufacturing imports from outside as well as inside the EU and, paradoxically, particularly rapid growth of penetration in some sectors where external trade barriers exist (textiles, clothing and footwear, motor vehicles, and electrical goods). Even in the field of anti-dumping policy, where the Community has been very active, the incidence of provisional duties is no higher than a decade ago and there is no clear trend to an increase in investigations. The agreement to introduce simple majority rather than qualified majority voting will, however, make anti-dumping measures easier to activate in the Council of Ministers.

The 1992 process, with the scrapping of national trade barriers under Article 115, has made access a little easier for non-EU suppliers, as has the simplification of procedures. But the effects are complex depending on the balance of 'levelling down and levelling up'.[7] The national quotas for Japanese car imports, for example, have been replaced by informal understandings which seem to be liberalizing but may not be in practice.[8]

The outcome of the Uruguay Round does suggest a commitment to liberalizing external trade policy, especially in relation to the one sector which, more than any other, has justifiably given the Community a protectionist reputation: agriculture. But there are also signals of a contrary nature; particularly the threats – from France – to pursue a more aggressive trade policy against 'low wage' economies.

Economic liberalization and transformation in eastern Europe

The end of communism in eastern Europe has had enormous implications. From the standpoint of this chapter there are two main trends to be assessed: the progress of eastern Europe in making the transition to market economies and the response of the EU to the emergence of states which are variously seen as clients, competitors and opportunities.

The evidence of economic transformation in eastern Europe is now clear. First, after a decline in GDP of not much less than 20 per cent, and much bigger falls in industrial production, output recovery is apparent in several countries – Poland, the Czech Republic, Hungary and Slovenia. Poland is growing briskly – perhaps by 5 per cent in 1993. The former USSR and Yugoslavia (except Slovenia), by contrast, are far from bottoming out. Second, consequent upon macro-economic stabilization, inflation is falling sharply in many countries in eastern Europe – though not yet in the ex-USSR or Slovakia. Unemployment rates are rising everywhere and are well into the teens, except in the Czech Republic.

Third, some longer-term structural changes are striking. By the end of 1992 the private sector accounted for 32 per cent of Polish industrial output – and a higher proportion of retail, construction, road haulage and agriculture. The private sector in Hungary then accounted for 37 per cent of GDP, and a fifth of industrial output. Even in Russia, Layard estimates that the private sector now accounts for 20 per cent of employment, and the privatization programme of Chubais was proceeding rapidly in 1993.

It would, however, be foolish to glamorize the process or to underestimate the problems still to be faced, not least in the former USSR and Yugoslavia where transformation has scarcely begun, outside of Slovenia, Estonia, Latvia and Russia. Despite stabilization, there is still double-digit inflation or worse. Throughout eastern Europe the necessary bankruptcy or retrenchment of state enterprises has yet to be fully felt by the labour force or absorbed by the banking system whose balance sheets are stuffed with worthless assets. The more sophisticated aspects of modern western capitalism – legal enforcement of property rights and trust in commercial transactions, competition policy, broad and deep capital markets, accepted systems of corporate governance, and advanced telecommunications and IT infrastructure – are still largely on the drawing board. The political underpinnings of economic reform are not fully secure, most obviously in Russia.

Some lessons have been learned. Radicalism pays. The Polish 'Big Bang' approach to stabilization has led to the earliest and strongest recovery in eastern Europe. The Czech voucher privatization scheme (and the Russian variant) seem to have worked, at least in broadening private ownership rapidly.

A further conclusion stems from the fact that the different paths taken by Poland, the Czech Republic and Hungary seem to have produced broadly similar profiles of recovery. In the early stages of transformation, what governments do may not be as important as getting out of the way, so long as they control the printing presses and maintain order. We shall probably now see more differentiation of experience with different approaches to the medium- and long-term policy issues: competition (phasing out subsidies; trade liberalization; currency policy; privatization); the regulation of competition as it affects financial institutions, services and labour markets, including the role of wages policy; and social safety nets and income distribution.

The process of economic integration with western Europe is proving no less problematic than domestic transformation. East European exports to the West were declining in 1993. Eastern Europe's shares of the EU's imports are still way below what they were in 1980, let alone what they could be in a 'normal' set of market-based trade relationships.[9] Several problems are short term: the recession in western Europe; a phasing out of loss-making exports; drought; and an uncompetitive exchange rate in Poland and Hungary. Potentially more serious is trade friction with western Europe. The Community has caved in to protectionist lobbies who have demanded special 'safeguard measures', especially for 'sensitive' items – mainly textiles, agriculture, steel and aluminium. Special quotas, tariffs, anti-dumping duties and health regulations have been deployed.

One of the most damaging (if unquantifiable) instruments is the threat of 'contingent protection'; between 40 per cent and 60 per cent of the exports of east and central Europe are potentially caught by EU barriers over and above the common external tariff.[10] After the Copenhagen Summit there is to be a more rapid phasing out of quotas and tariffs but the concessions are negligible in respect of contingent protection and in the sectors that matter: steel, textiles and agriculture.

Economic integration with the West is not solely a matter of trade. But there are reports of a drying up of flows of direct foreign investment in Hungary (by far the largest recipient). Political uncertainty, half-hearted privatization (e.g. in Hungary and Poland) and flagging exports to the West have all played a part in discouraging new inflows into eastern Europe. Seen from the admittedly poor vantage point of only three years experience, the prospects for a rapid and successful integration with the West of the economies of eastern Europe (let alone the Balkans and FSU) are very uncertain.

Economic liberalization within the West

A common thread in the EU Single Market and in market reform in the East is a liberalization revolution in economic ideas. There is widespread belief in the merits of competition, deregulation, and private ownership as the dominant mode of production. Liberalization still has a long way to run in the West.

First, privatization is no longer a British eccentricity but is becoming a major fact of life in France, Italy and Spain, and starting from a smaller public sector, Germany. Hitherto sensitive areas like telecoms, energy and airlines, where Community-wide liberalization has been held back by national state monopolies, are being opened up to competition. Public procurement barriers also diminish as state concerns go private.

Second, there has been a shift to less state intervention in industry. The Community is no longer keen to help 'lame ducks' and to 'pick winners'. State aids to manufacturing fell substantially at the end of the 1980s, especially in the UK, Spain, France and Greece, primarily for financial reasons. The Commission has reflected this shift in its 1990 policy paper, 'Industrial Policy in an Open and Competitive Environment'. The French attempt to introduce a stronger industry policy commitment into Maastricht largely failed. The 'Cresson clause' (Article 130) remains, but it is subject to unanimity rather than qualified majority voting and is prefaced by the statement: 'this title does not provide a basis for the introduction by the Community of any measures which may distort competition'.

Third, Community competition policy is promoting internal competition and not EU 'champions'. Articles 85 and 86 of the Rome Treaty, which prohibit, respectively, cartels and abuse of dominant monopoly positions, have been predominantly interpreted in a liberal sense; the De Havilland-Aerospatiale decision was a landmark case. German insistence that EU merger control be exclusively based on competition considerations is captured in the latest merger regulation (Article 2.3), though only very large mergers are considered by the Community.

Fourth, liberalization is driving Community policy, too, in respect of factor markets. The scrapping of restrictions on capital movements was largely completed in 1990 and, despite some temporary capital controls in Spain and Ireland, the principle of free capital flows is now entrenched (indeed, mandated by the Maastricht Treaty). Capital mobility has accelerated the freeing of the European market for financial services where cross-border establishment and cross-market securities investment rather than arm's-length trade are the norms.

The 'liberalization revolution' is, however, mostly absent in one sensitive area: labour markets. There is effective freedom of (private sector) labour movements within the EU, facilitated by the move to mutual recognition of national professional and vocational qualifications under the Single Market. But actual cross-border mobility is actually very low. When last counted (in 1985) other EU nationals were only 2.5 per cent of the German labour force, 1.9 per cent of the British and almost nil in Italy. There has, moreover, been a severe tightening of immigration controls on lower-cost labour from outside the EU. The lack of liberalism shows itself also in the debate over the Social Chapter. The argument that demand for labour might be related to its cost – direct and indirect – to the employer has not, until recently, penetrated Community thinking on labour markets. Prompted in part by British recalcitrance, however, the most recent ideas to emerge from Brussels on the employment crisis suggest at least the possibility of more flexible thinking.

The response of global business

Foreign direct investment (FDI) is an important driver of international competition in general and European integration in particular. In the 1980s, FDI globally grew more rapidly than trade by a factor of three, and more rapidly than GNP by a factor of four.[11] In the shorter period of 1984–9, intra-EU FDI flows alone grew by 800 per cent and inflows from outside the EU by 300 per cent. There is a connection between economic integration and FDI flows.[12] The abolition of customs controls and harmonization of standards, and the Single Market, have increased the attractions of an integrated market. These include economies of scale with a concentration in favoured sites; risk diversification; better access to distribution networks; and optimization of location following the abolition of exchange controls and the free right of establishment. The Single Market should lead to more inward investment, as well as to mergers and acquisitions within Community countries and across Community borders.

There are several key features of the Community's FDI flows. First, a high and growing proportion is in the services sector (over 60 per cent in the late-1980s). Second, the main recipient of FDI, by far, has been the UK – with 40 per cent over the 1989–91 period – though France has a large and growing share despite the resentment displayed over investment competition (Hoover and alleged 'social dumping' by the UK). Third, the main (marginal) supplier of FDI in recent years has been Japan – with around a third of new flows going to the UK, and 80 per cent of the total to non-manufacturing activities, mainly banking and insurance. Some inward FDI was to preempt trade barriers though studies have down-played this motivation.[13]

One lesson from the past is that FDI flows can change very rapidly in reaction to perceived changes in the business environment. The upsurge in Japanese investment in the EU and the investment boom in the services sector may have been peculiarities of the late 1980s. In the 1990s a factor to watch may be a portfolio shift in response to developments in markets in East Asia and eastern Europe which are growing more rapidly than western Europe. This could lead to a slowdown in inward investment to the EU and a spurt of long-term capital outflow. This in turn could provoke some intense and fractious competition among Community countries for inward investment.

An emerging west European economic geography

Western Europe is far from homogeneous. The approach of member countries to both deepening and widening will be heavily influenced by whether they judge the process of integration to be working in their favour. And, within countries, regions with a distinctive identity will pose the same question. What can we conclude from recent trends?

First, there is a slowly evolving common European infrastructure, one consequence of which is to make frontier areas less peripheral. By 2010, there will be a high-speed rail network linking almost all of western Europe (with the Eurotunnel and the Scandinavian link in place). There is already a dense grid of interlinking networks for oil, gas and electricity (linked also to eastern Europe). The Single Market will, in time, remove most of the political barriers to road transport. National deregulation is (slowly) opening up telecommunications. Cost and convenience, not politics, will dictate firm location.

There are different strands of thought in economic geography which emphasize, on the one hand, a polarization into 'growth poles' of economic activity and, on the other, a 'catch up' by areas of relative poverty. The EU experience is mixed. The new (and poorer) southern European members grew, on average, faster than the EU average on joining the Community, though Greece has been falling behind since 1980. A study of regional and national inequalities in western Europe suggests that there was convergence in the 1960–75 period – though this may since have reversed.[14] The emergence of strong growth areas in southern France, eastern Spain, northern Italy and southern Germany contradicts the conventional wisdom of a decade ago that western European growth would be concentrated within a triangle connecting Paris, the Ruhr and the English midlands.[15] The relatively successful performance of the Irish economy also suggests that peripheral location is not an insurmountable handicap.

A more pessimistic view of centre-periphery relations was taken by those who predicted that deeper integration would marginalize areas of agricultural and industrial decline.[16] They point to a widening gap opening up between the most successful and least successful areas within the Community.[17] There are other disparities of a more subtle kind: between the growing concentration of high-tech industries and high value-added, creative services in metropolitan areas and other areas, which may be close by, which have very little such activity.[18] In any event the scale of the EC's regional funding operations designed to counter spatial inequalities is derisory: just over 0.2 per cent of EU GDP for vocational training and infrastructure projects outside the agricultural sector.

The vulnerability, perceived or real, of peripheral areas has two major implications. The first is to intensify competition between low labour-cost areas in southern Europe and those in developing or east European countries. The second implication is the shaping of future monetary integration to avoid the dangers for the EU periphery of an early move towards locking nominal exchange rates.[19] Hitherto this concern has been reflected in the demand for large compensation – 'solidarity'- payments. But the mood of fiscal expansiveness which surrounded the original discussion of solidarity payments has evaporated and a more likely implication of core-peripheral tensions in the EU is that they will act as a brake on monetary integration.

This discussion also has implications for eastern Europe. The argument for speedy integration with western Europe is based on southern European experience: that provided there is a mechanism for adjustment (the real exchange rate), integration will lead to 'catch up' rather than a further polarization. But there is clearly a danger. East European countries could face severe internal regional problems as a consequence of accelerated liberalization within a more integrated European market. The Czech Republic and western Poland may benefit from close proximity to the German market, but Silesia and the eastern border areas of Poland and Slovakia could face serious regional decline.

Conjunctural crisis or deeper crisis?

There is a sense of crisis in the Community. This crisis is symbolized by the breakdown of the ERM in September 1992 and then, more comprehensively, in August 1993. There are, in essence, four overlapping problems: the cyclical slowdown in western Europe; the trend for the EU to grow, on average, less rapidly than the US and much less rapidly than East Asia; the emergence of large-scale unemployment; and the failure to achieve the degree of convergence in monetary and fiscal policy to make early monetary union credible.

When Britain contemplated membership of the Community in the 1960s and early 1970s, an important motivation was the belief that relative decline could be reversed by integration with what was then seen as a dynamic, rapidly growing market. Ironically, the long British debate about relative decline and loss of 'competitiveness' is now a European debate. In the 1980s, the EC grew, annually, by 2.3 per cent (Germany by 2.1 per cent), less than the US, and much less than developed or developing Asia (the UK managed 2.5 per cent p.a.). Among other worrying indicators is the deteriorating trade balance in high-tech products (an export import ratio of 0.8 as opposed to 1.1 in 1980); and the decline in the EU's share of world manufactured exports, the value which has slipped from 22 per cent to 18 per cent since 1980. The Single Market initiative was designed to re-energize the Community. But any early impacts have been overshadowed by the recession.

Even taking into account cyclical recession and relatively slow growth, the EU's unemployment rate – now averaging 11 per cent – reflects a labour market which is significantly more rigid, and labour which is more costly in wage and non-wage cost terms, than the US, let alone east Asia. EC employment has remained virtually constant since the mid-1960s despite economic growth averaging over 2.5 per cent while employment grew 70 per cent in the US and 40 per cent in Japan. The problem has been belatedly addressed in the Delors report to Heads of Government in December 1993.

Rising unemployment and lack of competitiveness have a common cause: real wages have risen more rapidly in the EU than Japan or the

US despite slower output growth. Policy could now go in several directions. One is in the direction of a 'British model' of labour market deregulation, diluting minimum wage legislation, unemployment benefits and job protection. But much political capital is invested in the ideas of the Social Chapter at national and Commission level. Deregulation may be unfeasible politically, or slow, in which case the problem of unemployment may deteriorate further. This could lead in turn to a further souring of public attitudes towards competing 'low cost' labour outside and inside the Community.

Political and institutional deficits

An underlying trend within the international economy, and not only in Europe, has been the 'globalization' of business activity, through capital flows and trade, which has outstripped the capacity of governments to cooperate in order to handle externalities and provide international public goods.

In some respects the EU has advanced considerably in providing cooperative structures; indeed the argument about 'subsidiarity' reflects a concern that the Community has been over-zealous in centralizing decision-making beyond what is required to handle spillovers between member states. The Community may have got the balance about right for competition policy[20] but may have gone too far towards centralization of policy-making in certain aspects of environmental policy and labour market policy.[21]

Institutional development, however, has fallen short both of the Community's own objectives and of the likely benefits in macroeconomic policy coordination. Here, the central concern is the failure of the EMS.[22] The debate will continue to rage over the achievements of the ERM: whether six years of nominal exchange-rate stability conferred tangible benefit and how much of the decline in inflation rates in Europe can be attributed to the ERM (as opposed to weak commodity prices, US dollar weakness and relatively weak economic growth). Debate will also continue over whether the crisis in the system was caused by accident (the strains placed on the system by German reunification); pilot error (failure to realign quickly enough); design fault (the inherent instability of adjustable peg systems in a world of free capital movements); or sabotage (Anglo-Saxon speculators; the Bundesbank failing to support the pound).

A central reason for the failure was the lack of convergence in monetary and fiscal policy: in particular the inability, as perceived by the markets, of EMS members to match Germany's commitment to maintain a low inflation and of all members, except Luxembourg, to observe fiscal convergence objectives. Which of the several options is now chosen for the ERM to EMU process will significantly affect the progress towards European economic integration as a whole.

European economic scenarios

Among the various trends considered above, liberalization was dominant in the 1980s, and this coloured the approach to the Single Market, enlargement, competition policy, and (despite some lapses) external trade policy. It has also dominated the policy agenda in eastern Europe. There are, however, several different or counter tendencies: the political reaction against economic liberalization in some countries; the pressures in western Europe for a protectionist response to external competition; and a reassertion of national and regional identity.

Alternative possibilities provide the basis for different stories of how Europe's future could evolve. The essential elements of three possible scenarios are contained in Table 6.1. Clearly, many variations and nuances are possible; but these seem particularly plausible.

The idea of a *fortress Europe* has long been discussed (and feared by those who might find themselves outside). How might it happen and what form could it take? Several forces could push the Community to look inward and create external barriers: rising unemployment and social tensions within the EU and the success of political movements in scapegoating foreign (non-EU) workers and imports; serious political and economic setbacks in eastern Europe which undermine the belief that much of the East can be integrated economically with the West; and a growing conviction that western Europe's falling behind Japan and the United States in the more advanced sectors of technology must be met by a common – but dirigiste and mercantilist – European response.

The 'fortress Europe' idea has obvious protectionist features, but is also concerned with promoting 'competitiveness' through internal competition. In this scenario, internal competition is strengthened by stripping away remaining barriers to the Single Market and by developing common infrastructure. Political cohesion is seen as crucial to the success of the EU project resulting in generous regional funding (which helps rich applicant members – Austria, Sweden – to gain admission). It also reinforces a strong taboo against 'undercutting' Community standards.

The most difficult task is getting EMU on the road again. This is achieved by other members accepting German conditions for monetary management, by the temporary exclusion of problematic members who fail – modified – convergence criteria (notably, Greece) and by the use of capital controls to ease an early return to narrow bands by EMU adherents along the lines advocated by Delors.[23] An ability to accept EMU rules facilitates the early membership of Austria, Sweden and the Czech Republic.

Externally, the emphasis is on stronger trade protection. Admission of the EFTAns helps to strengthen the most protectionist features of the CAP and the enthusiasm for tariffs against social and environmental 'dumping'.

There are, however, two fundamental difficulties with such a scenario. The first is that, quite explicitly, it creates a new dividing line across Europe between western insiders and eastern outsiders. It is possible that one or two countries – notably the Czech Republic – would cross the dividing line, but Poland would not, nor the countries of central Europe. Economic transformation would be dealt a severe blow. The spill-overs for the west – in particular, attempted mass migration – would be met by stern controls, deepening the divide even further.

The other difficulty is that a fortress Europe would heighten tensions between existing members. There would be serious differences about the use of protectionist measures. There would be increased trade diversion costs and arguments about who should bear them (especially if current tentative attempts to align European and world farm prices are abandoned). There would also be adjustment problems within an accelerated monetary union for the economically weaker members of southern Europe – and possibly Britain. There must be serious doubts about whether a fortress Europe could work over the long term without leading to some form of fragmentation.

Fragmented Europe is a scenario which has no advocates. But it could happen. Mr Delors is fond of the image of the bicycle which topples over when it is no longer pedalling forward. In this scenario he is proved right.

The trigger for this scenario could lie in some of the events which also create fortress Europe. For example, different approaches to trade

Table 6.1 Three European scenarios

	'Fortress' or 'Mercantilist' Europe	'Wider Europe' or Multi-speed Europe	'Fragmentation' or the Return of Nationalism
Themes	External protection Strong but managed competition Market deepening Maastricht lives	Wider European Economic Space Expanding membership Free trade Subsidiarity Variable geometry	Retrogression from Single Market Inter-member disputes Popular resistance to integration
Members	Selective. Clearly defined. 12 + Austria (possibly Czech Republic and Sweden) – Greece	Expanding Membership/Associate status blurred Many overlapping European Communities	'Empty chairs' Semi-detached members (UK?)
External economic relations	Strong 'commercial defence' (Euro 301; anti-dumping) Support for 'strategic industry' 'Green tariffs' Protection against external 'social dumping' EC bilateralism; not GATT Tough migration controls	Free Trade Area including Russia, Turkey 'Deep integration' – Single Market – for widening group (20?) GATT disciplines CAP unwinds	External disputes lead to internal friction (e.g. agriculture) Reversion to Article 115 National quotas National bilateralism (e.g. Germany-Russia agreement)

Continued

Table 6.1 *Continued*

	'Fortress' or 'Mercantilist' Europe	'Wider Europe' or Multi-speed Europe	'Fragmentation' or the Return of Nationalism
EMU	Maastricht with small modifications Capital controls on extra EC transactions Accelerated for lead group (incl. Italy)	Small lead group (6?) accelerated EMU Second tier in wide bands Third tier of floaters	No progress Competitive devaluation
Rule-making for Internal Market	Harmonization to minimum standards	Mutual recognition. Competition among rules	Rule breaking Aggressive competition for capital – standards cut
Competition policy	Strong EC powers re mergers/cartels/state aids Support Euro-champions	EC/EFTA model for reconciling national policy Support GATT code	Weak EC National champions
Tax	Strong move to harmonize VAT, company tax	No harmonization GATT code on company tax	Tax competition to attract investment

Continued

Table 6.1 *Continued*

	'Fortress' or 'Mercantilist' Europe	'Wider Europe' or Multi-speed Europe	'Fragmentation' or the Return of Nationalism
Social policy	Strong move to extend harmonization and defend minimum standards. Common front against external 'social dumping' Strong EC cohesion/social funds	Minimal harmonization except portable benefits and mutual recognition.	Internal friction over 'social dumping'
Networks	Ambitious plans for Euro-wide infrastructure Strong Euro-preference (telecoms; civil aviation; construction contracts)	Emphasis on privatization/ deregulation of national monopolies	National monopolies

policy lead to unilateral quotas by some members which are then reinforced by trans-shipment restrictions on intra-EU trade, or by bilateral agreements with third parties in defiance of Community rules. Enlargement is aborted for the Scandinavians by domestic pressures. There is no progress in enlargement to the East.

The implementation of the Single Market is patchy with many examples of non-implementation and foot-dragging over public procurement. Monetary union never happens. The British 'opt-out' from monetary and social policy proves to have the effect its European critics feared: a cycle of competitive devaluation and competitive bidding for capital inflows through low corporate tax rates and the cutting of labour standards. 'Subsidiarity' becomes a pretext for ceding no sovereignty, even where there are European-level externalities. Governments express national concerns through 'empty chair' policies or use of veto powers. Policy is blocked for long periods in difficult areas. Frictions reach such a pitch that intra-EU trade flows are seriously affected both by official action and by public reaction (attacks on foreign lorries; blockages of road and rail links). Fragmentation would involve a resurfacing of nationalism in eastern and western Europe.

The *wider Europe* scenario, by contrast, captures the current mood of flexibility in Community arrangements. Two ideas are central. One is 'variable geometry': different members and associates integrating in different spheres and at different speeds. The other is 'subsidiarity': accepting a hierarchy of rule-making authorities in which the Community has a strong, but not dominant, role between global and national institutions.

The wider Europe scenario reflects current UK thinking but has wider support. The key is eastern Europe. The success of trans-formation in the east is seen as politically and economically crucial to Germany in particular. This leads the Community to make the necessary concessions on access and promises of eventual membership. The concept of a wider European Economic Space takes firm hold.

EMU becomes possible once it is recognized that the current membership of 12 is not an optimum currency area[24] but that an inner core of five or six (Germany, Benelux, Austria and probably France) may be.

The success of the GATT Round helps to establish the legitimacy of global economic governance, and multilateral trade, and new nego-tiations provide rules for competition policy, trade and environment and corporate taxation on a much wider basis than the Community.

All of this emphasis on widening is deeply deplored in Brussels and Paris but the redeeming feature for them is that Europe is much more than 'a mere free trade area'; for those like-minded and compatible countries, closer integration, including monetary union, presses on, faster than in a Europe of 12 moving at the same speed. It is only in this way that the interests of eastern and western Europe, and of those favouring rapid deepening and those more cautious about sovereignty, can be reconciled.

Towards wider Europe

Of the three scenarios sketched above, only 'wider Europe' offers eastern Europe the prospect of integration with the West. It is probably also the only sustainable long-term future for western Europe: one which reconciles different capacities and levels of enthusiasm for deeper integration.

Enlargement and trade policy

A major element in widening is flexible enlargement to the north, east and south. The first and (economically) least problematic aspect of enlargement is the inclusion of the EFTAns. Many of the economic impacts of enlargement to include EFTA are being felt, in any event, as a result of the formation of the European Economic Area. This gives EFTA countries full integration into the Single Market (except for agriculture). Economic analysis had suggested that such integration would raise EFTAn GDP by up to 5 per cent but have little impact on the EU.[25] Further integration through full membership would have ambiguous consequences. It would force EFTAns to liberalize their agriculture but would have the considerable cost for the EU of adding three to five more countries with an interest in high-cost, subsidized and protected agriculture (probably Austria, Sweden and Finland; possibly Norway and Switzerland). EFTA would, however, be a net contributor to the EU budget (by up to 15 per cent of the present total, on current figures).

Enlargement to east and central Europe (the CEECs) faces more formidable political obstacles. Potentially one of the largest economic benefits to western Europe from a wider Common Market would be immigration;[26] an idea that would create apoplexy among many politicians in the EU. There are also potentially large net gains to western (as well as eastern) Europe from demolishing precisely these barriers to eastern exports – notably agriculture – which are most politically sensitive.[27]

Simulations suggest that 'regular' trading patterns uninterrupted by trade barriers, including those in agriculture, could raise the EU's exports to the five CEECs fivefold[28] or ninefold[29] in the long term. The potential gains from trade in terms of growth stimuli are substantial, even for the EU, and would be augmented by complementary capital flows. The June 1993 agreement by the Community to provide better market access, involving faster dismantling of trade barriers and leading to eventual membership, goes a small way towards recognizing these possibilities.

There are, of course, adjustment costs from liberalizing the EC's import regime. There is also, potentially, a large opportunity cost to the EU from a failure of the eastern European transformation process: collapse of democratic governments, heightened instability and rearmament.[30] The issue is that if eastern Europe is to transform itself economically and politically, it has (among other things) to be able to export freely to the West. All the above arguments also apply, in varying degrees, to the various parts of the former Soviet Union and the Balkans, which are looking to freer trade with the EU if not to membership.

The Community will also not be able to defer for ever a closer relationship with Turkey (and the smaller Mediterranean applicant members). Turkey has already responded to the opportunities offered by the EU market (merchandise exports to the EU as a proportion of GDP are greater than for Italy or Spain and about the same as for the UK). As with the CEECs, the key issue is market access but Turkish experience has also shown that eventual promise of membership, even if remote, is politically and psychologically important. Beyond Turkey is the Maghreb whose relationship with western Europe could be as mutually beneficial as is Mexico's with the US if free trade could be established (as King Hassan among others has argued).

In a wider Europe, such challenges will be met through a phased extension of membership to those ready for fuller responsibilities and Free Trade Area-type agreements with a wider group of countries of the east and south. Such a process can help prevent a deepening of integration leading to an inward-looking bloc, rather than broader liberalization.[31] But the best remedy is a strong commitment to multilateral GATT processes which will remain the main forum for

EU external trade policy. Hitherto, the EU's protectionist bark has been worse than its bite, but the EU has sharp teeth and they could do long-term injury to Europe itself.

Monetary integration

The main step to deepen integration will come from resumption of the progress towards monetary union. Despite disruption of the ERM, the European Monetary Institute has been established and the restored DM-franc parity underlines the continuing commitment to monetary union.

It will be argued that a wider Europe requires floating exchange rates since such a system gives flexibility to accommodate external adjustment requirements among a varied group of countries. Even for countries which do a lot of trade with each other, the negative impact of exchange-rate volatility on trade is modest and can be hedged against in the market.[32] US-Canadian dollar-floating has not been seen as a barrier to NAFTA. The counter argument is that fluctuations do matter, especially in respect of investment and discouraging risk-taking.[33] There is a danger of floating being regarded as competitive devaluation, attracting retaliation and trade protection.

There is more current interest in the idea of an ERM continuing with wide bands: an arrangement which has the advantages (and disadvantages) of floating, with the additional feature of cooperative monetary policy to stay within the wide bands. Unnecessary instability is reduced, albeit with the risk of speculative attack at the band limits. There are many variants of this approach, ranging from those which emphasize explicit target rates and strong intervention, and use of interest rates, to defend the bands[34] to informal and weakly defended bands.

A third option is to try to return to the EMS of narrow bands, while strengthening defences against speculative attack of the kind which overwhelmed the old system. Capital controls could be used under the safeguards provisions of the Maastricht Treaty and the EU capital liberalization Directive. These could range from Mr Delors's ill-defined threat to impose temporary capital controls on non-EU 'speculators', to taxing the foreign exchange profits of commercial banks operating within domestic jurisdiction, and the use of temporary margin requirements on financial institutions with open positions in foreign exchange.[35] Any system of capital controls, however, meets the objection that they will either be ineffective and evaded or effective and risk suppressing the necessary correction of misaligned rates.

Finally, there is the possibility of an accelerated jump to EMU. This satisfies the essential aims of monetary integration – while cutting out the difficulties associated with managing an adjustable peg, particularly over the long transition envisaged in the Maastricht Treaty.[36] Experience of the EMS strengthens the judgment that monetary union, like pregnancy, is not something it is possible to have a bit of.

The EU as a whole is not an optimum currency area, especially if it is enlarged to the east.[37] There is no flexible, Euro-wide, labour market. The burden of the adjustment, in the form of unemployment in economically weaker regions of the EU, would be severe or the compensating assistance would be implausibly large. The plunge could, however, be taken – initially at least – by an 'inner group'[38] which does constitute an optimum currency area and which accepts the disciplines involved.

The most promising immediate way forward may be through a coordinated approach to monetary and fiscal policy, and to achieving a common level of price stability, placing less emphasis on the exchange-rate mechanism itself.[39] If common macro-economic policy is shown to be credible, it would then be feasible to move quickly to lock exchange rates, at least for an 'inner group'. There are numerous possibilities for defining the membership of the inner group and the modalities of its operation and its relationship with the other tier (or tiers) which could be based on a wide-band EMS (or a hierarchy of degrees of free floating). But it is only through a flexible arrangement of this kind that it will be possible to reconcile the wish of some countries to integrate more closely with the necessity for opening the Community to a larger membership.

Conclusion

In a wider Europe there will be considerable, and quite unavoidable, tension between 'deepening' and 'widening'. There is no simple choice between the two. There are legitimate arguments for further deepening of the EU integration process.[40] The crucial test is whether or not this is done in a way which obstructs the widening of market access, and membership, to the east (and south). What will have to be created is a process of economic integration that is much more flexible, in timing and membership, than in the past.

Notes

1. David Mayes, 'The External Implications of Closer European Integration', *National Institute Economic Review*, 4, 1990.
2. A. Jacquemin and A. Sapir, *The European Internal Market: Trade and Competition*, OUP, 1989; and Alan Winters, 'Britain in Europe: a survey of quantitative trade studies', *Journal of Common Market Studies*, 25, 1987.
3. Bela Balassa and L. Bauwens, 'The determinants of intra European trade in manufactured goods', *European Economic Review* 32, 1988.
4. A. Sapir, 'Regionalism and the New Theory of International Trade', *World Economy*, July 1993.
5. B. Balassa, 'Trade Creation and Diversion in the European Common Market', in B. Balassa (ed.), *European Economic Integration*, North Holland, 1975, Mayes, *op.cit.* and Jacquemin and Sapir, *op.cit.*
6. J. Haaland and V. Norman, 'Global Production Effects of European Integration', CEPR Discussion Paper 669, 1992; Robert Baldwin, 'The Growth Effects of 1992', *Economic Policy*, 9, 1989; and P. Cecchini, *The European Challenge: 1992*, Wildwood House for European Commission, 1992.
7. Kym Anderson, 'Europe, 1992 and the Western Pacific Countries', *Economic Journal*, 101, 1991; and S. Arndt and T. Willett, 'Europe, 1992 from a North American Perspective', *Economic Journal*, 101, 1991.
8. Peter Holmes and Alasdair Smith in 'The EC, the USA and Japan: the trilateral relationship in the world context' in D. Dyker (ed.), *The European Economy*, Longman, 1992.
9. Carol Hamilton and Alan Winters, 'Opening up international trade in Eastern Europe', *Economic Policy*, 14, 1992.
10. Jim Rollo and Alasdair Smith, 'The Political Economy of Eastern European trade with the European Community: why so sensitive?', *Economic Policy*, April 1993.
11. DeAnne Julius, 'Liberalisation, Foreign Investment and Economic Growth', Shell Briefing Paper, March 1993.
12. G. Yannopolous, 'The Effects of the Single Market on Japanese Investment', *National Institute Economic Review*, 4, 1990.
13. Stephen Thomsen and Phedon Nicolaides, *Foreign Direct Investment: 1992 and Global Markets*, RIIA, 1990.
14. Mike Dunford, 'Socio-economic trajectories, European integration and regional development in the EC' in D. Dyker (ed.), *The European Economy*, Longman, 1992.
15. Bice Dotti, 'Two Heartlands for Development', Department of Economic Studies, Pirelli, Milan.

16. T. Padoa-Schioppa, 'The EMS: a long-term view' in F. Giovazzi, S. Micossi, M. Miller (eds), *The European Monetary System*.
17. T. Cutler *et al.*, *The Struggle for Europe: A critical evaluation of the European Community*, Berg, 1989.
18. P. Beckouche, 'French "Hi-tech" and space: a double cleavage' in G. Benko and M. Dunford, *Industrial Change and Regional Development*, Belhaven, 1991.
19. Barry Eichengreen, 'Is Europe an Optimum Currency Area?', NBER Working Paper, 3579, 1991.
20. Damien Neven, Robin Nuttall and Paul Seabright, 'The Economics and Politics of European Merger Control', CEPR, 1993; and Horst Siebert and Michael Koop, 'International Competition versus Centralisation', *Oxford Review of Economic Policy*, Spring 1993.
21. David Begg *et al.*, 'Sensible Centralisation', *European Economic Perspectives*, CEPR, December 1993; and Stephen Smith, 'Subsidiarity and the Coordination of Indirect Taxes in the EC', *Oxford Review of Economic Policy*, Spring 1993.
22. David Begg and Charles Wyplosz, 'The EMS: recent intellectual history' in *The Monetary Future of Europe*, CEPR, 1993.
23. Barry Eichengreen and Charles Wyplosz, 'The unstable EMS', CEPR Discussion Paper 817.
24. Philip de Grauwe, 'The Political Economy of Monetary Union in Europe', CEPR Discussion Paper No. 842, 1993.
25. Richard Baldwin *et al.*, 'Is Bigger Better?: The Economics of Enlargement', *Monitoring European Integration*, 3, CEPR, 1992.
26. Richard Portes, 'The Impact of Eastern Europe on the European Community', Birkbeck and CEPR (mimeo), March 1992.
27. Rollo and Smith, *op.cit.*
28. Zhen Kun Wang and Alan Winters, 'EC Imports from Eastern Europe: Iron and Steel', CEPR Discussion Paper, 1993.
29. Susan Collins and Dani Rodnick, 'Eastern Europe and the Soviet Union in the World Economy', Institute for International Economics Paper 32, 1991.
30. Jim Rollo and J. Stern, 'Growth and Trade Prospects for Central and Eastern Europe', NERA Working Paper, May 1992.
31. Gary Hufbauer, *Europe 1992: An American Perspective*, Brookings Institute, Washington, 1990.
32. Martin Feldstein, 'The Case Against EMU', *The Economist*, 13 June 1992.
33. Alan Winters, 'Threats to the Single Market', *European Economic Perspectives*, CEPR, October 1993.
34. John Williamson, 'Equilibrium Exchange Rates, an Update', Institute for International Economics, Washington, 1990.
35. Eichengreen and Wyplosz, *op.cit.*
36. Peter Ludlow, 'Beyond Maastricht', Centre for European Policy Studies, Brussels, 1993.
37. David Begg, 'Neither Deeper nor Wider Union', *European Economic Perspectives*, CEPR, October 1993.

38. Samuel Brittan, 'The Urgent Need For a Firm Inner Core', *Financial Times*, 26 November 1993.
39. David Currie and John Whitley, 'European Monetary Integration: what remains?', *International Economic Outlook*, LBS, December 1993.
40. Dieter Helm, 'The European Internal Market: the Next Steps', *Oxford Review of Economic Policy*, Spring 1993.

7

Can Liberal Democracy Span the European Divide?
Gordon Smith

The conditions of liberal democracy

One of the most striking developments in eastern Europe since the upheavals of 1989 is the swiftness with which western-style politics and institutions appear to have taken root. Can the hallmark of 'democratic stability' really be so rapidly acquired? Ironically, it is perhaps precisely the apparent ease with which the fundamental changes have been accomplished that may lead to doubts as to whether we can totally discard the old dividing line between eastern and western Europe.

There is an additional factor to consider: politics and political institutions in western Europe have themselves been subject to fundamental pressures, partly because of the effects of social and economic change, and not least because of the moves towards tighter political integration. Thus, if we choose to think of the new democracies of eastern Europe as fairly rapidly 'catching up' with western Europe, we have to suppose that they are easily able to work through – or even skip entirely – a whole set of evolutionary processes. Yet the countries of western Europe have themselves not found it easy to cope with change, and they have had all the political and economic advantages not available to eastern Europe.

Such problems of evaluation and comparison did not arise in past decades. Those who had almost exclusively concerned themselves with the liberal-democratic systems of western Europe or else with east European communist regimes could be reasonably sure that they were comparing like with like. As long as the sharp division between eastern and western Europe persisted, attempts to span the divide proved unprofitable. That applied to making comparisons by taking similar-looking political institutions in east and west at their face-value, as it did in looking for signs of a growing convergence in political systems, policy-making, and so on. Instead, it proved more rewarding to concentrate on 'intra-area' comparison which was justified by the quality of middle-range theory that was produced.

Eastern and western Europe then qualified as distinctive political areas, but there was never a perfect fit. For example, it was possible to include the Greek, Portuguese and Spanish dictatorships as part of western Europe on the basis that they belonged to non-communist Europe, and that criterion was taken to be of greater importance than their authoritarian character. The problem now is of a quite different order, since it is no longer the division of Europe that causes problems of definition, but rather the lack of any sharp delimitation at all.

There is, in fact, a distinct aura of fuzziness attached to the concept of a 'wider' Europe, since there is no clear cut-off at all. Thus, it is difficult to produce conclusive arguments for excluding all countries of the former Soviet Union, in particular the Baltic states, while at the same time including all those of east central Europe. In the absence of certain rules for delimiting the wider Europe, the best that can be done is to set out a number of fairly loose criteria. They have to be treated, *prima facie*, as being of equal importance, but none by itself can be regarded as either a necessary or a sufficient qualifying condition. A listing of generally applicable features includes: similarities of political regimes and socio-economic order; shared cultural heritage and historical experience; as well as geographical concentration. Other defining factors can certainly be added, especially ones that arise externally; there may be threats, constraints and pressures that act alike on a whole group of countries, alternatively they can quite voluntarily take on a common set of commitments.

Over-concentration on any one aspect has to be avoided, and yet it is inevitable that special attention should be given to the nature of a governing regime and to the political institutions that support it, and the characteristics of the west European political systems are naturally taken as the key points of reference, namely, the institutions and current practices of liberal democracy.

There are dangers inherent in this way of thinking. It can easily lead to the implicit or explicit assumption that the west European model of liberal democracy is the only one to be considered and that all deviations should at best be treated as transitional adjustments. Such a patronizing standpoint, a hegemony of values, postulates a single 'model' of liberal democracy that has little historical or comparative justification. It neglects important features of east European society and traditions that may lead to a different line of development, and it obscures the fact that our understanding of the forms and requirements of liberal democracy in western Europe is by no means uncontested.

If these reservations are put on one side, it is apparent that the minimum conditions for the establishment of stable democratic systems have been met for many of the post-communist states, certainly for the countries of east central Europe and possibly well beyond. Liberal-democratic constitutions have been adopted, multiparty systems are the product of open, competitive elections, governments are responsible to popular assemblies.

Yet these positive indications are all subject to qualification, and it would be unwise to base a firm judgement on the continuing viability of the political and party systems solely on the basis of a couple of national elections. Nor can the pretensions of a constitution be taken in isolation from political practice. Just how free are elections? Has the political influence of old political elites been eliminated? Have the changes in personnel and outlook been sufficient to underpin the establishment of an independent judiciary? These are empirical questions that can be settled only on a case-by-case basis. Moreover, the reputation a political system gains for democratic stability has to be earned over a number of years. It is only necessary to recall the experience of the Fourth French Republic and postwar Italy to realize that democratic stabilization can be a long drawn-out process.

Political transitions and the wider Europe

In seeking to apply the attributes of liberal democracy to eastern Europe, we encounter a central problem: that the post-communist democracies are still, to a varying extent, within the stage of transition.[1] The concept of a 'transition' may appear initially to provide a secure way of assessing political development, but any security turns out to be largely illusory. A political transition may be indefinitely extended or relatively brief, and there is no certainty as to when a transition is complete, alternatively as to when the regime is judged to have become consolidated. A similar problem affects the beginning of a transition: in formal terms, it commences with the downfall of the old regime and its replacement by the new democratic one, but substantial political and other changes may have already been taking place during the closing years of the former system, and, in a contrary direction, elements of the latter can persist despite the change of regime. Furthermore, it is precisely during the course of a transition that other factors – both social and economic – strongly affect its political direction and the eventual outcome.

In fact, the central meaning of a transition has to be interpreted as 'uncertainty'. In principle all changes that take place within it have to be seen as possibly reversible. Although the restoration of the *status quo ante*, in this case a reversion to communist rule, is most unlikely, a transition still has to be treated as open-ended with regard to its final outcome. It follows, too, that the arrival of the stage of democratic consolidation can properly be judged only in retrospect, not in the course of an ongoing process. These warnings all apply to the interpretation of the current situation of the new democracies in eastern Europe. It is rather too tempting to use the ideas of transition/consolidation by applying them in a conveyor-belt fashion, and thus to impute an unwarranted automaticity to democratic consolidation.

Insufficient attention may also be given to differences between individual countries in the timing and starting points of transition, even though, of course, the upheavals in eastern Europe were highly contagious and led to fundamental changes occurring almost simultaneously. The important distinction has to be made between 'fast-track' and 'slow-track' transitions. In the fast track should be counted those countries that had begun to make changes well before the ending of communist rule. These changes involved measures of liberalization which did not directly impinge on the political arena but which none the less provided the rudiments of a more pluralist society. Although there was a fairly general and growing tolerance of a 'grey' or secondary economy, those countries that were able to take the fast track had also preserved structures that ante-dated the communist dictatorship. Such 'structures' could be those relating to continuities in the legal system and in the treatment of private property, to the qualified independence enjoyed by the churches, and to the survival of certain economic and social interests, such as the farming community. Conversely, other countries that had experienced the most thorough-going effects of communist policies have usually taken a slower track (the Czech Republic being a notable exception), made only a partial break which is all the more pronounced to the extent that the effects of those policies on society are still apparent, and apart from anything else lead to a political culture less suited to the functioning of liberal democracy than those countries taking the fast track.

There is no 'normal' post-communist democracy or society, and for a variety of reasons they have all followed their own paths. The fastest track of all was taken by the former German Democratic Republic, and it demonstrates the difficulty of finding secure points of comparison. The most prominent feature was the rapidity with which a liberal-democratic consolidation – in the strict sense of being 'irreversible' – took place through the absorption of East Germany by the Federal Republic. At the same time, however, the process of democratic transition was not properly completed, and it can be argued that a 'cultural lag' resulted which has put a brake on Germany securing a firm sense of national identity. In the German case, the significant feature was the partially reversed sequence of transition and consolidation.

Exceptional as this development was, it underlines the argument that we should not use 'transition' in such a way as to suppose that the post-communist democracies are all destined to end up very much alike and only differing in how long it takes them to become stable liberal democracies. It is equally important to avoid making hasty assumptions about the comparability of western and eastern Europe until there is greater certainty as to how the democracies of individual states progress.

Transition: a 'double conditionality'?

The point was made earlier that the definition of a political area involves factors external to individual countries as well as those governing the nature of the political systems themselves. This twofold perspective – external/internal – also applies to the analysis of political transition. One would normally expect the emergence of fast- and slow-track performers to depend chiefly on a country's internal circumstances. But external constraints and opportunities – or their absence – can later have significant effects, outweighing differences of internal performance.

The external factors have been of particular importance for eastern Europe. On the one hand, after the removal of Soviet influence, they became free to chart their own course. On the other, there are several reasons for them to be attracted by the prospect of a closer attachment to, and conformity with, western Europe – just as the latter is concerned, as a matter of self-interest, to stabilize their democracies. The strength of the attraction derives from a powerful mixture of motivations affecting almost the whole of eastern Europe: economic, political, security and cultural. This combination leads to what can be termed a prospective 'self-definition', that is, a drive to be identified with western Europe. Yet we have to ask how certain this drive is and how realistic the expectations are.

Initially, the positive attractions of western Europe were supported by the 'negative reinforcement' supplied by the experience of communist rule. But this kind of support could not be expected to persist to the same degree, as memories of the realities of the dictatorship waned and as the harsh consequences of transition began to take effect. In comparison, at least some aspects of the old regime – job security and social services – came to be regarded by many in a more favourable light. Liberal democracy becomes an empty formula if it proves unable to provide the basis for satisfying economic and social needs. So the role of western Europe in giving economic and political support has assumed a critical significance.

The European Community can be likened to a 'gatekeeper', strictly controlling entry to western Europe, and EC membership as far as eastern Europe is concerned is tantamount to securing a permanent west European identity. The gatekeeper metaphor has merit, since the EC imposes a 'conditionality' on entry, made up of economic and political conditions: a reasonably well-functioning market system together with convincing evidence of democratic stability. For a country in the throes of transition, conditionality consists of a package of realizable aims. However, the precise terms of entry vary from one country to another, are not disclosed much in advance, and any 'timetable' is purely indicative – all reminiscent of Kafka's gatekeepers.

How the tool of conditionality can be used is best seen in relation to the three former west European authoritarian regimes of Greece, Portugal and Spain: they had to convince the existing members of the EC that they were capable of sustaining stable democratic government. It took some 12 years for both Portugal and Spain to gain entry after the ending of authoritarian rule, and yet the prospect of eventual admittance was in itself a stabilizing influence. Without it – and bearing in mind the relatively backward condition of their economies – the transition could have proved hazardous.

There are pitfalls in extrapolating their experience to the present situation of eastern Europe vis-à-vis the European Community. In Greece, Portugal and Spain, the market system had no discontinuity, business elites were in place, and the occupational structure, although tilted towards agriculture, did not differ markedly from the rest of western Europe; nor were there vast contrasts in social structure.

Unlike the total control sought by communist systems, large sectors of society were left alone.

In sum, the authoritarian regimes of western Europe fostered a kind of 'suppressed pluralism', and from an EC viewpoint it was sufficient to restrict its conditionality to the evidence of democratic credentials and the prospect of compliance with the *acquis communautaire* within a reasonable period after accession. Few of these favourable attributes initially applied to eastern Europe, so that one would expect the EC's conditionality to be in force over a much longer period. That is, however, only a part of the problem: the more intractable aspect is the situation of the EC itself.

There are numerous factors that together make it unlikely for the EC to assume the major role as the guarantor of democratic transition. It is doubtful whether the EC could cope with a wholesale enlargement to take in several east European states. Yet any piecemeal solution could exacerbate conditions for those left indefinitely on the outside, and yet that appears to be inevitable. The worsening economic conditions in western Europe and the unwillingness of EC member states to assume additional budgetary burdens is one factor, but another is the resistance of the less affluent EC states to agree to reductions in the support they now receive. Even if these problems could be resolved, there are others that would result from widening the Single Market beyond the EC and the EFTA members, since it is precisely those countries in the course of transition that have the lowest wage-rates in Europe, and their competitive ability would harm various industries in western Europe. In particular the problem of dealing with their agricultural produce within the Common Agricultural Policy would create havoc with EC finances.

What are the likely consequences if the EC route to securing a west European 'identity' is indefinitely postponed? In tackling this question, the second term of the 'double conditionality' is relevant: a continuing economic and social malaise brings with it the threat of political instability, a turning away from liberal democracy, and the prospect of mass migration into western Europe. This scenario sets limits on how severe the economic conditionality set by the EC can be.

The second aspect of conditionality with its implied warning from eastern Europe, 'enlarge – or else!', would force western Europe to take action to limit destabilization. It could be mitigated by measures such as the provision of security links with the West, and inward investment undertaken by firms and organizations such as the

European Bank for Reconstruction and Development. Individual countries – especially Austria and Germany – will take an active role in promoting links. Yet it is probably only to the extent that the EC is able to find ways of easing its political and economic conditionality, that the transitions in eastern Europe will take a benign course.

Society and politics: comparing 'like with like'?

In reaching judgments about the chances of democracy flourishing in eastern Europe, we have to take into account the substantial differences between western and eastern Europe at all levels of society and politics. The contrasts are substantial despite many formal resemblances in institutions and apparent similarities in some current trends.

Most western European countries have had the benefit of a relatively smooth evolution over a long period, at least since 1945 and in many cases for far longer. The strong social and political cleavages they inherited have gradually moderated; in that process, democratic stability was fostered to the extent that social cleavages were often 'cross-cutting', thus modifying the force of conflict and increasing the scope for compromise. Alternatively, as with the so-called 'consociational' democracies, political and institutional devices were perfected which helped lessen conflicts in highly segmented societies. Moderate social pluralism in western Europe is mirrored in a moderate political pluralism and by the longstanding political traditions – Conservatism, Liberalism, Christian and Social Democracy.

None of these characteristics apply to eastern Europe. The early formation of political parties necessarily ante-dated post-communist social changes, and in effect that has led to the grafting of political pluralism on to societies that had long been exposed to a process of proletarianization under communist rule: the cleavage bases for parties to develop in the Western mould have either simply not been available or else have not been exposed to moderating influences.

It is possible to put together an argument showing that a kind of 'convergence' can nevertheless be discerned. If, as appears to be the case, many of the old fault-lines in west European society are steadily being eroded – the weakening of class and religious cleavages are leading examples – then is there not already a similarity, given the weakness of these 'old' cleavages in many east European countries, albeit with the glaring exception of ethnic nationalism?

There is a misleading simplification in this formulation, since it neglects to take into account the difference of starting points. The absence of strong, existing cleavages in eastern Europe indicates societies that are still politically unstructured, and that is quite different from the situation in western Europe, where a gradual process of political destructuring is apparently under way. This latter process implies a weakening hold over electorates on the part of the established parties and the traditions they represent. The 'destructuring' of western politics is signified by the growth of partisan dealignment, increasing electoral volatility, and by the rise of new parties. Yet despite this evidence of flux, it is also remarkable just how successful these established parties have been in maintaining their prominence. Part of the reason is that the real extent of their decline is easily exaggerated: their *relative* loss has to be seen against the background of a substantial increase in the size of electorates in western Europe, and in fact the *aggregate* vote going to these parties has grown steadily over a long period.[2] This underlying stability still has to be acquired by those parties in eastern Europe that just at the outset have managed to attract a substantial following.

Electoral discontents and political extremism

Parallels may also be drawn between the apparent disillusionment with parties and their performance in both eastern and western Europe: people are inclined to support protest parties or at least those outside the political mainstream, are apathetic as shown by low turnout at elections, and readily turn to direct, even violent action. Admittedly, some of the symptoms are similar, but there are vast differences in the context. For east European states at the critical stage of renewed nation-building, it is a negative sign for the future that, after the first flush of enthusiasm for democracy faded, turnout at elections fell sharply. With widespread apathy, it is difficult to see how regimes can summon up a sufficient reserve of democratic support in the face of any future crisis.

Electoral apathy is also a problem in west European countries, but they can afford it more, and to a limited extent a lack of concern as to which parties form the government may indicate a degree of satisfaction with the functioning of the political system. In western Europe, too, any turning away from parties is compatible with the 'civic culture' thesis: most people regard 'other things' in their lives as more important than politics.[3] It is also the case that in strongly pluralist societies there is a multiplicity of ways of influencing political decision-making through economic interest groups and organizations promoting particular causes. In eastern Europe a civic culture has yet to form, and the institutional infrastructure of pluralist society has still to be established. In this situation a high level of non-voting may indicate a feeling of powerlessness which, with the onset of a severe crisis, could lead to an outright rejection of party democracy.

A more immediate danger for democratic politics is the rise of new, extremist parties and movements that directly challenge the existing political order. Yet – despite the prominent attention given, for example, to right-wing radical parties in western Europe their performance over the years has been uneven from one country to another and insufficient to threaten the established order. One reason may be that right-wing extremism relies heavily on a 'protest' potential, and it is difficult to maintain this kind of support over a long period.

In eastern Europe the potential for mounting strong attacks is far greater precisely because electorates are still largely 'unstructured' – and what structuring there is will be mainly determined by national and sub-national attachments. Nationalism is closely associated with extremist politics, and of all social divisions, the ethnic-nationalist cleavage is one of the most persistent. The appeal to national sentiments has proved all-important in the post-communist era because it helped to secure a basic consensus in the new democracies – 'anti-communism' only provided a transient, negative consensus. Yet the harmful effects are apparent: an otherwise socially rootless electorate can respond to the claims of rampant chauvinism and lead to an intolerance and suspicion towards national minorities. In western Europe, such expressions are confined to small usually right-wing parties; in eastern Europe the force of nationalism is an integral part of mainstream politics.

This contrast is worth making, particularly in relation to the concerns expressed in both parts of Europe by the prospect of large-scale migration. For affluent western Europe, the prospect of massive migration from poverty-stricken parts of eastern Europe arouses acute fears of social and economic tension. But this perception disregards the fact that, in the first instance, the effects are felt within eastern Europe itself, and success in halting immigration into western Europe simply leads to an intensification of the tensions elsewhere. Thus, the combination of heightened nationalism, negative attitudes towards national minorities, difficult economic conditions together with increasing immigration produces an explosive mixture leading to political destabilization and national conflicts – as has already become evident. Such a pattern of development is not seriously applicable to western Europe.

The problem of the left-right axis

In the search for a basis of political comparability between eastern and western Europe, reliance on similar names given to party formations – 'Social Democrats', 'Christian Democrats' and 'Liberals'- would be misleading. It is equally misguided to rely on a rough equivalence between such fundamental concepts as 'left' and 'right' as a way of classifying party positions and generalizing about the structure of party competition. As George Schöpflin has observed in relation to the strategy of playing the 'national' card on the part of the 'reformed' communists: 'The rise of chauvino-communism makes nonsense of the conventional left/right divide and requires a new ideological and party political classification.'[4]

These new lines of emerging political cleavages in eastern Europe necessitate re-thinking how we generalize about party competition. One significant contribution in this direction has been made by Herbert Kitschelt who not only provides a basis for generalizing about party systems, but at the same time illuminates the fundamental contrast between the orientations of party systems in eastern and western Europe.[5] Kitschelt argues that the driving forces behind party competition are competing values, and that leads him to give greater weight to politically determined cleavages rather than social cleavages. The two sets of values concern, first, the modes of resource allocation, and second, the clash between libertarian and authoritarian values. His major hypothesis is that:

> Unlike West European party systems, all East European party systems will be centred around a pro-market/libertarian versus anti-market/authoritarian axis. In contrast, West European party systems in the late twentieth century tend to be oriented toward an anti-market/libertarian versus pro-market/authoritarian axis.

If developments do approximately turn out to follow these divergent lines – as seen from a Western perspective, a partial transposition of the left-right axis – then there is a need to be wary of making interpretations of policies and political tendencies in terms of 'left' and 'right' in eastern Europe from a west European viewpoint.

Kitschelt's formulation has a particular significance in taking account of the political reactions to the economic problems of transition. Those countries that are quickly able to surmount the economic difficulties are likely to attract electoral support to the pro-market/libertarian axis and thus be well matched to what is still the *dominant ethos* (as distinct from individual party positions) of western Europe and the European Community. The countries that are unable to deal successfully with the economic transition could find that parties leaning to the anti-market/authoritarian axis become dominant in government. They would especially base their appeal on nationalism and national interests, and as the Polish 1993 election showed, reformed communism still has a leading part to play. An interpretation of party systems structured in these ways leads to an important conclusion: the old division between western and eastern Europe would be replaced by a new cut-off between those more successful in dealing with the transition – assumed to be east central European states – and most of the remainder.

Kitschelt's rendering for west European party systems – the anti-market/libertarian versus the pro-market/authoritarian – may be questioned, since parties belonging to the European left have, perhaps reluctantly, come to accept the market system, and the extent of 'authoritarianism' evident in parties of the right may be doubted. However, these caveats in fact say something about the nature of party competition in western Europe: that differences between parties on the left/right axis are rather small. Electoral volatility, issue-voting and dealignment are unsettling factors, but the outcome is in the nature of a 'centripetal turbulence'. Voters readily switch between parties, but only flirt with the extremes, and the competitive constraints facing the major parties make it hard for them to persist with the presentation of radical alternatives; they have to make a bid for the electoral middle ground.

The impact of the 'new politics' should be considered in this context: parties, such as Greens, and new social movements reject the 'old politics' associated with the left-right axis, based primarily on socio-economic issues. However, the major influence of these forces has been in putting new issues on to the political agenda, and pressing the established parties into action; but they do not have a destabilizing effect.

In contrast to the centripetal competition prevailing in western Europe, the new democracies of eastern Europe could experience a 'centrifugal turbulence' – high levels of electoral volatility, combined with a fragmentation and polarization of party systems. Kitschelt's version of the predominant axis of party competition in eastern Europe could result in the presentation of very sharp party alternatives; the consequences would be made all the more serious through the absence of the stabilizing influence of historical 'parties of government' (excepting, of course, the former communist parties). In this situation, radical and anti-system parties can flourish and, with them, the full syndrome of Sartori's 'polarized pluralism' – long absent from western Europe.[6]

The role of democratic constitutions

Against this background of political uncertainty, the new constitutions adopted throughout eastern Europe may be important guarantees of democratic stability. As one would expect in countries emerging from dictatorship, a leading priority was to guard against the emergence of authoritarian rule, and in constitutional terms that meant avoiding a concentration of authority and a fusion of powers. In the kinds of checks and balances adopted, there are many similarities with Western liberal democracies,[7] as, for instance, in providing for an independent judiciary, the 'rule of law', guarantees of individual rights, and the establishment of constitutional courts. On the party-political level, and in reaction against the communist one-party state, political pluralism has been encouraged – in some cases too successfully – through the adoption of generous proportional representation systems. Governing through broad coalitions, with the risk of unstable government, was preferred to using majoritarian electoral systems even though they could produce more stable and cohesive governments.

The parliamentary systems of government are to an extent modelled on those of western Europe, although they also draw on pre-communist traditions. In any event, however, parliamentary rather than presidential governing systems were instituted because they are more representative, especially in cases of coalition government, but also because presidential rule could lead to an undesirable concentration of political authority. Parliamentary government is the norm, but it is modified by significant powers given to presidents; the fact that most are directly elected means that they can intervene directly in questions of policy and government formation and in so doing draw on their democratic source of authority.[8] In different ways, Walesa, Havel and Zhelev, for instance, have been important stabilizing influences. The question, however, is whether this parliamentary-presidential combination represents a satisfactory long-term solution or whether it is more suited for dealing with the problems of transition; but even in the latter case there is the danger of a slippage towards personal rule. That may be avoided, but the other peril is a war of attrition, with the president pitched against parliament. That a fairly stable relationship can be forged is shown by the example of the Fifth French Republic, and its constitution helped put an end to the instability and party-immobilism of the Fourth Republic by virtue of the strong powers given to the presidency. Yet the fact that the presidential/parliamentary combination has worked may be largely due to the adaptive ability of French political parties, not to the constitution itself.

Too much reliance should not be placed on the new constitutions either to achieve an ideal balance or to resolve all kinds of political crisis. It is salutary to recall the difficulties of many European democracies between the two World Wars,[9] and in particular the fate of the Weimar Republic – the failure of a political system that had paid great attention to maximizing the democratic content of its constitution and had installed a variety of checks and balances. It combined proportional representation, a fragmented and polarized system, with an uneasy amalgam of parliamentary government and presidential power. Its checks and balances ultimately proved helpless to halt the process of democratic self-destruction.

Coping with the 'triple revolution'

What makes the ultimate outcome of the upheavals in eastern Europe still uncertain and comparisons with western Europe unsure is the combination of three fundamental and dramatic changes that have been taking place throughout eastern Europe, summed up by the concept of the 'triple revolution': democratization, nation-building, and the switch to the market system. This triple revolution – historically, probably a unique constellation – underlines the fact that the demands imposed by all three have to be faced *simultaneously* and, further, that their effects are all *intertwined*. Even though substantial progress may be made fairly rapidly in one direction, it can later be nullified by serious problems occurring in other directions.

It is for this reason that we should be wary of accepting, say, the initial success of democratization by itself as conclusive evidence that the transition has been safely negotiated. The firm implantation of the market system will be a lengthier process, and a chequered one, especially if large social groups lose out. Successful nation-building depends on the formation of a broad social consensus and a feeling for a common citizenship, but both will suffer if political democracy or the market system should falter. A pessimistic note is struck by Attila Agh:

> The traditionalist-nationalist-populist wave – in its two forms, extreme and traditionalist right – has been the biggest enemy of the implementation of democratic and European values in recent years. Therefore, a new opening, a 'second revolution' is needed to defeat them in order to have a real breakthrough towards Europeanisation cum democratisation.[10]

Once the scale of the problem associated with the triple revolution is fully taken into account, there can be less certainty as to the extent and speed with which the early, formal successes of democratization will be later followed by the anchoring of liberal democracy. Irrespective of precisely which Western model is followed, it is clear that the movement from the 'non-politics' of a state-society to a pluralist politics firmly rooted in civil society is unlikely to be easy or straightforward.

Notes

1. On various aspects of transitions to democracy in eastern Europe, see J. Batt, *East Central Europe from Reform to Transformation*, London: Pinter/RIIA, 1991; S. Whitefield (ed.), *The New Institutional Architecture of Eastern Europe*, Basingstoke: Macmillan, 1993; G. Pridham, G. Sandford and E. Herring, *Building Democracy? The International Dimension of Democratisation in Eastern Europe*, London: Pinter, 1994.
2. P. Mair, 'The Myths of Electoral Change and the Survival of Traditional Parties', *European Journal of Political Research* 1993, 121–33.
3. G. Almond and S. Verba, *The Civic Culture: Political Attitudes and Democracy in Five Countries*, Princeton: Princeton University Press, 1963.
4. G. Schöpflin, 'Culture and Identity in Post-Communist Europe', in S. White, J. Batt and P. Lewis (eds), *Developments in East European Politics*, Basingstoke: Macmillan, 1993.
5. H. Kitschelt, 'The Formation of Party Systems in East Central Europe', *Politics & Society*, vol. 20, no. 1, March 1992, 7–50.

6. G. Sartori, *Parties and Party Systems*, Cambridge: Cambridge University Press, 1976.

7. For a comparative assessment, see J.J. Hesse and N. Johnson (eds), *Constitutional Policy and Change in Europe*, Oxford: Oxford University Press, 1994.

8. See R. Taurus, 'Leaders and Executives' in S. White *et al.*, *Developments in East European Politics, op.cit.*

9. K.J. Newman, *European Democracy Between the Wars*, London: Allen & Unwin, 1970.

10. A. Agh, *Basic Democratic Values and Political Realities in East Central Europe*, Budapest: Hungarian Centre for Democracy Studies Foundation, 1993, p. 15.

8

The Rise of Anti-Democratic Movements in Post-Communist Societies

George Schöpflin

The rise of various authoritarian currents in the post-communist world, especially as exemplified in the electoral success of Vladimir Zhirinovsky in Russia in the autumn of 1993, has come as a distinctly unpleasant surprise for many in the West. Perhaps it should not have done. There were many warning signs and the West itself certainly encouraged anti-democratic forces by its seeming inertia in the face of authoritarian challenges. Still, many people in the West are unable to find an explanation for the apparent paradox that after 40 years of communism, sizeable minorities in the post-communist countries – possibly majorities – are opting not for liberal democracy but for another dictatorship.

The explanation for the success of anti-democratic movements in the post-communist world to be put forward here is that communism and its collapse have left a major hiatus in these societies and simplistic answers, such as those given by right-wing and left-wing authoritarianisms, inevitably sound more plausible to sections of these societies than the discourses associated with democracy. This argument is based on a number of assumptions: first, that the roots of the turn towards authoritarianism are to be sought not in the distant past, i.e. the 'return of history', but in the communist experience and its shortcomings, as well as in the post-communist experience and the expectations that the collapse of communism generated; second, that nationhood and nationalism are authentic political phenomena, not something that is foisted on an unwilling population; and, third, that the West could have had a far greater impact on the pattern of post-communist politics than it did. The chapter looks at the implications of the transformation, especially at the expectations of revolution and the failure of the end of communism to fulfil them; it examines the rise of populism; and it suggests reasons for the failure of the West, as well as assessing the consequences for the Western political landscape in terms of the rise of both ethno-nationalism and right-wing movements.

The partial modernization

There is a popular propensity to see the post-communist world as something unchanging, as societies that have been taken out of the deep freeze, in which the attitudes and prejudices that were current before the communist takeover have remained miraculously con-served and are now rampant. A moment's thought will show how silly this proposition is. It implies that 40 to 70 years of massive upheaval, the extension of the power of the state to encompass the whole of society, far-reaching industrialization, major demographic change, the introduction of mass education and the impact of the modern mass media have all left these societies unaffected. It does not need much reflection to see how implausible the deep freeze scenario is in the light of these changes. In reality, the first clues to the patterns of post-communism have to be sought in the particular nature of the modernization that these countries underwent as a way of understanding the types of societies that have emerged from communism.

In summary form, the central feature of communist modernization was that it was imposed from above and was regarded as alien by the bulk of the population. Although sections of society, notably the beneficiaries of communist modernization, might have begun by viewing the modernizing revolution positively and responded to the promise of a secular Utopia with enthusiasm, as the communist system decayed attitudes gradually changed and, particularly by those who ended up as the losers under communism as well as afterwards, modernity itself came to be rejected. In effect, as communism was seen to have failed and to have functioned to suppress rather than enhance aspirations, it discredited its secular objectives. At the same time, distorted and narrow perspectives of the West as a viable Utopia fuelled this failure.

Given this experience and the concentration of power in the hands of an elite that was increasingly seen as incompetent, significant sections of society felt excluded from the supposed benefits of modernity and were inclined to reject the entire package as alien. This implied that the elites that stood for modernity were themselves low in authority and found it difficult to sustain discourses legitimating democracy once communism had disappeared.

All this was exacerbated by the state of political innocence, not to say infantilization, in which the communist system kept society. Procedures were opaque, the use of power was arbitrary, routinization and predictability were at a discount and individuals were not encouraged to assume responsibility for the consequences of their actions. To make matters worse, communism promoted an attitude that to every question there was only one possible answer, all the others were false and, indeed, probably deliberately misleading ('falsifications'). This attitude was legitimated by reference to the supposed scientific nature of communism and the crude black-and-white world of a scientific epistemology that claimed to possess all the solutions. In all, the end of communism left these societies with very few guidelines that would serve them in trying to cope with the sudden demands that the introduction of democratic systems signified.

Another illuminating aspect of the communist experience was that it largely failed to create integrated societies in which the great majority of the population was broadly agreed on a particular set of values, in which there were no deep-seated cleavages, and in which horizontal communication between different sections of society, as well as vertical communication between rulers and ruled, functioned reasonably smoothly.

The tripartite division of society proposed by the Hungarian sociologist Gyula Tellér is a useful way of understanding the types of society produced by communism.[1] Tellér suggests that post-communist societies can be divided into liberal, communist and traditional segments. The first two need not detain us for long in this connection, except that their relative strength or weakness is obviously relevant to the size of the traditional segment. Tellér restricts his argument to Hungary, but it is applicable to other post-communist societies too. The liberal segment accepts the values of change, conflict that is mediated by institutions, markets, competition and individual responsibility. The communist segment was brought into being by the communist revolution and is necessarily dependent on the state. It prefers collectivist solutions to individualistic ones, but it also accepts that modernity in some form or another is the ultimate and desirable goal.[2]

The traditional segment, on the other hand, rejects modernity and is the strongest political and sociological base for the anti-democratic currents that appear to be gathering in the post-communist world. The characteristics of this segment derive from the shock it experienced through the enforced modernization of the communist revolution and its resistance to it, coupled with the renewed shock of the collapse of authority with the disappearance of the familiar markers of communism. Its members had failed to internalize the norms of communism but had come to accept the system of symbols, power and hierarchy associated with it, so that the end of communism impacted on them as a major crisis of meanings.

Traditional society can be described as defined by the area's rural past. Traditional peasant and, where appropriate, neo-feudal values survived the communist modernization, often in the face of the communist attempt at forcible transformation, and continue to motivate sizeable sections of society through cognitive categories that may not necessarily be the most suitable for the actual political conditions. Its ideas are strongly collectivist, negatively egalitarian or hierarchical, anti-intellectual, and distrustful of politics, seeing it as an alien and 'unclean' game. Thanks to its lack of political sophistication, it is vulnerable to manipulation by populist demagogues.

Elements of the past were conserved in the peasant mentality and mingled with those of the present, retarding it, refracting it and crucially leading to a situation where the aspiration for popular control of power was not the norm, but where a wide variety of illusions was entertained about what could be done *with* power. Where these illusions failed to materialize, explanations and comfort were sought in compensatory myths. These myths were of a total transformation, and could include aspirations to a very high level of material consumption, but being myth-derived without any sense of the intermediate steps needed to bring them into the real world.[3]

A further irony in all this was that the generally low level of political literacy had the automatic corollary of promoting the role of the state and dependence on it. As these traditional sections of the population found it difficult to come to terms with the complexity of industrial life, they were inevitably forced into a one-way relationship with the incomprehensible state and, willingly or otherwise, they were constrained into an acquiescence in *étatism*.

Although the emphasis in this section has been on the ex-peasantry, this term is used emblematically and the actual situation varies from country to country. Thus in Poland the peasantry was still very much a reality, largely because of the inability of the communist authorities to complete collectivization in the 1950s and 1960s. The impact of this still fairly traditional peasantry on Polish political life has been to introduce an element of unpredictability, impatient radicalism and unreliability into an already volatile political scene, as well as to provide a reservoir of support for a conservative Roman Catholicism. In the Czech lands, the absorption of the peasantry into industry took place much earlier, having begun before the First World War, but given the particular nature of Czech industrialization, a social formation was created that remained isolated from many of the technological and economic processes that might have favoured a more relaxed attitude towards mobility and change. The Czech working class was, therefore, deeply imbued with conservative values of hierarchy and immobility.[4]

In the former East Germany, the transformation was experienced in a more or less colonialist fashion, with West German values and institutions, as well as personnel, being superimposed on East German society. The attitude of the working class was resentful and dissatisfied, being determined to gain access to the symbols and reality of Western levels of consumption, but hostile to the methods imported from the West. Above all, the cognitive categories of the former East German population found it hard to cope with the new models of expected behaviour and the people tended to retreat into myths, resentment or apathy.

Possibly the most enduring feature salvaged from the rural past has been the deep distrust of the city. Communism imposed a terrible experience on traditional society, which it bore sullenly, unforgivingly and reluctantly, preserving what it could from the past, but changing in unperceived ways as well. This was an altogether different form of urbanization from that undergone by the West, which was much more organic and effected a fairly successful integration of the countryside by the city. The disappearance of communism thus meant an end to the sense of humiliation and, equally, provided an opportunity for revenge.

The particular irony of this is that whereas in the West communism was perceived as having created a world of especially soulless industrialization, remote from the Western experience, for the peasantry that underwent communist modernization, the distinction between the integrated Western process and the failure of the communist process was non-existent. In this sense, communist modernization was conflated with Westernization, coming to be seen as the triumph of the hated and sinful city over the pure and authentic values of the countryside.

The collapse of communism should logically have meant an easy return to those pure values, except of course that the clock cannot be put back and the semi-urbanized masses were thus ready to give an attentive ear to the ex-peasant intellectuals, who were making false promises of a simpler life. This ex-peasant intellectual stratum deserves special attention. Its members were recruited under communism and enjoyed the rapid upward social mobility that the system provided, but instead of embracing its values unquestioningly, they were repelled by it and had the articulateness to give voice to the lost world, not least because their vision of power was one of a simpler, more straightforward, more transparent set of relationships, where cause and effect were directly related.

The ideology voiced by this intellectual stratum is hostile to modernity, to industry, to the density and complexity symbolized by the city and in its most extreme manifestation could be observed in the war of Yugoslav succession. The senseless destruction of Vukovar, Sarajevo and Dubrovnik is best interpreted in this context as the ritual killing of the city. This Serbian example also illustrated something else that was evident to the outside observer – the futility of the war against modernity. But this futility was not at all obvious to the ex-peasantry, which was ready to believe its leaders that a better world was round the corner once its alien, sinful enemies had been extirpated. All this says a great deal about the superficiality of the communist modernization process, which failed to offer those affected enough of a material, moral or political vision to foster a thoroughgoing integration.

For the post-communist experiment in democracy, the existence of this sizeable, still collectivist-minded and homogenized traditional society does not augur well. Its broad attitudes towards a social and political system oriented towards complexity, change and choice have already been described. Its striking characteristic is its malleability, even manipulability and credulousness, as well as its hostility to opposing points of view. The sections of society that voted for Mečiar's HZDS in Slovakia, the Greater Romania party, the Smallholders in Hungary, the Bulgarian Socialist Party and, of course, the Peasant Parties in Poland can be regarded as having opted in favour of illusory solutions. They are bound to be disappointed with the nostrums purveyed by populist leaders and will continue to be a volatile element in the political spectrum.

The group was further marked by its economic marginality. It had failed to reach the level of existential solidity that had been achieved by the communist and liberal segments and was conscious that the post-communist transformation was likely to affect its members very negatively. With the severe cutbacks on collective consumption, the group was not only faced with the existential problem of attempting to cope with a diminished standard of living, but even worse, it had to devise new budgeting, earning and similar lifestyle strategies. In all processes of major change, the sections of society most vulnerable to demagogy are those who have attained a little, but see themselves as losing that little under the new order.

The actual economic transformation was impacting severely on various such groups. The inflation, the shock therapy, the new reordered status differentiation whereby previously low status individuals were unexpectedly doing well, all combined to accentuate the sense of loss and disenchantment among groups which had in any case very little patience with the kinds of change that were taking place and suspected their objectives.

The post-communist experience

The elites that took power from the communists in and after 1989 did so in the name of democracy. The slogan of democracy proved extremely effective in demobilizing loyalty to the communist system, largely because it was legitimated by tacit or explicit reference to the success of the West. The interpretation of the West that was current at both the elite and the popular level was, however, flawed. The West was not understood as a complex social, economic, political and cultural entity but as a political and economic success, which had won the Cold War. The externals of high levels of prosperity and sophisticated technology were regarded as the hallmarks of the successful competitor and it is no exaggeration to suggest that for many people 'democracy' was little more than an appendage to economic triumph. Thus their expectations were that the introduction of 'democracy' would automatically bring with it a Western level of prosperity.

In any case, the new political elites were handicapped by the struggle that they themselves had fought with communism. As in any extended conflict, the contending parties gradually acquire characteristics of each other and the democratic opposition was no exception. Inevitably, in having to fight a totalizing system, the democratic opposition, while placing great emphasis on human rights and democracy, tended to interpret these in a relatively homogenized manner. There were many individual exceptions to this proposition, but overall it is clear, not least from the writings of Václav Havel, György Konrád or Adam Michnik, that the counter-elite produced by communism tended to see society and democracy in rather simplistic and idealistic terms.[5]

The new democratizing elite was in any case so persuaded of the appropriateness of its democratic beliefs and of its own democratic credentials that it never seriously thought that democracy had antagonists. It proceeded to impose a democratic structure on post-communist countries without any attempt to consult the population though, to be fair, there were important external pressures that would have made non-democratic alternatives impossible to legitimate. In the post-1989 euphoria, the West was believed to be deeply committed to the maintenance of democracy throughout Europe and anti-democratic or non-democratic discourses were impossible to articulate at this time. Yet as soon as the impact of democracy began to be felt, it became evident that not all of society was as enthusiastic as had been thought.[6]

The ease with which President Iliescu of Romania was able to manipulate the Jiu valley miners to beat up students demonstrating in Bucharest in June 1990 was an early straw in the wind. The poor showing made by Tadeusz Mazowiecki in the Polish presidential elections of November 1990 was another.

The consequence of this was that the democratic elite's ability to run a democratic system was low. It proved reluctant to accept that in the real world of power politics, transactions were generally blurred and muddy and that the abstract intellectual and moral criteria that had been so effective in undermining communism – a construct legitimated by intellectual categories and therefore vulnerable to intellectual attack – were counterproductive in a democratic system.

This state of affairs had two outcomes. It resulted in the rapid re-emergence of the political sphere as the central area of all activity, coming to resemble the Soviet-type system that had just been defeated. This further meant that the social and economic aspects of the transformation were neglected while the new elites were busily engaging in ever more abstruse ideological and moral battles. Because the new system was legitimated by the language of democracy, society identified 'democracy' not as understood in the West, but as the seemingly irrelevant bickering, the empty contests for symbols and moral purity that had no bearing on everyday existence, above all with the rapid and continuing economic deterioration. The collapse and disintegration of Solidarity exemplified this process.

The second outcome was that the elite recruited from the democratic opposition was challenged or replaced by an elite that it never seriously thought existed, namely the nationalist-populist current. Although this was far from clear before 1989, with the benefit of hindsight it can be seen that traditional society was paralleled by a traditional elite. This traditional elite, while not untouched by the communist modernization, was resentful of it and emerged on the political scene hostile to both communist and equally to Western modernization.[7] It may have used the slogan of rejoining Europe but it was dreaming of a Europe that never existed. Certainly, it had no intention of accepting compromise, tolerance or even the complexity that had been brought into being by the lop-sided communist modernization. It was antagonistic to the proposition that under democracy, transactions were most successfully transmitted through a network of institutions; indeed, the total success it demanded was deeply detrimental to democracy.

What the conflict of these two elites – the democratic and the traditional – brought into being was a kind of political inflation that ran in tandem with the economic inflation. Words lost their meaning, the currency of the political discourse was devalued, the relationship between words and action, between speeches and policies, was obscure and as a result society grew yet more confused and resentful. Democracy was discredited as the new post-communist governments sought to deal with the multiple crises which they faced by the tried and failed method of over-regulation. Both the communist and the pre-communist traditions had been marked by this belief that issuing regulations, directives, instructions and the like was a substitute for action. The post-communist systems drew on these traditions heavily.[8]

In effect, political inflation created a state of affairs where the political sphere made ever-increasing demands on the economic and social spheres, offered little or nothing in return and when confronted by its own failures simply intensified the tempo. The reality was, however, that neither the administrative machinery nor the managerial competence of the elites nor the available technology was capable of coping with the mounting demands that the political sphere was making in seeking to subordinate all other spheres to itself.

In the first phase of post-communism, this traditional elite was successful in garnering considerable power, influence and status, though its political incompetence was rapidly exhausting its political capital. The Brazauskas effect – the success of the former communists now relabelled 'socialists' – was one response; the rise of populist nationalism was another.

These two currents were, however, distinct in most other respects.

What they shared was that they constituted responses to the chaos created by the interaction of the post-communist elites and the politically inexperienced populations. The success of the ex-communists could be attributed to elements of nostalgia, to the belief that at least the communists knew how to run things, to a desire for order, discipline and administrative competence, and to their emphasis on social welfare, which the post-communist elites tended to set to one side in the particular way in which they discussed the market. Crucially, the communists drew on the segment of society that they had brought into being, whereas the populists looked to traditionalism as their social base. The rise of populism was also closely associated with nationalism and it is to these two phenomena that we turn next.

Nationalism and populism

Some definitions are in order next if sense is to be made of populism and nationalism. Populism is extremely elusive, but it is most usefully understood as both a discourse and a set of policies. For the time being, the latter need not concern us in detail, because no avowedly populist government has come to power in the post-communist world, but populist policies involve an element of redistribution by using investment capital for consumption and introducing restrictions on foreign economic involvement. In political terms, populism is anti-individualistic and emphasizes movements rather than parties. The discourse and language of populism, however, have definitely made an appearance under post-communism.

For starting purposes, the definition to be followed here is that the heart of populism is to do with the use of political power without institutions. It involves a leader or an ideology in which there is a claim for direct access to the individual and an insistence that power, in order to be authentic, should be unstructured. In this context, the role of a charismatic leader can be very significant; certainly, legal-rational categories are rejected. In general, populist programmes offer their potential supporters more than they can deliver and seek to explain away their own failures, as well as those of the system or situation as a whole, by reference to scapegoats, usually scapegoats external to the community (these may be foreigners or an ethno-religious minority).[9]

Anti-intellectualism is evidently an important component of populism. There is a rejection of the complexity of society and socio-political interactions, and this is coupled with what may be a highly forceful rejection of the necessary complex explanations of what is happening. Under post-communism, the entire matter has been muddied by the behaviour of the post-communist elites as described above. This has created an intellectual and political gap through which populist solutions have come to appear attractive to the social categories vulnerable to this kind of over-simplified world view.

Conversely, this process may well have been strengthened by the sight of intellectuals unable or unwilling to abandon the epistemological certainties of the past in favour of a relativist world view by generating appropriate paradigms for societies equally incapable of making the shift. In this context, intellectuals may also be seeking to preserve the particular status that they have traditionally enjoyed in semi-developed societies, notably the status that derives from their roles as moral legislators.[10]

Other factors involved in the success of populist mobilization involve the nature of the relationship between the market and the consequent destruction of traditional communities, the impact of technological change and alien cultural influences. Populist mobilizers can use these factors as a resource and intensify the perceived authentic features of anti-modernism.

Some unique features of populism under post-communism derive from the particular legacies of communism, especially atomization and normlessness. These unique features can make it easier to initiate populist mobilization, because the processes of integration into the complexities of modernity were neglected or rejected by communism, leaving societies at the mercy of forces which they cannot readily comprehend. The role of exaggerated expectations in terms of consumption can also assist populist mobilization, in that these unattainable aspirations can be manipulated and channelled into backing for populist projects.

Nationalism is often closely associated with populism, indeed in many cases constitutes an integral part of it, but is all the same conceptually distinct from it. For purposes of this analysis, it will be argued that nationhood exists in a civic and an ethnic dimension. When reference is made in common parlance to 'nationalism', the ethnic dimension of nationhood is usually meant. Ethnic nationhood is an authentic experience, in that it has crucial functions in the maintenance of communities, in the definition of identities, in providing expression for the affective dimension of collective life and in the reaffirmation of communities through the symbols, rituals and liturgies of nationhood.

This last factor – the acting out of the affective dimension – is also what makes nationhood so powerful and so dangerous a political instrument. Ethnic nationhood is excellent for defining the nature of the bond between different members of a community and equally for marking the boundaries that differentiate them from other communities. But that is where the functions of ethnic nationhood end.

The proposition being offered in this analysis, therefore, is that while ethnicity is a real experience with genuine and legitimate functions in defining identity and expressing the underlying moral codes that have a strong constitutive role in the make-up of every community, ethnicity is worse than useless when it comes to matters properly in the civic dimension of nationhood. The civic dimension comprises the rules and regulations that govern the everyday relationship between rulers and ruled and the institutional framework through which these transactions are enacted – matters of representation, taxation, the institutions that mediate between government and society, and the codes of conduct that ensure that all are treated as equal before the law.

These matters are quintessentially settled by reference to reason and rational discourse. Ethnicity, by contrast, appeals directly to the emotions. When questions that belong properly to the civic dimension are transferred illicitly into the realm of ethnicity, the emotionality of ethnicity pushes reason into the background and matters are decided by passion.

Under post-communism, the civic sphere remains seriously underdeveloped. Even allowing for the devastation caused by communism in this respect, the institutional framework is weak and the level of trust in legislation and in the administration is low. Unlike ethnicity, the civic dimension of nationhood is not seen as authentic, with the result that citizenship becomes a matter of theory, façades and paper provision.

In these circumstances, it is understandable that sizeable sections of the population prefer to pursue their own interests and strategies of power than accept the constraints of legality. The losers in this jungle are easily tempted by politicians who offer them an easy redress.

The combination of these elements – a vulnerable population, a seductive public discourse that offers quick rewards and the pseudo-righteousness of nationalism – is tailor-made to erode democratic stability and, even more seriously, to undermine the self-legitimation of elites that continue to believe in democracy. The policy implications are that the ruling elites not in agreement with populist authoritarianism may well temper their policies in order to avoid isolation, or at any rate they may be inclined to move in that direction for fear that they would be isolated. There are countless examples of this kind of appeasement. The most striking is that of the democratic opposition in Serbia, which has concluded that an anti-Milosevic platform would be unviable without a strongly nationalist colouring; this has left Serbian politics in a situation where virtually all political parties use a heavily nationalist rhetoric.

A few words are in order as to the types of authoritarian dictatorship that might potentially be installed. The main characteristic that most of them are likely to share is that of charismatic or pseudo-charismatic leadership. They are not very likely, on the other hand, to attempt to establish a totalitarian or totalizing ideology with a totalitarian party; the legacy of communism coupled with the hostile international environment would make this difficult. This implies that islands of pluralism could survive behind an authoritarian system using a democratic façade. Their main legitimating discourses would obviously be nationalistic and possibly populist. They are only likely to become militarized if the country in question were to be involved in hostilities, as is the case with Serbia and Croatia, both of which are running a serious risk of the establishment of military dictatorships.[11]

Revolution and its legacies

The literature on the events of 1989 in central and eastern Europe and of 1991 in the Soviet Union is still at a loss as to how to describe what happened. Various terms like 'revolution', 'transition' or even the anodyne 'upheaval' are used.[12] The Western media have tended to use 'revolution' without much thought as to the deeper content of the word. However, in central and eastern Europe revolutions have a much higher prestige than they do in the West. Although there is still a touch of romance attaching to the French Revolution and traditionally the Western left was in thrall to the pathos of the Russian Revolution, by and large the West does not regard revolutions as desirable ways of effecting political change. For sizeable sections of society in the post-communist world, on the other hand, revolutions are seen as a valid and useful means of bringing about the transformation that normal political channels leave blocked. The weakness of civil society, the corresponding strength of the elites who have traditionally controlled the political sphere, not to mention the use of the legitimating force of revolutions by the communists, have created a discourse to which sections of society will listen.

The core of this argument is that the revolution which should have taken place to overthrow communism was aborted by an intra-elite deal, as a result of which society was excluded from power. In this line of argument, democrats and their backers in the West have colluded in a corrupt deal to side-step the millennial elimination of centuries of injustice and the creation of a new Utopia. It is noteworthy that in the initial period after the end of communism, the idea of revolution was largely discredited by its association with 1917 and with the communist seizure of power, but as the post-communist elites have failed to satisfy the sections of society looking for a radical improvement in their fortunes, revolutionary solutions began to appear more attractive.

Here again it is worth considering the thought-world of traditional society as a way into understanding these ideological constructs. The peasant mind-set was structured by its agricultural activities, its low level of technology, its dependence on the climate and hard manual labour, its economic marginality and consequent limited faith in the future, together with its restricted and largely negative contact with the state and the city, which it viewed as parasitical. Change was conceptualized as a radical transformation, in which everything that was bad would suddenly be turned into good. The inappropriateness of these cognitive categories to the complexity of the modern world needs no further comment.

Building on this mind-set, which was modified by communism but not reconstructed thoroughly for the reasons already discussed, the traditionalist elites have found themselves well placed to articulate a revolutionary ideology to appeal to a minority of society. What is especially noteworthy in this context is that the idea of revolution appeals to currents in the national tradition, the ones that reject compromise as contemptible and emphasize honour and moral purity as the most desirable criteria in politics.

The combination of resentment of the new on grounds of loss of status and economic deprivation with the legitimation derived from revolutions as the ideal method of effecting political change is distinctly uncomfortable and counterproductive from the perspective of democracy. Despite the lessons of history that revolutions generally produce authoritarianism rather than Utopia, the tenacity of the revolutionary dream is such that it offers a serious challenge to those committed to gradualism in politics.

The impact of the West

The democrats who took power from the communists had high expectations that their experiment would receive immediate and substantial support from the West. Given their idealism, which had in any case been fuelled by decades of western statements, they believed firmly that the end of communism would be greeted not merely with verbal backing, but with active measures. Indeed, there was a kind of widespread and somewhat naive faith that these new democracies would be able to 'enter Europe' in a very short space of time. 'Entering Europe' was equated with membership of the European Community, with the arrival of large sums of investment capital and the opening of western markets to their products, with political integration and incorporation into the western security system. It all resembled a vague idea that entering Europe was rather like going into a bar, where the landlord would greet one with open arms and press a drink into one's hand.

Reality was, as has been evident, very different and much less favourable. Disregarding the first few months of euphoria, the West's attitude towards the end of communism was hardly one of unalloyed welcome and became more one of sour grapes. The comfortable world of the Cold War with the certainties and verities of the confrontation with communism was over and the West found itself in a major crisis of identity that it has still to resolve. The end of communism may have removed one particular security problem – the danger of thermo-nuclear war with the Soviet Union – but this has been replaced by a host of others with which the West is in no position to cope, whether politically, economically or intellectually.[13]

Not only is the structure of international organizations set up to cope with the problems of the Cold War ill-suited to deal with post-communism, but western Europe has found itself in a twofold dilemma. The end of the Cold War has placed the question of the distribution of power and the nature of democratic institutions on the domestic agenda of most if not all these states, the fate of Italy being the most vivid illustration, while at the same time the security vacuum in central and eastern Europe has posed a question of strategy to which they have no answer precisely because their domestic politics are in a state of turmoil. The economic recession has simply made this situation worse, because investment capital that might have gone to central and eastern Europe is not available, even while domestic pressure groups impose restrictions on imports from the post-communist world.

Equally seriously, the West has watched or even turned away from the gathering chaos that appears to be enveloping the post-communist world. At the heart of the problem is the proposition that the territorial dispensation made at the Paris Peace Settlement of 1918–20 and largely reaffirmed after 1945 has been brought into question as the post-communist governments and politicians seek to raise political capital by resorting to irredentism. As far as the West is concerned, the post-First World War settlement is sacrosanct and the attempts to alter it are viewed with dismay, distaste and contempt. There has been very little effort made, notably in Britain and France, to understand the motives of those seeking change and to formulate policies based on such an understanding.

In reality, by accepting the reunification of Germany, an action that was based solely and exclusively on the national principle, the West tacitly rehabilitated that principle throughout the post-communist world. It was quite pointless for western spokesmen to say, as they did, that the German case was an exception – a precedent is a precedent. Others are now busy claiming that the precedent applies to them too. German policy predictably was alone in having a clearer comprehension of what was involved, but after the recognition of Croatia and Slovenia, the other countries of the West have buried their heads in the sand and are refusing to acknowledge the national principle in international politics. A final factor in this mix was that the West seemed to be mesmerized by what was happening in Russia and was ready to subordinate the interests of the central and eastern Europeans to its Russian policies, for example by effectively blocking access to western security arrangements to the Visegrad countries.

Indeed, by its inactivity over the war of Yugoslav succession, the West encouraged nationalists in the belief that nothing would happen if they applied measures like ethnic cleansing to their economic problems. Even accepting the difficulties raised by possible military intervention, western passivity remains puzzling. Declarations of principle in support of democracy, moral support for democrats and proclamations that the West would offer security backing to fledgling democracies would have helped to boost morale and de-legitimate authoritarianism, by encouraging the central and eastern Europeans in their perception of 1990 that there really was no alternative to democracy. None of this has actually happened, and the consequence has been an increasingly active right-wing authoritarianism that has come to recognize that the international climate is not as hostile to its projects as it once appeared.

The prospects for right-wing authoritarianism have improved

considerably since the collapse of communism. After the initial rather naive democratic euphoria, the obstacles to democratic transformation became evident and the attendant social problems came to provide fertile ground for extremist movements of both right and left. For the time being, left-extremist movements remain weak because of the memory of the communist period, but the revival of the left, with the success of ex-communist parties, came much sooner than most observers would have predicted.

The rise of the right was similarly unforeseen and creates serious dilemmas for democracy, because it raises the prospect of Weimarization as a possible scenario for some of the post-communist countries. That pattern of development would engender insecurity in central and eastern Europe, something that would impact most strongly on Germany, Austria and Italy. The possibility that the western alliance itself would be undermined cannot be excluded as one possible outcome. Another result of the rise of the right in the post-communist world was that it found imitators in the West. The example of small states like Slovenia gaining their independence has evidently been watched with interest in, for example, Catalonia and Scotland, and such methods as genocide against the Muslims of Bosnia have been a source of encouragement to racists in the West.

The overall pattern, however, was that the insecurities and instabilities left by the end of communism would persist for many years, that the reintegration of Europe would be a much harder process than was envisaged in 1989–90, that the domestic travails of the post-communist systems would receive little in the way of support from the West and that appeasement of right-wing authoritarianism would only encourage it to grow by giving it a semblance of acceptability.

Notes

1. Gyula Tellér, 'Döntés elött: politikai vita', *4x4 oldalas: Szabad Demokrata tájékoztató*, no. 44, 4 November 1992.
2. I make this argument in somewhat greater detail in George Schöpflin, 'Culture and Identity in Postcommunist Europe', in Stephen White, Judy Batt and Paul Lewis (eds), *Developments in East European Politics*, London: Macmillan, 1993, pp. 16–34.
3. Some of these issues are discussed by Piotr Sztompka, 'The Intangibles and Imponderables of the Transition to Democracy', *Studies in Comparative Communism*, 24:3 (September 1991), pp. 295–312.
4. Miroslav Petrusec, 'A posztkommunizmus mint szociopolitikai fogalom

és probléma', in Václav Belohradsky, Péter Kende and Jacques Rupnik (eds), *Politikai kultúra és állam Magyarországon és Csehszlovákiabán*, Turin: Giovanni Agnelli Foundation, 1991, pp. 87–105; and Jacques Rupnik, 'The Roots of Czech Stalinism', in Raphael Samuel and Gareth Stedman Jones (eds), *Culture, Ideology and Politics*, London: Routledge, 1982, pp. 302–19.

5. See Václav Havel, *The Power of the Powerless*, London, 1985; and *Disturbing the Peace*, London, 1990; Adam Michnik, *Letters from Prison and Other Essays*, Berkeley, CA: University of California Press, 1985; György Konrád, *Antipolitics: An Essay*, tr. R. Allen, New York: Harcourt Brace Jovanovich, 1984.

6. Andrzej Tymowski, 'The Unwanted Social Revolution: Poland in 1989', *East European Politics and Societies*, 7:2, Spring 1993, pp. 169–202.

7. There is an excellent assessment of the Hungarian case in István Márkus, 'Utórendiségünk: gyökerek és gyümölcsök', *Valóság*, 34:5, May 1991, pp. 1–23.

8. Attila Ágh, 'A kiábrándulás kora', *Valóság*, 36:10, October 1993, pp. 62–73.

9. This analysis of populism draws on the discussions at the workshop on 'Populism in Politics and the Economy' held at the Central European University, Budapest, 2–3 April 1993 and especially the paper delivered by András Bozóki, 'An Outline of Three Populisms: United States, Argentina, Hungary'.

10. Zygmunt Bauman, 'Intellectuals in East-Central Europe: Continuity and Change', *Eastern European Politics and Society*, vol. 1, no. 2, Spring 1987, pp. 162–86.

11. László Lengyel, 'Útközben: Magyar politika az ezredfordulón', *Politikatudományi Szemle*, 2:2, 1993, pp. 112–34.

12. My own views are set out in George Schöpflin, *Politics in Eastern Europe 1945-1992*, Oxford: Blackwell, 1993, pp. 253–5.

13. See *inter alia* several of the essays in Soledad García (ed.), *European Identity and the Search for Legitimacy*, London: RIIA/Pinter, 1993.

9

The Breakdown of Welfare Regimes and the Problems for a 'Social' Europe

George Kolankiewicz

As pressures mount on the welfare state in western Europe and welfare provision in eastern Europe is under stress, a European *underclass* has emerged which threatens the legitimacy of both west European integration and transformation in east central Europe. This chapter argues that a social dimension of European construction is essential if these issues are to be addressed.

Social Europe in context

A combination of economic recession, burgeoning unemployment and demographic shifts has served to drive European welfare systems into profound difficulties. Increased costs in all types of welfare regimes, be they conservative, liberal or social democratic,[1] have led to growing resistance from employees and employers and tax payers at all levels. Pressure for combining public with private provision has led to a convergence of responses from embattled welfare systems which in turn may feed into the formulation of a common European social policy.

As the OECD countries have continued to give way to the newly industrialized nations in terms of their shrinking industrial base as well as their purchasing power, the consequent shift to services and high value-added products has had severe consequences for employment. With services representing over 20 per cent of world trade, the GATT agreement of 1993 will only serve to intensify these tendencies. Thus the gap between skilled and less adaptable labour will grow. Redistributional conflicts around the allocation of structural funds will intensify as regions decline. In this sense the Delors infrastructural project is a far-sighted attempt to provide a Euro-Keynesian solution to simultaneously providing jobs, boosting competitiveness and fostering European regional integration.

The popular portrayal of a *European underclass* common to all member states represents in a shorthand form those who are 'excluded' (*les exclus*) or 'marginalized' by the processes of the Single Market and European unification.[2] Do the 50 million European inhabitants living below the poverty line, defined as half the national average level of income, or the 3 million homeless have any stake in the European process? Could they become divorced from and then actively opposed to not just the European idea but the mainstream of their own societies?

There is little doubt that the visibility of homelessness, poverty, vagrancy, unemployment and low pay as well as the attendant crime and personal insecurity have quickly diluted the post-1989 triumphalism of the Western industrialized countries. Post-Fordism and the pressure on welfare provision have put the focus sharply on the 'new urban poverty.'[3]

What is clear is that the new poverty affects a widening range of the population with greater economic insecurity (not just migrant but indigenous blue-collar workers, the unskilled and women and young people) and reproduces itself in new forms, particularly in single-parent families.

In Europe as a whole one in five children is now born outside of marriage; the proportion is 50 per cent in Denmark and a third in the UK and France. Fifteen per cent of women between the ages of 20 and 39 live alone, and women earn 30 per cent less in the retail and manufacturing sectors. This points to a new set of social processes with effects not just on the labour market but on the very fabric and texture of social life.[4] Rates of marriage have declined in all the countries of the EU, particularly in Italy and France, while divorce rates have risen. When women choose to marry they now do so almost two years later than ten years ago and as late as 27 in Denmark. In the UK 10.1 per cent of women between 20 and 39 years of age are single parents.

There is a considerable debate as to the relationship between single parenthood and the conditions for the growth of an underclass. When the former is associated with social isolation, poor housing and labour market inequality (not to mention racism) as well as exclusion from full rights of social citizenship, then it is not surprising that their poverty, welfare dependency and social insecurity come to be associated with underclass status for themselves and their children.[5]

There is a well-founded concern that absolute as well as relative poverty is re-emerging and that long-term unemployment transmitted from one generation to the next is producing a form of marginalization which European integration will intensify and not diminish. As the EC's 'Social Europe' report says: 'There is a very real danger . . . that the internal market will make certain sections of the population more vulnerable.'[6] Unemployment is scheduled to reach 12.25 per cent by mid-1994 whereas youth unemployment has risen dramatically to 19.6 per cent. Europe is not working for these people.[7] This situation represents the erosion of the European project from within, an undermining of the legitimacy of a united Europe within the generation which will have to carry forward the new agenda.

To this extent, western Europe shares the same problem as post-communist societies where significant groups of citizens have little or no interest in continued marketization. In the most prosperous of post-communist states – the Czech republic – 36 per cent of the employed population are seriously concerned over unemployment, although it actually stands at a mere 3 per cent. They are mainly the older, less-educated and small-town residents.[8] They and their counterparts have voted in ex-communists in Poland and Hungary and shown an upsurge of support for left parties in general, threatening to derail the train of reform in these countries – not to mention the voice of the excluded in Russia in the December 1993 elections.

Changes in political mentality in both sets of countries among their political elites as well as their populations may, however, lead to a renewed emphasis on social policy intervention and provide a common plank for European widening and integration. Both groups of countries will have to pay greater heed to their losers and not assume a preponderance of support for their respective projects.

Briefly put, therefore, both Eastern and Western Europe face the problem of legitimating an economic order, one national, the other transnational, which until recently was seen as self-legitimating. In a global situation no longer dominated by a bipolar vision and where socialist class-based rhetoric and sociological reality provide no easy discourse for such legitimation, the political classes have to provide a formula, in Mosca's sense, which will give a moral rationale for subordination to programmes of reform. In both sets of societies the reforms have no clearly defined outcomes, have an unfolding destination and demand a degree of trust from the populations involved commensurate with the scale of the transformations.

In this context the over-arching drive to expanded membership from 12 to possibly 25 without shoring up past achievements is perceived as at worst fantasy and at best a substitute for dealing with the urgent problems of EMU and foreign policy enactment and more specifically with the political goals of European union. It may be the corollary of the east central European (ECE) countries' ideology of 'rejoining Europe' which substituted for spelling out the costs of transition from communism. For west Europeans the wider Europe substitutes for examining what the eventual goal of European union involves; for the ECE rejoining Europe substitutes for understanding what the reality of European Union association and membership involves in terms of social costs. It is here that the social agenda, until now the step-sister of market integration, may suddenly come into its own. To the extent that social Europe introduces the human dimension it may provide the moral impetus to unification programmes which have run out of steam.

However, such an emphasis on caring for the socially excluded and marginalized could be internally inclusionary but externally exclusionary. It would care for the insiders at the expense of the ranks of outsiders and provide fuel to those who see in this another dimension of fortress Europe.

Western Europe has effectively sealed itself off from eastern immigration by creating *de facto* migration control zones out of adjacent countries. Poland, for example, has several hundred thousand migrant workers, chiefly from the former Soviet Union, annually working either legally or illegally on building sites and farms as well as in the role of domestics or even in skilled jobs.[9] Whether these migrant workers are a portent of a longer-term process brought about by a surplus of labour in the FSU or simply reflect relative currency values is not clear. Nevertheless it does indicate that a fortress Europe has different consequences for those just outside its walls than for those further afield.

New sources of social cleavage?

The underclass phenomenon raises certain key questions for the future of the European process. To what extent is the nation state a continuing key actor in maintaining and creating social structures, outside of globalizing and homogenizing tendencies? Following on from this, to what extent can Europe erode the inequalities maintained by the nation-state and intervene in the political process through which class and other inequalities are institutionalized and reproduced? To answer these questions it is first necessary to ask whether class is still a determinant of social inequality or whether it has now been superseded in advanced capitalist societies by other forms of cleavage.

Some argue that in advanced industrial societies, class distinctions have become less rigid.[10] Thus hierarchy rather than class, status rather than labour market have become the important factors in determining political action and allegiance. The welfare state, occupational diversification, growing affluence, changing party dynamics, dual labour markets associated with new labour market distinctions have all contributed to the decline of class politics and a lesser role of class in explaining political action.

Pakulski[11] has identified five changes behind the decomposition of classes. It is useful at this stage to signal how processes which in the West are associated with class decomposition and reformation are in the post-communist East linked with highly specific processes of class formation.

Privatization

The first change Pakulski identifies is massive privatization and small business proliferation within the context of a global economy, trade liberalization and markets. The privatization of the state sector, of housing stock and of utilities such as telecommunications is doing more than simply blurring property rights boundaries: the possibility of privatizing Germany's state-owned banking sector is seen as going to the core of the 'social market' regulation in that country and the introduction of competitiveness into the Swedish welfare state goes to the very heart of the Swedish model. More indirectly the privatization of municipal housing stock has been identified as one of the obstacles to anti-poverty programmes.[12] There are also broader processes at work dividing sections of the white-collar 'service class' professionals from managers within the context of the post-Fordist flexible firm.[13]

Research identifying assets with classes and in particular property assets with the *petite bourgeoisie*, organizational assets with managers and cultural assets with professionals is useful in understanding class formation in the newly marketizing ECE societies. In post-communist societies mass privatization through vouchers or small-scale privatization from below is constituting classes *ab initio*, both a class of employees and one of entrepreneurs. The manner in which various forms of political, social and cultural capital (including organizational assets, networks of dependence and information and educational qualification and knowledge) are converted into economic capital provides one way into understanding who becomes a capitalist, and more generally how a middle class[14] is shaped from the admixture of intelligentsia, state employees and small businesses and who emerges as 'loser' and 'winner' from the transformation process.[15]

There is a real possibility that two societies are being formed in these post-communist systems:

> About two thirds of adult Poles have adopted the 'hedgehog' strategy: they have cut down on their use of electricity, hot water and heating, renouncing personal pleasures, repairing old things rather than buying new or else looking only for bargains (or Russian bazaars), they seek support in the family, eat their savings and do not pay rent and other bills, have no concrete life goals and live ever more frugally from day to day. The remaining one third of society, chiefly the young and the educated, apply a diametrically different strategy of the 'fox': they look for and find better paid or additional work, they set up their own businesses or invest in shares, they raise or change their qualifications and skills, and set themselves concrete life goals to be realised. *These are two separate societies but – contrary to western class systems or eastern caste-clan systems – they are completely mixed together.*[16]

As such, the market led to the initial collapse of old ties (even families) and the reformulation of new groups.

At the elite level in the ECE countries a powerful managerial class with communist pasts and international ties will co-exist with an emerging capitalism and new capitalists and further complicate property rights.[17] In Hungary, for example, whereas the new political class has emerged from the professional and intelligentsia backgrounds, the new economic elite has been recruited from the ex-communist technocrats who nonetheless had fewer organizational assets than their nomenklatura counterparts. The latter have generally done least well since political capital has not transferred easily in these societies. Where ex-communist parties are in power, as in Poland, this political capital has had to be buttressed by cultural and economic capital.[18]

Here the growth of the divide between the public sector and private sector employees within conditions of tight budget constraints may override traditional class divisions. Teachers and medical personnel may increasingly support the political choices of the statist left to the extent that they cannot escape into private education and medical practice. Likewise, property ownership is not necessarily an accurate indicator of political proclivities in countries like Poland. Here entrepreneurs and peasants supported ex-communist parties and their allies rather than more overtly liberal parties.[19]

There are no easy assumptions to be made as to the course of class formation and political action in the post-communist countries. What is clear is that the structural legacies of the redistributive state could be more permanent than transition theory assumed. In particular the link between forms of property and political tendencies is unclear.

Convertibility of credentials

Secondly it is argued that the importance of educational credentials and more generally of cultural capital weakens the power of market forces and property and therefore intervenes in the old class divisions. In post-communist societies the manner in which the state intelligentsia is able to adapt to the market for culture and competition for funding as well as to function within professions and occupational groupings will have considerable impact on the salience of class. In many cases credentials such as higher education and forms of expertise developed within the planned redistributive economy cannot easily be converted into similar positions within the market. Accountancy, the law as well as minor professions provide common credentials but often individual personal predispositions rooted in family background, e.g. mother's occupation, may determine the inclination to entrepreneurship.[20]

Social citizenship rights

It is possible that in advanced industrial countries the generation of substantive citizenship rights such as positive discrimination and affirmative action could further undermine the role of market forces and class position in determining life chances. Furthermore it is state-protection which will defend large categories of producers across the class divide and thus create industry or sectoral-based solidarity.

In ECE countries substantive social citizenship in terms of rights to work and to own a share of the enterprise accompanied the return to favour of post-communist political parties. Whether such a collective interpretation of citizenship rights will serve to assuage the effects of class inequality or actually limit their propagation remains to be seen. What is evident is that the state continues to figure predominantly in the determination of life chances.[21]

Producer-consumer tensions

Mass consumption creates a tension between individuals and groups as consumers and producers of both goods and services. The impact on the ability of trade unions to mobilize on higher wages is obvious.

The corollary of this for trade unions in east central Europe is the tension between defending employee-producer interests in the subsidized vestiges of state-owned industry and agriculture and defending the interests of the new consumers for modern goods and services. This represents a clear cleavage between single-issue class parties, supporting either worker or peasant interests, as opposed to the more generalized commitment to privatization, the market and European membership. Solidarity was the *locus classicus* of such a division of interests. The ex-communist PSL government has opted for protecting agricultural producers against foreign imports, raising prices to consumers by between 2 and 5 per cent.

Declining corporatism

Alternative sources of identity formation, the so-called 'imagined communities' (ecological, lifestyle, regional, etc.), have helped to dilute class identity and given greater salience to new social movements. It is, however, in the decorporatization and de-alignment of political structures in western Europe that the major change lies. The dissonance between corporatist arrangements and partisan politics cemented earlier in the twentieth century and the tensions generated by socio-economic differentiation mentioned above underlie the tectonic shifts and realignments in western Europe. The New Europe is a factor in this renegotiation and realignment. The degree of corporatism prevalent in collective bargaining is generally recognized as one of the factors influencing the level of unemployment in OECD countries.[22]

It is possible that Euro-corporatism may replace the declining levels of national neo-corporatist structures.[23] But for the time-being a 'hybrid model lying somewhere between the deregulated market economy and the corporatist social economy' is the most likely outcome.[24] In the ECE the arrangements of the transition, often neo-corporatist in nature, may yet be replaced not by new politics but by traditional left-right alignments. However, if class identity is short-circuited by limitations on the formations of markets and civil society flourishes then perhaps these countries may miss a historical stage and move into classless politics and social structure.

Pakulski's schema is countered by those who argue for the continued influence of class in structuring political consciousness as well as life chances. UK researchers have concluded that class continues to be as much a source of ideological conflict in the 1980s as it was in the 1960s. Class-based politics has declined because of the contraction of the working class and not because of its socio-political distinctiveness, confirming the view that just because parties have shifted to the larger middle class, this does not of itself imply the end of class interests as such. The effects of other social cleavages in determining political consciousness have not been at the expense of class differences.[25]

In effect, the argument is that the birth of new sources of inequality does not imply the death of old ones.[26] For these observers the existence of long-term unemployment and low-income localities of multiple deprivation, extended marginalization and exclusion point to the resurgence of class, not to its demise.

Although the debate continues it is apparent from what research can be mustered that the overlap between class and status, race, ethnicity and gender varies across nation-states. Although nation-states may share certain socio-structural trends, the continuing differences in institutions, political dynamics, and the ability of the states to modify social inequality mean that 'class relations within nations . . . still mediate relations between nations.'[27]

Poverty and the making of a European underclass

This section addresses the issues of poverty and unemployment as they affect both western and eastern Europe and the extent to which they highlight new social cleavages or the persistence or even intensification of old divisions.

The new poverty affecting western Europe involves an increase in the long-term unemployed, greater insecurity of employment, indebtedness and homelessness. It is also on the agenda of political parties, and of trade unions which, with declining membership, now have to include the problems of the unemployed. Local government is likewise a new actor, as are poverty lobbies.

These trends affecting poverty have to be read with the proviso that among western countries 'cross-national variation in income inequality seems to have become somewhat larger in the late 1980s compared with the beginning of the decade' and that therefore there has not been a convergence among western countries. A further rider is that research in the Eurobarometer countries has indicated that national cultural traditions may strongly mute or intensify the expression of satisfactions and discontents.[28] Moreover, a multitude of social mechanisms alleviate the consequences of changes within industry, welfare provision, education and employment. Naples, despite rising unemployment and increased reported poverty, displays a 'strengthening of the dynamics of social consensus': on the one hand, kinship solidarity and reciprocity and, on the other, the informal economy mitigate the effects of economic change.[29] The obvious relevance of this form of survival to the countries of ECE needs to be remarked upon. Indeed Rose has referred negatively to the 'Neapolitanization' of the economy in post-command econ-omies.[30] In Hungary the continued reliance of households on the informal economy is not only due to the inertia of the previous activity in the second economy or to traditionalism but 'because people are rational and they rely on deeply socialised behavioral patterns, skills and networks'.[31]

Even taking these considerations into account, Eurobarometer surveys show that two-thirds of the populations of ECE countries believe that their standard of living has declined since 1989. A third felt it would continue to deteriorate and another third thought that it would not improve. In fact in one study 52 per cent of Hungarian respondents recognized that their household finances would get worse over the next 12 months.[32]

Some poverty studies have indicated that genuine hunger and poverty are related to a restructuring of consumption patterns especially towards more expensive but available consumer durables and away from foodstuffs. Only 3 per cent of Poles in their subjective assessment believed their situation had improved over the past five years. Yet car ownership between 1989 and 1991 rose by 22 per cent.[33] Likewise, 40 per cent of adults claim to have no savings at all and yet bank deposits in the first half of 1993 compared with 1992 rose by between 14 per cent for domestic currency and 9 per cent for foreign currency holdings.[34]

These qualifications aside, there is little doubt that economic reforms in the ECE countries are creating a section of society which has suffered considerable material cutbacks, sees little prospect for inclusion into the rewards of economic growth and retains the prospect of long-term multiple deprivation. In particular, multi-children families, often with an invalid among them, are often ignorant of where to seek help.[35] Income redistribution in Poland, for example, has favoured pensioners (often those who have taken early retirement) and private entrepreneurs at the expense of workers and farmers.[36] It is among the employed rather than the unemployed that many of the new poor are to be found since in all countries of the region the minimum wage was reduced quite drastically (except Poland where it increased by 3 per cent in 1992).[37] Although income re-stratification has occurred over the past five years, it appears that people have not changed their ranking of social positions. In any case, perceptions of occupational prestige change over a longer time scale. Certain groups received wages below the social minimum, such as one in five women workers in the private sector. In fact 12.4 per cent of those employed in the private sector were paid less than the social minimum and overall 60 per cent of all Polish employees received pay below that required to sustain two persons.[38] Given that the non-state sector of employment is now greater and has much reduced trade union cover, this represents a key group in society.

Almost as an afterthought, those ECE countries to the fore of economic reform have now recognized that the social dimension has to be built into any model of economic transformation. Whether this lesson is too late for the ECE reformers it is too early to say.

Poverty is compounded by poor lifestyle, low health levels and the inability of the health services to provide adequate care.[39] The health crises inherited by most of the post-communist countries have intensified and low-income families have been hit by the combination of privatization and re-organization in this sector. In Hungary 'a third of those aged between forty and fifty nine suffered from a chronic illness or a physical or mental deficiency'.[40] Environmental degradation further compounds the problem, with low male life expectancies and high infant mortality rates. Poland has seen its highest drop in birth rates since the war, reflecting the intense economic pressures on households. Societal pressures have also seen suicide rates increase after 1989, and youth in particular both in the East and West appear to be affected.

The dynamics of poverty in the post-communist societies indicate the new cleavages being created by the market and their impact upon the political system. Given that it is mainly young people under 25 years of age with higher education living in larger conurbations who are wholeheartedly in favour of reforms in the ECE countries, it will be some time before a constituency of support emerges. At the other extreme are the 25 per cent of households in Poland that now depend on social assistance, which is itself being cut, particularly housing benefit and provision of goods and services in kind. Poland has at least 200,000 homeless and shares its casualties of the transition with its neighbours.

In the meantime both in eastern and western Europe images of poverty will continue to be used to demand a 'socialization' of the over-economicized processes of transformation. The question is to what extent ECE countries will accept this level of impoverishment of themselves and their fellow citizens.

Unemployment in the EC: dealing with the underclass

While the ECE countries are in the process of creating a class of outsiders who are unable to manage the demands of transition, the EC is developing policies to integrate its 'outsiders', largely to be found within its 17 million unemployed and more specifically among the 40–50 per cent of these without work for over a year, without at the same time undermining the rights of the secure 'insiders'. The aim is to provide flexibility with security and deregulation without economic deprivation, by creating low-paid jobs instead of unemployment.

Rising unemployment across the EU is recognized as threatening economic and monetary union. The problem of increasing numbers of unskilled male workers displaced through new technologies and production processes is not alleviated by the growing flexible, atypical largely female employment. Active labour market policies involving (re)training of the unemployed and the school-aged as well as restraints on unions are among the remedies offered. If widening pay differentials and an increase in the proportion of insecure jobs as well as in unemployment point to more volatile and diversified labour markets, then countering this involves a level of intervention which is currently beyond the EU remit. A coherent social policy could, however, provide a basis for acceptable EU involvement.

Research has shown that the equation of part-time work with the marginalization of employment for women only really holds in Britain. France and Germany, although having different gender regimes, vary little in terms of employment conditions. Likewise in terms of pay differences between men and women, European countries vary among themselves. This points to one of the factors other than class associated with determining life chances. The precariousness of women's employment has increased, as has labour force participation, because of the exclusion of women from the political process.[41] Since women, as both recipients and employees, are more dependent on public policy and state agencies this may foster their political mobilization.[42] Further deregulation could jeopardize those gains that have been made.

Unemployment in the ECE countries: an underclass in the making?

Although the EU figures are not as high as in the majority of ECE countries, Spain's unemployment, for example for the under-25s, nonetheless stands at 37.9 per cent against 19.6 per cent for the EU as a whole. Can the unsatisfactory initial experience of employment among youth of both East and West undermine the future legitimacy of their respective projects?

With unemployment rates ranging from 32 per cent in Albania to 15.7 per cent in Bulgaria and to a mere 3 per cent in the Czech republic, both parts of Europe face a second common problem which goes to the very heart of their programmes. The problem appears to have taken on the same sense of urgency in the EU as in those countries facing it for the first time. Long-term unemployment is a key to identifying the potential winners and losers of the trans-formation processes and thus the social basis for the new politics.

Unemployment is obviously a major factor in poverty (although not the only one). For example in Poland not only does it affect one in five households, but they are those in which 60 per cent of all children are found. Nearly 60 per cent of all the unemployed in Poland are under 35 years of age and at a critical point in the demographic cycle. Of 14.3 per cent Polish unemployed, 2,700,000 in total, over 1.2m have been unemployed for over a year and 13 per cent for over two years.[43] Unemployment is calculated as lowering household income by at least 30 per cent.

Alongside young people, who are disproportionately affected by unemployment in all the countries of the region (over 80 per cent of the unemployed in Romania were under 40, and 45 per cent in Bulgaria under 30), women took the brunt of unemployment, especially in Poland and Romania. In the latter case social capital of a kind was also involved in keeping a job. Connections and influence counted considerably and women, who made up 60 per cent of the unemployed in Romania, have fewer of these.[44]

In Poland less than 10 per cent were involved in active programmes for the unemployed and 5 per cent were in public works programmes. Vocational training falls well below western efforts, which are themselves the subject of criticism and have a negligible impact. As in the West this has led to regional approaches to unemployment with special retraining schemes and incubators for small business development. But it is those who fall outside the unemployment register and become dependent on welfare – some 30 per cent of the total unemployed in Poland – who have the least chance of returning to the labour market. It is they who may not just fuel the second economy but also intensify social pathologies of a personal or public nature, such as alcoholism or criminality, and thus produce an underclass which at best may accompany the growth of market-capitalism and at worst may undermine its very foundations.

The social policy dimension

The introduction of a social dimension to Europe through the Social Protocol has raised not just a question of providing a social policy to underpin the European labour market but also the broader issue of the normative integration of these employees into Europe's Single Market.

Whereas the Protocol has to date excluded interfering in the nationally determined balance of power between labour and employers, it is evident that a form of Euro-corporatism is increasingly driving the European agenda[45] as much as the growing pressure for EC-level regulation of labour markets and their consequences.

Although it is accepted that labour market conditions are linked to national political histories and values, there is 'scarcely any area of public policy in which there is a greater need for a far-reaching, radical and European-wide debate than social policy'.[46] This is not to suggest that the German, Italian, French and British welfare regimes will somehow grow together organically since there is little common ground for such convergence. More likely, the EU may create a *parallel* welfare state[47] alongside national forms of welfare provision. In particular there are activities which contain the bases of a shared social policy. Structural funds involve income transfer not just between regions but between social groups and the Delors proposals are further evidence of this. The European Regional Development Fund, not to mention the CAP as well as the anti-poverty programmes in place since the 1970s have led to the conclusion 'that at best it is possible to identify the seeds of welfarism in the operation of programmes with other ambitions and in the form of rather minor welfare programmes.'[48]

The social dimension will also be brought about by multinationals requiring consistency for their planning and investment strategies. At least two processes are generally identified, both requiring a harmonization of standards. Firstly, the labour market is itself undergoing fundamental changes. Secondly, transnational business and transfrontier worker mobility require the coordination of rules and regulations for both employer and employee alike.[49]

Whether this is achieved through harmonization or coordination, that is through the approximation of national laws, through control over the degree of variation[50] or through a combination of these two, depends on the internal political complexion of the countries involved. But in the main Europe's social dimension will continue to represent an expression of national political processes rooted within nation-state identities rather than of supranational ones.[51] ·

There can be little doubt that the question of poverty, its popular perception and political resonance has made it a European concern both at micro and macro level. Both the Poverty III EC Programme and the Social Exclusion 1994 Programme reflect the desire of the Commission to highlight the problem of poverty and thus bring the social chapter of the Maastricht agreement to centre stage. At the same time there is official reticence in admitting the existence of anything as semi-permanent as a European underclass.

For its part, survey data indicate quite clearly that of all the issues under the heading of social affairs, the fight against poverty is considered the most appropriate for EC action.[52] That poverty should have become a west European issue, raised from private, national or local concerns to its public transnational status, is probably best explained by the redistributive connotation of EC funding (whether this be in structural funds or the CAP).

If the growing opposition to further European integration in some EC member states, not to mention the growing minority of opponents in post-communist countries, is to be defused it may well be in the form of concessions in the area of European citizenship rights. The perceived casualties of European economic and political integration (whether real or imagined) have to be incorporated through the extension of substantive rights to the benefits of continued economic union. In fact there is a feeling that the EC will have to move from largely industrial citizenship concerns associated with labour markets and workplace decision-making to broader areas of citizenship, particularly social citizenship.[53]

Conclusion

With the recognition that the 'new security' in Europe has a socio-economic dimension rooted in the labour market, as well as military and political aspects,[54] the social dimension of European integration has received the highest affirmation. It is recognized that the level of social exclusion created through unemployment is unacceptable. Therefore seeking national as well as transnational solutions to unemployment and poverty, as well as to exclusion based upon race, gender and even region, is as high a priority as monetary union.

The structural sources of inequality and deprivation have global as well as regional dimensions which economic liberalization will only intensify. Class inequalities associated with markets and status inequalities tied to welfare policies retain their nationally specific features regardless of the common pressures that beset them. How any set of policies can be elaborated and imposed taking this multi-layered interdependence into account appears a daunting task.

Yet the European project involves not only the interests of consumers and voters but also of social citizens who have the right to participate meaningfully in the new European order.

Notes

1. The generally accepted ideal types of welfare regime clusters characteristic of capitalist societies are contained in G. Esping-Andersen, *The Three Worlds of Welfare Capitalism*, Cambridge: Polity Press, 1990.
2. The announcement of the social exclusion five-year action plan by the EU to tackle at the grass-roots level the problems facing those disadvantaged in housing, health and social integration is a political response within a social policy format, *The Week in Europe*, 23/9/93.

3. E. Mingione, 'The New Urban Poverty and the Underclass: Introduction', *International Journal of Urban and Regional Research*, No. 2, 1993.
4. *The Week in Europe*, Eurostat, 2/12/93.
5. For an excellent overview of the dimensions of the underclass phenomenon see: Lydia Morris, *Dangerous Classes: The Underclass and Social Citizenship*, London: Routledge, 1994.
6. *Social Europe – Second Report on the Application of the Community Charter of the Fundamental Rights of Workers*, Supplement 1/93. Part one, pp. 13–14.
7. *Eurostat* 8/9, 1993, pp. 44–5.
8. RFE/RL Daily Report 14/10/93.
9. T. Wolf, 'Czarna liczba obcych', *Życie Gospodarcze*, 26/12/93.
10. T. Nichols, S.M. Lipset and M. Rempel, 'The declining political significance of social class', *International Sociology*, vol. 8, no. 3, September 1993, p. 313.
11. J. Pakulski, 'The dying of class or of marxist class theory?', *International Sociology*, vol. 8, no. 3, 1993, pp. 284–5.
12. 'Internal Market. Current Status', *Community Social Policy*, 1/1/93, p. 115.
13. M. Savage *et al.*, *Property, Bureaucracy and Culture: Middle Class Formation in Contemporary Britain*, Routledge, 1992.
14. *The Formation of the Middle Class in Transition Societies*, Estonian Institute of Future Studies, Tallinn, 1993.
15. While recognizing the limitations to the easy use of a term derived within a specifically economic context it would appear that Bourdieu's forms of capital can help in understanding the strategies adopted by groups in dealing with inherently new economic, political and social realities. P. Bourdieu, 'The Forms of Capital', in J.G. Richardson, *Handbook of Theory and Research for the Sociology of Education*, Greenwood Press, 1986, Chap 9.
16. J. Czapinski, 'Szczęście w nieszczęściu', *Wprost*, 26/12/1993. This is a summary of social psychological research carried out between 1991 and 1993 in Poland on individual attitudes to the consequences of economic and political change.
17. For a view of the complexity of class formation when tied to privatization at both micro and macro level see A. Agh, 'Europeanization through privatizing and pluralization in Hungary', *Studies in Public Policy*, no. 211, Glasgow 1993.
18. For an interesting first account of work in progress see I. Szelenyi and S. Szelenyi, 'Changing patterns of elite recruitment in post communist transformation: first results from a Hungarian study', Paper presented 16/9/93, CEU, Prague.
19. 'SLD zyskał u wszystkich', *Prawo i Życie*, 21/9/93.
20. See Gyorgy Lengyl and Istvan Janos Toth, 'The spread of entrepreneurial inclinations in Hungary', Paper presented to the ESRC East-West Programme Workshop, Budapest: University of Economics, 25–8 March 1993.

21. For an earlier version of this argument see G. Kolankiewicz, 'The reconstruction of citizenship: Reverse incorporation in Eastern Europe', in K. Poznanski (ed.), *Constructing Capitalism: The re-emergence of civil society and liberal economy in the post-communist world*, Westview, 1992.

22. M. Burda, 'Unemployment, Labour markets and structural change in Eastern Europe', *Economic Policy*, April 1993.

23. J. Greenwood, J. Grote and K. Ronit, *Organized Interests and the European Community*, London: Sage, 1992.

24. See E. Kirchner, 'Interest groups, the European Commission and parties: their influence on European industrial policy in the years ahead', Paper submitted to the FINE Teilnetzwerk Project on 'Macro-Change-Makers', European Institute for Public Administration, March 1993.

25. G. Evans, 'The decline of class divisions in Britain? Class and ideological preferences in the 1960s and 1980s', *British Journal of Sociology*, vol. 44, no. 3, September 1993.

26. Hout, Brooks and Manza, 'The persistence of classes in post-industrial societies', *International Sociology*, *loc. cit.*, p. 270.

27. H. Silver, 'National Conceptions of the New Urban Poverty and the Underclass: Introduction', *International Journal of Urban and Regional Research*, no. 2, 1993, p. 349.

28. A. Inkeles, 'Industrialization, modernization and the quality of life', *International Journal of Comparative Sociology*, 1–2, 1993, pp. 13–15.

29. E. Mingione and E. Morlicchio, 'New forms of urban poverty in Italy: Risk path models in the North and South', *IJURR* 1993 *loc. cit.*, p. 423.

30. R. Rose, *Toward a Civil Economy*, Studies in Social Policy No. 200, Glasgow, 1992, p. 17.

31. E. Sik, *From the Second Economy to the Informal Economy*, Studies in Public Policy No. 207, Glasgow, 1992, p. 27.

32. Central and Eastern European Eurobarometer, EC Commission, February 1993, Fig. 5.

33. M. Luczak, 'Polska bieda', *Wprost No 27* 1993.

34. J. Malysz K. Duczkowska-Malysz, 'Kondycja gospodarstw domowych w I kwartale 1993', *Życie Gospodarcze* 2/5/93.

35. It is almost a national press pastime in Poland to go and look for the poor. When they are found the picture is as harrowing as it is differentiated. See A. Leslawski, 'Bieda spogląda w oczy', *Polityka*, 25/12/93.

36. S. Gomulka, 'Poland: glass half full', in R. Portes (ed.), *Economic Transformation in Central Europe. A Progress Report*, CEPR, 1993, p. 204.

37. *Employment in Europe. Central and Eastern Europe*, EC No. 4, May 1993.

38. Z. Jacukowicz, 'Praca czy płaca?', *Życie Gospodarcze*, 15/9/93.

39. A. Mozowski, 'Chory jak Polak', *Polityka*, 25/9/93.

40. For an overview see 'Health care crisis. Eastern Europe and the former USSR', *RFE/RL Research Report*, vol. 2, no. 40, 8/10/93.

41. C. Lane, 'Gender and labour markets in Europe: Britain, Germany and France compared', *The Sociological Review*, no. 2, 1993.

42. Julia S. O'Connor, 'Gender, class and citizenship in the comparative analysis of welfare state regimes: theoretical and methodological issues', *BJS*, vol. 44, no. 3, 1993.
43. I. Lisek, 'Walka. statystyków z bezrobociem', *Tygodnik Popularny*, 3/10/93; I. Dryll, 'Bezrobocie-bez programu', *Życie Gospodarcze*, 25/4/93.
44. D. Ionescu, 'Unemployment: Romania's number one social problem', *RFE/RL Research Report*, vol. 1, no. 22, 29 May 1992.
45. J. Greenwood, Grote and Ronit, *Organized Interests and the European Community*, London: Sage, 1992.
46. P. Ludlow, *Beyond Maastricht*, Centre for European Policy Studies, Working Document, no. 79, Brussels, October 1993, p. 37.
47. A. Cochrane and J. Clarke, *Comparing Welfare States. Britain in International Context*, London: Sage/OU, 1993.
48. *Loc. cit.*, p. 252.
49. *Social Europe. Second Report on the Application of the Community Charter of the Fundamental Social Rights of Workers*, Supplement 1/93, Part One.
50. E. Meehan, *Citizenship and the European Community*, London: Sage, 1993, p. 67.
51. P. Lange, 'Maastricht and the Social Protocol: Why did they do it?', *Politics and Society*, vol. 21, no. 1, March 1993, p. 29.
52. *Eurobarometer*, 39, Fig. 3.5.
53. S. Garciá, 'Europe's Fragmented Identities and the Frontiers of Citizenship', in S. Garciá (ed.), *European Identity and the Search for Legitimacy*, London: RIIA/Pinter, 1993, pp. 24–6.
54. See reference to President Clinton's speech in Brussels referring to the three pillars of European security, *Financial Times*, 10/1/94.

10

Security for Europe

Trevor Taylor

Introduction

How is security in all of Europe to be assured after the Cold War? Satisfactory answers have not yet been agreed to this question, although many governments and individuals in the former communist bloc clearly feel that their current situation is uncertain and disturbing. Although Soviet dominance has gone, there are too few structures of reassurance in central and eastern Europe. While there is little immediate sense of threat in many cases, there is also little sense of what could offer protection should a threat arise. Ideally, many in central and eastern Europe would like their security relations to have a similar cooperative and reliable character to those perceived among west European states. One of the most impressive features of western Europe, indeed of the North Atlantic area, is its character as a 'pluralistic security community',[1] where the threat and use of force plays no part in inter-state relations. International relationships among the developed states of the northern hemisphere have been described as 'post-modern', having broken free of traditional struggles for power and concentrating on cooperation for economic, social and political gain.[2]

It is argued here that convincing and widely accepted answers have been elusive with regard to security in the newly liberated parts of Europe partly because the questions involved raise such fundamental issues about the nature of international relations. An appropriate starting point is in the Cold War itself, which had global scope but was focused on Europe.

The European security order during the Cold War

The Cold War system was notable for its clarity. The Soviet Union dominated eastern Europe in military, political, economic and social terms while seeking with its armed forces to maintain a capability quickly to overrun western Europe in the event of (a western-induced) war.[3] While Moscow's doctrinal position on non-conventional weapons varied somewhat over the years, at several stages the Red Army envisaged the early use of chemical and even nuclear weapons to achieve its goal of a quick victory in Europe. The West for its part formed a successful alliance based on the US to deter Soviet aggression and, if necessary, to defend against it. NATO too had its debates about nuclear weapons and, after acceptance of flexible response as NATO doctrine in 1967, increasingly sought to place a greater share of the burden of deterrence on conventional forces, though with only limited success.

The key to the stability of the system was the lack of real interest on either side in using force to change the *status quo*. The high human and material cost which would have been involved was certainly a disincentive. In the early 1950s, some in the West talked about 'rolling back' the Iron Curtain but the idea of doing this by force would never have won popular endorsement. Some analysts stress that the presence of atomic weapons was of decisive impact on the attitudes of leaders and peoples.[4] Thus the system withstood various challenges including several crises over Berlin, the Hungarian and Czechoslovak crises of 1956 and 1968 respectively, the French withdrawal from the integrated military command of NATO after 1967, and a more or less continuous technological and quantitative arms race.

When the system broke down, as it did after 1988, it was mainly because of changes in attitude within the Soviet Union with regard to the increasingly doubted hostility of the West, the growing costs of maintaining the Soviet empire at a time when economic growth in the communist part of Europe was lagging behind that of the West, and Soviet military awareness that any effort to overrun western Europe was likely to be unsuccessful.

Emphatically clear in the Cold War security system was that the states of central and eastern Europe were victims rather than beneficiaries. At the height of the Cold War, not only did they suffer Soviet occupation and political domination in peacetime, in a major war the central Europeans particularly would have been the likely targets of any initial western use of tactical nuclear weapons.

At the same time, the states of western Europe had good reason to be content with the Cold War stand-off, with the exception of the Germans, who had to suffer the division of their country, and to a lesser extent the French, who worried constantly about American domination. West Europeans, by spending between 3 per cent and 5 per cent of their national products on defence (but without coordinating their spending particularly well), could reliably keep Moscow at bay. While many were reluctant to spend more on defence than the minimum necessary, and NATO experienced a more or less constant debate on burden-sharing, the volume of resources devoted to defence did not prevent most west European countries from achieving a very satisfactory rate of economic growth and overall prosperity. West Germany, which enjoyed a remarkable recovery from the devastation of 1945, had particular cause for satisfaction in this respect. Also the United States did not seek a massive economic price from or exact close political control over western Europe in exchange for its conventional help and nuclear guarantee. Indeed, not all west European states even needed to ally with the US in formal terms.

Clearly many individuals found the price of living with the constant possibility of nuclear war to be high in stress and even in moral terms, as the important peace movements of the 1980s revealed, but the great majority of westerners remained confident of their future.

Perhaps most important, the countries of the North Atlantic area developed exceptional relationships with each other, becoming a pluralistic security community. Britain, France and West Germany had to worry constantly about the military capabilities of the Soviet Union but not at all about those of each other. Britain and France even independently developed their own nuclear forces without creating any sense of threat to each other.

Western European security after the Cold War: expanding a security community?

Particularly significant for the post-Cold War period is the uncertainty as to the real foundations of the west European, indeed the entire North Atlantic security community. While the Cold War was in place, the west Europeans could enjoy the existence of that sense of community without asking too persistently about its basis and whether it might disappear. With the end of the Cold War, some doubts and uncertainties have become exposed.

There are two major schools of thought. On the one hand is the argument that the cooperative and friendly attitudes of governments and peoples have been built from shared values and cultures[5] and from the interdependence and contacts brought about by a massive network of beneficial economic and social interaction. In this perspective, associated particularly with the thought of Karl Deutsch[6] and his followers, the European Community/Union has been and is the engine helping peoples and states in the region to become ever more integrated so that war among them becomes both impractical and unthinkable. This perspective tends to stress that west European integration processes are already irreversible, and indeed generate many pressures for further cooperation and supra-national decision-making. Integration theorists sometimes recognize the possibility that integration may stall and may even be pushed into reverse but they basically expect progress ('spill-over') to prevail, albeit at a slower rate than some would like.

Subsumed within this school for the purpose of this chapter are those who argue slightly differently, placing emphasis on the impact of the international institutions which facilitate integration and on the economic benefits which those institutions bring.[7]

On the other hand is the argument of the 'neo-realists' that states in an international anarchy naturally tend towards mutual suspicions and rivalry, regardless of the contacts between their peoples. In this perspective, the decisive element determining state behaviour is the absence of a central authority in the anarchic state system.[8] This means that no state can be reliably constrained other than by countervailing power, normally of a military or economic nature. Thinkers in this school believe that west Europeans cooperated as they did in the past 45 years or so mainly because failure to do so would have meant their domination by the Soviet Union. In addition, a significant American presence in Europe helped west Europeans to put aside their traditional fears of each other. The observation that best encapsulated this perspective was that the purpose of NATO was to keep the Russians out, the Americans in and the Germans down.

Those who hold this perspective argue that the end of the Cold War will probably also mean the end of the west European security community, especially once the US decides to withdraw its forces from Europe. Led in intellectual terms by John Mearsheimer,[9] this group has much in common with those who argued that even during the Cold War the west Europeans could not cooperate effectively on defence without US leadership and encouragement.[10]

The contrasting nature of these assessments is clear. One asserts that the west European security community is stable and able to withstand external shock. The other says that traditional rivalries and behaviour patterns might well reappear. Evidence as to which argument carries most weight with politicians and bureaucrats is predictably ambiguous, but significantly there has been some recognition that the 'neo-realists' might just have a case. In particular there have been a series of warnings stressing the need to maintain existing Western coalitions and the real possibility that defence might become 're-nationalized'.

Much of this debate must appear artificial to many east Europeans, who simply see western Europe as secure and themselves as floating in a cold, dark, uncomfortable security vacuum, but from a west European perspective the true basis of west European security determines not just the attention which west Europeans can make available for the East, but also the effectiveness and time-scale of what western Europeans can do for their neighbours.

In perhaps over-simplified terms, if the pressures stressed by the 'neo-realists' are perceived to be very strong, west Europeans will probably devote most energy to maintaining their own cohesion and solidarity, holding on to what they have got, rather than worrying about expanding the area covered by their security community. On the other hand, if the Deutschian optimists are correct, and the west European security community is built on a network of economic and social contact rather than on the presence of both an external threat and guardian, it follows that the west European security community cannot be extended overnight merely through inter-governmental agreement: eastern Europeans must over time become drawn ever more closely together through a diverse range of contact, both with each other and with west Europeans. This will take some years to build up with much help needed from the European Union (EU).

Neither of these perspectives on western security cooperation are particularly appealing to states in the East, yet their relevance and importance is plain. There is a need for reflection on the fundamentals of the western security system before its possible role in the East can be assessed.

Expanding the area of guarantee

Since major questions will remain about the place of force in interstate relations in the former communist bloc in future, one possibility is that the West should extend the area covered by its alliances, to protect at least some east European states from aggression. Certainly Czechoslovakia, Hungary and Poland became keen on NATO membership almost as soon as they became independent and their enthusiasm did not dim.[11] Other states including the Baltic countries and Russia itself have expressed interest.

By the autumn of 1993, something of a head of steam had built up in favour of allowing at least the Visegrad three or four into NATO sooner rather than later. Both the German foreign and defence ministers had argued in this direction, and so had NATO Secretary-General Wörner. There was also some support for this in the US Congress, articulated notably by Senator Richard Lugar.[12]

In favour of a wider NATO membership were several arguments. One was that NATO membership should bring political stability in the country concerned and would encourage peaceful, cooperative relations between that country and its neighbours. Also, NATO membership would give an assurance of security that would encourage foreign investors and thus economic growth. Should Russia again become a hostile, assertive power, an expanded NATO would have the advantage of defending against it further east. More negative reasons in favour were that NATO needed to remain relevant to contemporary problems to survive (east European insecurity was certainly a contemporary problem); that it was hard to say no to democratic, market economy states, given Article 10 of the North Atlantic Treaty; and that Germany, as the government keenest on a widened NATO, would lose enthusiasm for NATO (and for having foreign forces on its soil), if the Alliance did not meet German preferences.

Many but not all of the points against widening membership in the near future concern the expectation that Russia would not like such a change and would react in a manner inimicable to European security as a whole. Notwithstanding that President Yeltsin accepted briefly in the summer of 1993 that Poland and others were sovereign states free to make their own alliance choices, it remains the case that many nationalist and military elements in Russia would see an expansion in NATO's membership as a threat. There would be the real possibility that Moscow might then seek to reassert control over the Baltic states and Ukraine in particular, almost as a *quid pro quo* for the Western move eastwards. Increases in the Russian defence budget would be likely, making economic growth in Russia more problematic and perhaps increasing the chances of civil war in Russia, with all that would imply for the control of 30,000 nuclear warheads. Russia might well decide to withdraw from the North Atlantic Cooperation Council (NACC), where it is often politically isolated in the face of complaints from the Baltic states, for example. Without the NACC it would be hard for the West to promote useful changes such as the democratic, civilian oversight of defence in Russia and cooperation on peace-keeping. In early 1994 Russia was ambivalent about signing a Partnership for Peace agreement with NATO; Russia would probably not do so if NATO's membership was enlarged. Finally Russia might decide to abandon arms control and disarmament commitments such as the Conventional Forces in Europe Treaty.

There are also points related to the realist perspective. In the period between 1945 and 1989 the western states were clearly unwilling to fight to save democracy in Hungary (1956) or Czechoslovakia (1968), not least because west Europeans and North Americans could enjoy an adequate degree of prosperity and security even though the then Soviet Union appeared powerful. Thus ratification of a widening of NATO's membership might well run into trouble in national legislatures, most obviously the US Congress. North Americans and west Europeans became accustomed and almost comfortable with the assertion that they should defend all West German territory, if necessary with nuclear weapons. They might not feel the same about Poland, especially if Poland was only thinly linked in economic and social terms with western Europe.

Widening NATO's membership in the 1990s would be very different from during the Cold War when Greece and Turkey joined in 1951, Germany and Italy in 1955 and Spain in 1982. Once the door opens again, it may be hard to close as ever more countries struggle to come through. Slovakia would probably want the same benefits as the Czech Republic, Lithuania, Estonia and Latvia already want NATO membership, Romania and Bulgaria are interested and while Ukraine currently says it wishes to remain neutral, it has made repeated demands for guarantees of its territorial integrity. Periodic Russian interest in eventual NATO membership has also been apparent and the more states NATO took in, the harder it would be to refuse a democratic, reforming Russia.

If the three central Europeans (or four including Slovakia) were brought in on the clear basis that expansion was a one-off exercise with no others to follow, the consequence might be to reassure the new members but it would do little for the security of other parts of Europe including the former Soviet Union whose stability and peaceful development is much in the interest of the West. The expansion would be viewed at best as a means of providing Germany with a *cordon sanitaire*.

On the other hand, if an expansion to include central European states was seen as the start of a process of NATO widening, there would be no obvious limits on where it might end. Looking at changing NATO's membership as a process, in the autumn of 1993 thought was being given in Europe to specifying criteria for joining NATO which would always mean Russia would be excluded and would ensure no new members were taken in prematurely. Three criteria were suggested: new NATO members would have to be (i) market economies; (ii) reliable liberal democracies and; (iii) prospective members of the European Union. This last was seen as the one to keep out Russia, despite its incongruous nature. (The US, the most valued member of NATO, could never be in this category, nor could Canada. Perhaps the most vulnerable NATO member, Norway, still appeared to be rejecting the EU membership in 1993, while the EU kept Turkey at arms length despite Ankara's wish for membership.)

Were the sole criteria to be a market economy and liberal democracy, Russia might become a credible NATO candidate if things go well there. 'I think we would all agree', a State Department official has observed, 'that admitting Russia would fundamentally change the nature of the Alliance'.[13]

Quite how the Alliance might change in the long run is, however, unclear. Certainly Russian membership would rule out the possibility that the Alliance could ever be invoked by another NATO member against Russia: the NATO commitment is for collective defence rather than collective security. On the other hand, to join NATO Russia would also have to agree to the peaceful and cooperative behaviour called for in Articles 1 and 2 of the North Atlantic treaty, thus possibly reducing others' sense of insecurity about Moscow.

If Article V (providing for collective defence and a security guarantee) remains the most important element in NATO, then Russian membership would lead to western involvement in the defence of Russian territory, perhaps against threats from China or the Islamic world.

On the other hand, if NATO's main mission changes to providing the training and organization necessary for forces from both sides of the Atlantic to work together effectively in combat and a range of other military operations, and to arranging the political consultation which might make joint military activities feasible, Russian membership would mean that NATO gained access to potentially large and capable forces for deployment on peace-keeping and perhaps peace-enforcing missions around the world. Such a re-orientation of NATO is being seriously considered, not least because of the widespread appreciation of the military value of preparations made by NATO in the context of defence against the Soviet Union when NATO states undertook major multilateral military operations in Kuwait and Yugoslavia.[14] Sustaining the cooperative capabilities of western forces will not be easy given the range of missions which are currently under review and the fact that such missions can be expected to involve an *ad hoc* rather than pre-determined group of NATO states.

The east central Europeans are taking part in the NACC's efforts to increase its members' efforts to improve its members cooperation in peace-keeping preparations[15] and are all signing Partnership for Peace agreements. However, they are less interested in NATO as a forum for discussion or as a training organization for external intervention forces and most interested in the guarantee it provides. Clearly, for NATO to provide a credible guarantee for new members, it would have to make appropriate military preparations and plans. Certainly it would seem unwise to expand NATO's membership until at least outline answers had been agreed to issues such as what role should nuclear weapons play in an expanded NATO, where would (air-launched) nuclear weapons need to be deployed in Europe, would foreign forces ever need to be stationed in the new members, would appropriate exercises to reinforce new members be allowed under CSCE confidence-building agreements, how would NATO's command structure need to be amended, and how would new members fit into NATO's new emphasis on multinational forces. NATO should not commit itself to doing something without having some idea as to how it might do it. These points underline the inadequacy of some half-way measures which have been suggested, such as making the central Europeans associate NATO members or giving them a security guarantee without Alliance membership.

Of course, the assumption that NATO should be able to help defend its members at least for some time using conventional forces only assumes that NATO would include a criterion of inherent defensibility as a qualification for NATO membership. Such a criterion would, however, rule out Estonia and Latvia as potential members since they could not easily be defended against their large neighbour. They would need to rely either on a cooperative security relationship with Russia or, more difficult to envisage, on a deterrent based on weapons of mass destruction or even preparations for protracted guerrilla warfare.

All this suggests that NATO should not change its membership until it has decided what its long-term main mission will be, whether any expansion will be one-off or the start of a process, what the criteria for membership should be, and how the disadvantages of a wider membership can be minimized.

Enlightened rationalism

The arrangement with established concern for pan-European security is the Conference on Security and Cooperation in Europe (CSCE). The CSCE approach to international security reflects thinking about international relations different to that of either the integrationists or the neo-realists. The CSCE applies the views of those who feel that the true, long-term interests of states normally can be reconciled, that decision-makers are capable of action which serves the long-term interest of their societies, that the benefits of cooperation rather than confrontation are too valuable to refuse, and that justice is an objective reality (and is not the product of particular cultural norms). In short, the CSCE reflects the idealist tradition in international relations.

Central in much of this thought is that democracies are much more inclined towards such rational and peaceful behaviour than are other forms of government such as dictatorships and autocracies. In other words, the prospects for interstate relations are much affected by the quality of intrastate political arrangements.

Also important in the idealist tradition is the idea of progress through learning and experience, as actors come better to appreciate the benefits of cooperation rather than confrontation.[16]

Emphasizing the CSCE's contribution to European order means asserting that the most promising short-term option for central and eastern Europe may be to work for interstate relationships based on avoidance of the threat and use of force to change the *status quo*. Instead there should be agreed stress on the value of peace, cooperation, mutual respect for interests of others, international law, ethical norms of behaviour, defence transparency, arms control, and so on. Over time, there is reason to hope that governments will increasingly appreciate the value of this approach. To date, the essential elements in the CSCE process have been that governments discussed and agreed on how they ought to behave with regard both to other governments and to their own citizens, reviewed regularly how well they had lived up to their past commitments, and discussed how existing agreements could be strengthened and extended. The Paris Charter of November 1990 and the July 1992 Helsinki Document were the most recent products of the CSCE process of agreement-building, and have meant the CSCE acquiring a small staff to deal with human rights and conflict prevention in particular.

The CSCE is the forum through which the West can work most easily in diplomatic ways for the establishment and consolidation of cooperative and peaceful behaviour throughout Europe. The ill-defined Balladur Plan of 1993, which developed through the EU Council of Ministers into a proposal for a multi-dimensional European security conference to agree a 'Stability Pact for Europe' including minority rights, should sustain the diplomatic momentum. The West should not seek to control security in eastern Europe by widening the area of NATO membership, but it cannot afford to stop trying to manage security in the region.

Collective security and likely security problems

If stress is to be laid on the CSCE as a means of reinforcing through diplomacy the potential of states for cooperative and peaceful behaviour, some account has also to be taken of those who decide to dismiss such an orientation and to rely on force to gain their way. Thus, it can be argued, the CSCE should have a collective security dimension under which it organizes the punishment of aggressors.

For much of this century considerable thought has been devoted to the possibilities for collective security in Europe.

In previous periods collective security efforts have failed partly because of rivalries among the states which might have enforced them: Britain and France were reluctant to punish Italy in the 1930s over the invasion of Abyssinia because Italy was valued as a possible ally against Germany. In the Europe of the 1990s, however, collective security looks impractical, in so far as it may require the use of armed force against an aggressor, because the states needed to enforce collective security lack the willpower (and to some extent the military means) to do what is necessary because of the likely human and material costs involved. The states of the UN Security Council, including Britain and France, have persistently voted for measures regarding Yugoslavia which they have been unwilling to make stick, of which perhaps the most telling was the designation of 'safe areas' in Bosnia in the summer of 1993.

In view of the western failure to prevent the rule of force in the interstate and intrastate relations of the former Yugoslavia, it is worth outlining what an effective collective security system would have to involve in political-military terms.

In the mid-1980s, John Steinbruner wrote about the requirements for conventional deterrence, showing that states initiate war only when they expect a quick (and so low-cost) victory.[17] Thus the road to reinforced deterrence should be that which makes the prospects of a successful surprise attack less favourable. His reasoning appears to be relevant for the possible enforcers of a collective security system as well as for would-be aggressors. States can be expected to punish an aggressor with military force only, if (as was the case with Iraq with regard to Kuwait) important, tangible interests are at stake and there is a good chance of a quick military victory.

This has clear implications for force structures. If aspirations for a collective security system are to have any credibility, western Europe needs to have forces which can be used for other objectives than self-defence and which are capable of rapid movement and periods of high-intensity warfare. These criteria suggest that many more professional forces need to be prepared and equipped with armour and firepower.

Since it is just such forces which are capable of successful surprise attack and the capacity to seize ground quickly, there needs to be a source of reassurance that they will not be used themselves for aggressive purposes. The best such source would be to ensure that major units have a multinational character which would mean that more than one government, perhaps several governments, would have to agree to their use.

Both the need for multinationality and the requirement for more professional forces imply that serious combat by west European states should not be the exclusive preserve of the traditional martial countries, Britain and France. It is encouraging that Belgium and the Netherlands have decided to professionalize their armed forces but major questions arise about what Germany, Italy and even Spain could contribute. Currently they have only small forces which could be deployed overseas in combat roles and would then need extensive logistic and other support from other states.

In addition, the armed forces of east European states must be taken into account, but the current reality is that they are undergoing significant change and reorganization away from their Moscow-dominated past. They also have many fewer resources available for defence than have their western neighbours. They cannot be expected to offer much to collective combat efforts, although they should be able to help considerably with less-demanding missions towards the peace-keeping end of the spectrum.

Talk of multinational operations raises many military questions about training and command and control. While particular arrangements would have to be made for every operation, as noted above an ongoing defence planning role for NATO, using also the North Atlantic Cooperation Council, should be to organize matters so that North American, west European and, as time progresses, east European forces possess the capability to fight alongside each other. This means maintaining and developing common procedures and operational concepts and doctrine. It means procuring standard and interoperable equipment where appropriate. It means the maintenance of multinational headquarters and ensuring through exercises that coalition action will work if called for.

The most sensitive state to involve would be Russia as the UN/NATO experience in Sarajevo in February 1994 highlighted. There are several reasons to suggest that preparations should be made to enable Russia to act militarily with other European states. First, it has significant and useful professional military capability. Second, it is likely to be less reluctant to act than western Europeans in the cases of aggression in the former communist bloc, because it will feel its national security is at stake. Third, increased contact of the Russian armed forces with their western counterparts can be used to generate increased appreciation among Russians of western democratic values, including the legitimacy of democratic civilian oversight of national defence. Fourth, excluding Russia would enhance Russian feelings of separation, even isolation, from the rest of Europe, and of paranoia that Europe or rather the North Atlantic area was organized principally against them. Finally a collective security system as described could not work against Moscow and so there would be little harm in treating Russia as a 'policeman' rather than a potential criminal from the beginning. Russia is too large in space and military capability to be quickly overrun.

Politically there also would have to be clear acceptance in a European collective security system that aggressors will be punished rather than just being forced to give up their ill-gotten gains. Government leaders ordering aggressive action must expect to lose office and even their freedom. This means that the normal aim of a collective security operation should be to occupy the territory of the aggressor, perhaps even occupy its capital, to seize control of government, and to arrange for a new government quickly to be elected.

Two important things need to be noted about a prospective collective security system for Europe as sketched out above. The first is that we are very far from having the elements of such a system in place.[18] The political will to make such a system work is clearly absent because Western governments do not judge their interests, most obviously in the former Yugoslavia, to be sufficiently threatened to sacrifice significant numbers of Western lives in combat. The West is ready to make economic sacrifices through the imposition of sanctions against Serbia, but it is not ready to fight it. It may be ready to offer troops to underwrite a settlement in Bosnia, but it will not use force to punish aggression, except from the air, which should mean minimum human costs for the West. Whether or not this judgement is sound or short-sighted is debatable, but it is certainly the stance which NATO states have adopted.

Thus, any collective security element in the CSCE must probably place greater emphasis on non-military punishments of an aggressor state, and in particular on economic sanctions. While in many ways these may be less effective than the use of force, they are probably the strongest action which will prove feasible. Because their role should be to deter aggressive behaviour in general, and not simply to change the behaviour of a state which has already committed an aggressive act, they must be used to penalize an aggressor over a significant period of time.

However, a second point is even more serious: early in this chapter an analysis was presented of the fundamentals of Western security cooperation. Essential also to the evaluation of any structure for pan-European security is an assessment of the likely problems, risks and threats which such a system may well have to face. In such an assessment, it becomes clear that collective security, which requires the agreed identification of an aggressor, will sometimes and perhaps often seem irrelevant.

Using the somewhat conventional but contentious view of security as issues involving the threat, use and control of armed force, there is first the possibility that Moscow will again become assertive and aggressive, seeking to dominate by force its immediate and less immediate neighbours. This is the possibility which alarms the states most anxious to join NATO (including Lithuania). In the West, an aggressive Russia is widely seen as a future possibility but it is not accepted as a future certainty.[19] Moreover, Russian military strength is clearly nowhere near that of the former Soviet Union and in some ways the West has more to fear, in the way of proliferation dangers, from a weak Russia rather than a strong one. NATO is the optimum body for the containment of Russia, but the states which could well be threatened first by Russian aggression (such as Ukraine, Estonia and Georgia[20]) are not at the front of the queue to join the Alliance. In principle at least, a pan-European collective security system might help to deter Russia. Arguably, NATO and the European Union already make a contribution here since, even with their existing memberships, they ensure that Russia could never hope to dominate Europe as a whole and that any Russian aggression would meet a firm, coherent response, one element in which might be an expansion of the Western Alliance commitments.

A second possibility is that individual bilateral relations among the liberated states of the East could deteriorate. The basis for peaceful relations between states such as Hungary and Romania, Lithuania and Poland, and Hungary and Serbia, is not yet deeply rooted or even clear. A collective security system again might help to deter a resort to interstate violence and again NATO and the European Union help to assure Western cohesion.

Finally, however, there are many dangers arising from the plethora of ethnic conflicts and rivalries which can be identified in the former Soviet empire broadly defined.[21] Many of these are 'domestic', albeit with some international implications where the identification of an international aggressor may not be an issue and where agreement on the aggressive party in a domestic conflict may not be possible.

There may not be much that either collective security, an alliance such as NATO, or even diplomacy may be able to do about some such issues other than try to contain their effects. Northern Ireland, Cyprus and the Basques remain problems within the West despite its plethora of security structures. Arguably, membership of alliances and other bodies may exacerbate problems: Greek membership of the EU and NATO has not helped these bodies to handle Yugoslavia and arguably Greece would have been less inclined to be so obstructive on many aspects of UN policy towards Yugoslavia had it not enjoyed the reassurance which its NATO and EU membership brings.

In the messy central and eastern Europe of the 1990s, the number of cases where there is a clear aggressor which can be quickly punished is likely to be small. Particularly in the former Soviet Union where so many borders lack legitimacy among local peoples, the designation of an aggressor is likely to prove elusive: Armenia would appear a credible candidate in the light of its fighting in Azerbaijan, but there have been no moves in the UN Security Council or the CSCE to condemn it. In cases of civil wars such as those taking place in Georgia, the specification of an aggressor is all the more problematic.

Conclusion

The West has clear interests in the stability and development of the formerly communist parts of Europe, including Russia. A stable, developing East offers economic opportunities, reduces the need for Western defence spending and brings the possibility of security cooperation with new partners to enhance global order. A conflictual East will bring economic costs and dislocation to the West (including perhaps loss of vital gas supplies from Russia). It could cause serious refugee problems which in turn could bring harsh measures in order to secure frontiers. There is also the possibility of environmental damage in the West from fighting in the East. But none of this means either that the West will 'pay any price' to manage east European security, or that the West can wave a wand, sign magic cheques and treaties or send troops to bring peace, somehow extending the west European security system into a pan-European system.

The first and most obvious conclusion to emerge from this analysis is that there are no easy fixes to building security in central and eastern Europe including the territories of the former Soviet Union. The economic and social integration believed to underpin a pluralistic security community cannot be put in place overnight; expanding NATO membership would generate further difficulties and would help only a few states, and the factors needed for a collective security system could not be easily created.

The immediate emphasis must therefore be placed on the idealist aim of progressively building cooperation, on diplomacy working on a multilateral basis through the CSCE and also the North Atlantic Cooperation Council, which provides a regular opportunity for private political discussions as well as generating specific cooperative activities in areas like peace-keeping and civilian defence management.

Moreover, the EU and wider Western economic cooperation with the East must have a central role in building a wider 'Deutschian' security community over the longer term. The granting of aid and the provision of access to Western markets should serve to constrain behaviour (since aggression could then be expected to involve the loss of valued economic assets), to make conflict less likely (since economically growing societies should be less vulnerable to ethnic conflict), and to build the economic and social links which would give credibility to subsequent Western security guarantees and provide the foundations for an extension of the Western security community.

This is not a counsel of despair, since on the interstate level European relations are not significantly deteriorating and in many cases are improving. Slowly Russian troops are coming out of the Baltic countries and both Latvia and Estonia could have no Russian troops left by the end of 1994, especially since the dispute over the Skrunda radar site in Latvia seems to have been resolved[22] (Russia will keep it for four more years, probably manned by 'civilians', and then it will be dismantled after a four-year period). At the executive if not always at the parliamentary level, even Russia and Ukraine are able to reach difficult agreements, and the strategic missiles in Ukraine are being taken back to Russia.

It is neither accurate nor useful to assert the existence of a security vacuum in eastern Europe. If the societies in the region can develop economically, and if the West can provide prudent military aid and advice (which is far from certain),[23] the states of the former Warsaw Pact will increase their capacity to defend themselves without alarming their neighbours. CSCE-based arms control and confidence-building measures (with consultations and discussions perhaps being as important as agreements) should ensure that this can occur. Developments through the NACC, NATO's Partnership for Peace initiative, Western European Union cooperative efforts with the Baltic states, the Visegrad states, Romania and Bulgaria, multinational units such as the envisaged Baltic battalion[24] and armaments cooperation not tied to any institution should all help to ensure that the reorientation of defence structures in much of eastern Europe takes place within an international cooperative rather than a purely national environment.

The extension of the formal Western alliance system is a matter of timing and the obvious timetable to aim for involves the rapid integration initially of the Visegrad countries into the EU around the end of the century if possible. EU aid and market access have a key role to play. The new EU members will be eligible for WEU membership and at that stage should also have NATO membership available to them. If the US guarantee and presence is to play a key role in west European security, it makes no sense for west European states to have defence commitments on their own continent in which the US is not also involved. By the end of the century, a multitude of links – military, economic, social, political and cultural – should have been established between the West and the former communist world in Europe, and the position in Russia will have become clearer. Either its democracy will have become reinforced, its economy growing and its foreign policy as respectful of the sovereignty of others as are the policies of Western countries, or it will have reverted to intimidation and authoritarianism. In the one case, it too will clearly want to work closely with NATO and perhaps even join. In the other, it will be a threat which the West will again have to contain.

Currently, however, Europe's worst conflicts are clearly ethnic and internal to states, although many have important interstate implications. The urgent need is therefore for progress and consensus in the difficult area of minority rights where the Council of Europe may be able to bring a new legally binding dimension. On questions such as rights to citizenship, it may well be that the west European states will have to make changes to their own practices in order that a uniform regime can be built up across Europe as a whole.

In international political terms the biggest potential problem in Europe is clearly Russia, but Russia is also potentially a positive force for order. It will take time to instil in the basic outlook of Moscow decision-makers that the Baltic states, Georgia, Ukraine and others are sovereign states which should not be intimidated and it is only through contact with the West, through the CSCE and the NACC as well as many bilateral links, that Russian psychology will be changed. However, stressing that it will take a while to improve further a difficult situation should not mean that the great progress made to date should be overlooked. Russia, having hung on to its nineteenth-century empire longer than any west European state, has finally abandoned it very quickly and with little bloodshed. West European states still see themselves as having particular influence in many of their former imperial territories and so cannot blame Russia for feeling similarly about its empire. The Western challenge is to make sure that Russian efforts to exercise influence involve cooperation, persuasion and rewards which bring benefits to the former imperial territories, rather than threats, the use of force and intimidation.

If diplomacy and the cooperative rationalism of the CSCE approach must be relied on in eastern Europe for the short and even medium term, in the longer term pan-European security can move to being founded on economic development and integration, bringing political stability based on liberal democracy and on full membership of the range of European cooperative institutions, including the EU and, for those that seek it, the WEU and NATO. At these stages too it is important that Russia should not be excluded. Whether or not Russia needs to be a member of the EU is not a question in need of imminent resolution. However, it is necessary from the beginning to appreciate that Russia must eventually either be integrated into Europe or defended against.

Notes

1. A term emerging from the work on integration of Karl Deutsch, see K. Deutsch, S.A. Burrell, R.A. Kann *et al.*, *Political Community and the North Atlantic Area*, Princeton, Princeton University Press, 1957.
2. See Chris Coker, 'Post-modernity and the end of the Cold War: has war been disinvented', *Review of International Studies*, vol. 18, no. 3, July 1992, pp. 189–98; R. Cooper, 'Is there a New World Order?' in S. Sato and T. Taylor (eds), *Prospects for Global Order*, London, RIIA, 1993, pp. 8–24.
3. The USSR denied aggressive intent during the Cold War but saw the need to be able to initiate conventional or nuclear war once conflict, because of western drives, became imminent and unavoidable. MccGwire, among others, distinguishes between the defensive character of Soviet military doctrine at the dominant socio-political level and its offensive nature at military-technical level. See M. MccGwire, *Perestroika and Soviet National Security*, Washington, Brookings, 1991, ch. 2, especially pp. 12–16; see also D. Leebaert, *Soviet Military Thinking*, London, George Allen & Unwin, 1981; and J. Baylis and G. Segal (eds), *Soviet Strategy*, London, Croom Helm, 1981.
4. For instance Coker observes that 'The atom bomb concentrated man's thoughts on his own existence more than anything else in the twentieth century', *op. cit.*, p. 195.
5. Such shared values should make the foreign policies of others more predictable and so less susceptible to crises caused by surprise. In addition, policy-makers should empathize with the goals of others who share their values. This, however, is an argument indicating that all states with similar values and ideologies should have cooperative relations. As relations show, for instance between the Soviet Union and China and between the Baathist states of the Arab world, this is often not the case. However, the normally peaceful nature of relations among pluralistic democratic states has been widely observed.
6. See Karl W. Deutsch, S.A. Burrell, R.A. Kann *et al.*, *op. cit.* For analysis of integration theory as a whole, see Charles Pentland, *International Theory and European Integration*, London, Faber and Faber, 1973.
7. See Bruce Russett and Harvey Starr, *World Politics: The Menu for Choice*, New York, Freeman, 1992, 4th edn, pp. 379–96.
8. The neo-realist perspective is fundamentally associated with Kenneth Waltz, *Theory of International Politics*, Reading, Mass., Addison-Wesley, 1979. See also R.O. Keohane (ed.), *Neorealism And Its Critics*, New York, Columbia Univ. Press, 1986.
9. John Mearsheimer, 'Back to the Future: Instability in Europe After the Cold War', *International Security*, vol. 15, no. 1, Summer 1990, pp. 5–56.
10. The German journalist Joseph Joffe has been firmly drawn to this view, and re-stated it in 'Collective Security and the Future of Europe', *Survival*, vol. 34, Spring 1992, pp. 46–8.

11. With the split-up of Czechoslovakia, Slovakia was a less enthusiastic NATO candidate than the Czech Republic, but if the Czech Republic got into NATO, Bratislava would probably want to follow suit.
12. See Richard Lugar, 'NATO: Out of area or out of business', Washington DC, US Senate Media Release, 24 June 1993.
13. S.A. Oxman, 'NATO in business to stay', speech of 12 August 1993 published by USIS, US Embassy, London on 17 August, pp. 5-6.
14. See the Biden-Roth amendment approved in the US Senate on 13 September 1993, Congressional Record, S11493.
15. See the NACC Workplan for Dialogue, Partnership and Cooperation 1994, issued by NATO Press Service, Brussels, 3 December 1993.
16. See especially Norman Angell, *The Great Illusion*, London: Heinemann, 1911.
17. John Steinbruner, *Conventional Deterrence*, Ithaca, New York: Cornell University Press, 1983.
18. See Joffe, *op. cit.*
19. See, for instance, the qualified pessimism of Robert D. Blackwill in 1993 in a speech ('Why there will be no strategic partnership between Russia and the West') at Chatham House on 2 December 1993. Blackwill was the joint author with Graham Allison of the 'Grand Bargain' with Moscow proposal in the spring of 1991; 'America's stake in the Soviet future', *Foreign Affairs*, Vol. 70, No. 3, Summer 1991, pp. 77-98.
20. Georgia under President Shevardnadze appears to have been forced into joining the Commonwealth of Independent States in the autumn of 1993 by Russian support, later toned down, for the rebels of Abkhazia.
21. See, for instance, 'That other Europe', *The Economist*, 25 December 1993-7 January 1994, pp. 17-20.
22. 'Russian pull-out talks stall', *Jane's Defence Weekly*, 18 December 1993. By the end of 1993 there were no Russian troops in Lithuania, 12,000 in Latvia and 3,000 in Estonia.
23. NATO governments have proved reluctant to invest many resources in the NACC and funds for Partnership for Peace could well be scarce, see 'Money is Next Hurdle in Integrating East Europeans', *Defense News*, 13-19 December 1993.
24. 'Baltic battalion to form in '94', *Jane's Defence Weekly*, 27 November 1993.

11

Can Institutions Hold Europe Together?

Peter van Ham

The purpose of this chapter is to trace the development of international institutions in Europe in relation to the changing power of the state. It asks whether institutions can cope with the threats of fragmentation which have emerged after the end of the Cold War.

The chapter first examines the contribution of International Relations theory to explaining the nature of cooperation and institutions. Thereafter it provides a concise historical overview of the development of several international institutions in western Europe, before examining how these institutions have been affected by the end of the Cold War. It concludes with an evaluation of the prospects for conflict and cooperation in post-Cold War Europe and the role which international institutions may play.

Institutions and international relations theory

The French philosopher Joseph de Maistre remarked in 1796 that '[h]istory proves unfortunately that war is in a sense the habitual condition of mankind, that is to say that human blood must constantly flow somewhere or other on earth; and that for every nation peace is no more than a respite.'[1] This, however, leaves unexplained the occasional instances of collaboration between states and even more so the institutionalized forms of cooperation among them. Although discord and conflict may be the normal state of affairs among states, it is important to gain insight into what may explain cooperation.

Cooperation may partly be explained by democracy. When peoples and states have the chance to openly work out their problems, conflicts may be easier to resolve. Part of the explanation may be economic growth, for when states have an ever bigger cake to divide, conflicts are likely to be fewer. This chapter will argue that the most important factor explaining cooperation is the process of institutionalization which has characterized Western Europe since 1945. Numerous institutions have pulled west European states together over the past four decades, creating frameworks of economic, political and military cooperation in which extreme nationalist policies are discouraged.

West European institutions developing closer economic cooperation and integration include the European Union (EU), the Benelux and the European Free Trade Association (EFTA). The Council of Europe has been set up 'to promote increased unity and quality of life in Europe'; the Conference on Security and Cooperation in Europe (CSCE) – which also includes the United States, Canada, Russia and countries of the former Warsaw Pact – has focused on military, economic and human rights issues. The North Atlantic Treaty Organization (NATO) and the Western European Union (WEU) are collective defence organizations. These are institutions with a very different functional scope and domain. They have all been constructed during the period of the Cold War and have, to variable degrees, experienced difficulties in adapting to the changed post-Cold War Europe.

It is clear that institutions are themselves phenomena which require an explanation. Why would countries be willing to constrain their freedom to act by joining these institutions? International Relations theory has formulated several explanations of which neo-realism and neo-liberal institutionalism have been the most important. Both theories are schools of thought offering a certain perspective on international affairs which incorporate different questions and assumptions about the basic units and crucial forces shaping world politics.

Neo-realism, neo-liberal institutionalism and regimes

The assumptions of realist political theory are threefold. First, states are the major actors in world politics. Second, states function within an anarchic international system which conditions their behaviour. Third, states will pursue their national interests in a rational way.[2] Realists argue that power and security are like oxygen to states: deny it to them for even a short while, and all other issues – ranging from trade to human rights – are revealed as secondary. These tenets were first developed into a scientific theory by Kenneth N. Waltz (who labelled it neo-realism). Waltz argued that the structure of the international system (which is either bipolar or multipolar) shapes state behaviour, although states with different capabilities will behave in a different way. All states strive at the least to preserve their national sovereignty and at the most to dominate the world.[3]

Neo-realists deny the conventional belief that states with common interests usually act together to further those common interests collectively. The lack of a supranational body both willing and capable to provide and enforce rules of state behaviour makes international cooperation exceptional and always ephemeral. They further contend that this lack of cooperation is bound to result in conflicts. They argue that states' attempts to increase their power and security unilaterally is bound to set off spirals of tensions, suspicions and hostility. This results from the so-called 'security dilemma' which all states face: that in most cases an increase in one state's security will automatically and unintentionally reduce that of other states. In practice this has led to economic protectionism and arms races. Neo-realists further maintain that international institutions have little effect on state behaviour and can do little to ameliorate the security dilemma. They consider institutions as epiphenomena, since powerful states may ignore rules and even change the arrangement itself when they do not like the expected results. Neo-realists often quote the Greek historian Thucydides to the effect that 'the strong do what they can, the weak suffer what they must'; a postulate to which inter national institutions are not expected to form an exception. They argue instead that institutions only reflect the distribution of power, and that Great Powers dominate alliances and institutions, which may, in some cases, even add to their overall strength. More importantly, they assert that Great Powers operate within these institutions only as long as these are of some use and continue to serve their national interests. When this is no longer the case, they are likely to reduce their commitment, or even abandon them.

This neo-realist school of thought has been challenged from several sides. Some have claimed that new actors in world politics are becoming increasingly important, such as specialized international agencies, labour unions, multinational corporations and transnational groupings.[4] Others have claimed that states are hardly unitary actors and do not necessarily act rationally.[5] These critics – ranging from functionalists to representatives of the interdependence school – consider neo-realists overly pessimistic about the prospects for international cooperation. They point out that swelling trade and financial flows make cooperation among states imperative. Ernst Haas has stated that international institutions like the EC were 'the appropriate regional counterpart to the nation-state which no longer feels capable of realizing welfare aims within its narrow borders.'[6] Functionalists have maintained that participation within international institutions may influence the perception and articulation of the state's national interests, and may even, in the long term, redefine the character of the nation-state itself. Those who cherish federalist visions argue that history is a record of progress towards ever larger units, and that the state system – which was codified in 1648 at Westphalia – will one day be replaced by an order comprising greater, regional units.

In the early-1980s, a number of scholars challenged neo-realism on its own ground, accepting tenets like international anarchy and state-centrism, but claiming that international regimes may nevertheless promote enduring cooperation.[7] This so-called neo-liberal institution-alist school accepts most of neo-realist assumptions but contends that the anarchical nature of world politics can be mitigated by insti-tutions that provide legitimate and effective channels for reconciling states' national interests. They claim that the order in west European economics and politics can largely be attributed to the growth of multilateral institutions. These institutions, they maintain, have helped states identify their common interests, have boosted the flow of reliable information, and have provided effective procedures for settling disputes. The most important contributions of neo-liberal institutionalism can be summarized in three central ideas.

First, international institutions are more difficult to build than to maintain. It is argued that western international institutions have mainly been erected with the assistance of the United States, which in its role of benign hegemon provided the impetus to cooperate, helped in formulating regime rules and guarded against breaches of these rules.[8] Some maintain that the creation of new institutions may be facilitated by the atmosphere of mutual trust created by the existing ones. Robert Keohane has claimed that institutions will be easier to create in 'dense policy spaces', since *ad hoc* agreements in such areas are likely to interfere with one another unless they are based upon a common set of rules and principles.[9] This may partly explain the compact web of institutions in western Europe as well as the relative scarcity of institutions in many other regions (e.g. Africa).

Second, international institutions facilitate agreements among governments (and other actors, such as firms). Cooperation becomes easier since institutions create the conditions for orderly multilateral negotiations and facilitate linkages among issues. Bargaining and log-rolling become commonplace, and states acquire a vested interest in maintaining these institutions. Since states participate within these institutions over a long period of time, governments have fewer incentives to cheat. Within these institutions, reputations of reliability can be established and common interests among states may thus be more easily realized.[10]

Third, international institutions may not be able to control what policies Governments pursue, but they do assist them in pursuing their national interests through cooperation with other states. It is argued that states' perceptions of their national interests change because of participation in international institutions. Since states value these institutions, they refrain from adopting unilateral policies which may be disruptive. The main reason for their restraint is (as Arthur Stein has argued) that the 'institution may be required again in the future, and destroying them because of short-term changes may be very costly in the long run. Institutional maintenance is not, then, a function of a waiving of calculation; it becomes a factor in the decision calculus that keeps short-term calculations from becoming decisive.'[11]

West European institutions during and after the Cold War

Institutional density varies among regions of the world, with Western Europe being exceptionally well endowed. During the Cold War, western Europe has developed what may be called an *institutional complex*, in which economic, political and security relationships are relatively intense. As a result, a number of states perceive their national interests in such a way that major problems cannot be reasonably analysed and solved apart from one another.[12] One of the questions is what explains the construction of this institutional complex in western Europe after the Second World War? A related question is what effect the end of the Cold War will have on institutions and institution-building for both western Europe and the continent as a whole?

The Cold War as catalyst

The increase of tensions between the United States and the Soviet Union after 1945, and the subsequent outbreak of the Cold War, played a crucial part in west European institution-building. The EC (and its predecessor, the European Coal and Steel Community – the ECSC) may be considered as an 'economic alliance', established to fence off the external menace of Soviet communism and to contain and manage the internal threat of renewed German militarism. These factors were also important in setting up NATO, which, according to its first Secretary General, was meant to 'keep the Russians out, the Americans in, and the Germans down.'

The embryo of west European economic integration can be found in the conditions set by the American Marshall Plan, which specifically asked for a *comprehensive* European recovery plan, *collectively* framed by the west European nations, based upon the principle that all participating European countries assumed *joint* responsibility for making the programme work. It also called for the setting up of some permanent institutional organs for utilizing the aid according to plan. The instrument of United States assistance was thereby wielded as an economic lever in order to promote a sense of European unity. The Dutch scholar Ernst H. van der Beugel has argued that '[f]rom the moment of the launching of the Marshall Plan, it became apparent that European integration was a major objective of American foreign policy . . . It pursued this aim primarily within the framework of its stand against Communist aggression.'[13] One of the other objectives of the ECSC was to pool the French and West German primary resources (coal and steel), which would make war between these countries almost impossible.

The Cold War's bipolar structure therefore provided two crucial external pressures for west European states to cooperate. First, the acuteness of the Soviet threat temporarily overshadowed primal conflicts among west European states. Second, the predominance of the United States worked as a catalyst for west European integration since the major burden of military and economic security was shouldered by Washington. Without America's leadership and determination, it is very doubtful that west European governments would have been able to overcome mutual distrust. Both external factors facilitated West European states to overcome their collective action problems.

Western Europe's institutional complex after the Cold War

During these 40 years, west European states constructed an institutional complex which patterned their relations on a wide range of policy issues. This process has been a slow and arduous one, with three steps forward and two steps back, as in an Echternach procession. Institutionalization took place in the relative peace and quiet of Cold War politics until 1989. But in the five 'post-Wall' years that have followed, west European countries have rethought their commitment to institutions such as the EU, NATO and WEU, and these institutions have been obliged to adjust themselves to new realities.

These developments have raised two basic questions. First, are these west European institutions sturdy enough to survive the centrifugal forces which characterize post-Cold War dynamics? A range of new challenges has been added to the agendas of the EU, NATO and WEU, which call for new approaches and sometimes radical changes of strategy. Not surprisingly, states participating within these institutions do not always agree on how to address these new challenges. There is fear that major actors like Great Britain, France and Germany will be suspicious of each other over policy towards central and eastern Europe, former Yugoslavia, as well as the former Soviet Union (FSU). When these countries start to redefine their national interests in relative power gains and formulate their foreign policies using different geopolitical concepts, the institutional complex will come under greater pressure and might eventually even start to unravel.

Second, are these institutions, in their current form, still relevant to solving the main economic, political and security problems of Europe *as a whole*? Past decades of the Cold War were dominated by concerns about a massive invasion of Warsaw Pact troops and global thermonuclear war, but western policy-makers now worry about a myriad of less tangible threats to their security. Instead of one 'clear and present danger', the post-Cold War period is characterized by diffuse perils including resurgent nationalism, minority problems, the threat of uncontrolled mass-migration and nuclear proliferation. Western institutions have to adjust to these new circumstances, and strategy as well as policy must be tailored to manage new crises and conflicts. These institutions also have to deal with applications for membership from formerly neutral countries and countries previously in Moscow's sphere of influence. With the end of the division of Europe, the EU is negotiating its enlargement with Austria, Sweden, Finland and Norway. NATO may also contemplate extending its security community eastward. But will it be possible to incorporate these countries into the west European institutional complex without significantly altering its structure and character?

This second set of questions will be dealt with in more detail in the third section of this chapter.

Here we will first examine the centrifugal (as well as centripetal) forces working on west European institutions during the 1990s.

Fragmentation

Although the Cold War division of Europe was an unjust one, it did provide peace and stability of some sort. No shots were fired between East and West during the Cold War (although many were killed in proxy wars in the developing world). The violent breakdown of Yugoslavia and the military clashes in Russia's backyard would have been unthinkable (as well as unlikely). Why this is so has been explained by neo-realist scholars who argue that stability can best be provided in a bipolar world.[14] In 1990 John Mearsheimer asserted that Europe is heading for instability, being substantially more prone to violence than during the past 45 years.[15] Mearsheimer's strict neo-realist analysis may not be shared by many, but it does provide the main elements of the fragmented Europe scenario (which Hugh Miall has set out in Chapter 1), expecting the erosion of the west European institutional complex and the spread of violent conflicts in the rest of Europe.

The basic thrust of the argument is that the demise of the Soviet Union and the relative decline of the United States' economic and political power (i.e. the shift from bipolarity to multipolarity), will significantly increase uncertainty and instability.[16] There are several reasons for this assumption. During the Cold War, both the United States and the Soviet Union were concerned with conflicts and sources of instability all over the globe since these might result in gains or losses for either of them. In a multipolar world, on the other hand, dangers are diffuse and responsibilities are ill-defined. Moreover, it is often not clear who forms a danger to whom, and the incentive to regard all disequilibrating changes with concern and react to them appropriately is therefore weakened.[17] Conflicts are more likely since there is no longer a clear-cut demarcation of spheres of influence between two Great Powers, but instead a number of Great Powers exist in a volatile configuration of world politics. It is also argued that by virtue of their superior strength (economic as well as military), bipolar Great Power dominance simplified international relations.[18] Indeed, the Cold War confirmed the premise that the two Great Powers managed their relations with allies and, by using their preponderance of power, provided leadership within their alliance. Since both former hegemons currently seem to lack the economic and political capabilities as well as the political will to pacify emerging conflicts, such conflicts may be more difficult to contain.

These centrifugal forces are likely to be at work in both western Europe and in the East. In the West they are expected to make cooperation more difficult; in the East they may even result in military conflict. The period after the signing of the Maastricht Treaty has illustrated the nature of post-Cold War intra-western conflict. After a short spell of Europhoria, western Europe has again returned to a period of Europessimism. Although a manic-depressive attitude to the process of European integration has never been a healthy one, it is obvious that there are some reasons to be glum. For example, problems with ratification in several EU countries have indicated that the enthusiasm for far-going integration may not be as wide as previously assumed. The quantum leap towards an Economic and Monetary Union (EMU), which was planned in Maastricht, was put into doubt by the breakdown of the European Exchange Rate Mechanism (ERM) in late August 1993. Although the economic recession affecting large parts of the industrialized world also played an important role, western Europe has especially suffered from the negative consequences of Germany's unification. Although tightening credit conditions may have been prudent policy to limit the budget deficit and inflation after monetary union in Germany, it proved to be detrimental to economies in the rest of Europe.

Western Europe's failure to contribute to a solution to the Yugoslav war has seriously discredited its ambitions to arrive at a Common Foreign and Security Policy (CFSP), and has indicated that EU members are still mainly consumed by domestic preoccupations. The war in former Yugoslavia was the first major test case for western institutions to see whether they were suited to cope with post-Cold War conflicts. One of the main objectives of the Maastricht Treaty was to develop a CFSP for the EU, and the case of Yugoslavia was at first considered an opportunity to demonstrate that western Europe could indeed act decisively and speak with one voice. The then president of the EC, Jacques Poos, commented in late-June 1991: 'This is the hour of Europe. It is not the hour of the Americans.'[19] However, solving the Yugoslav conflict proved too demanding a task, not only for the EC, but later also for NATO and WEU, whose member states became absorbed by arguments over the use of military force. The failure of western institutions to respond adequately to the atrocities taking place in former Yugoslavia is already well documented. For those who were sceptical of the effectiveness of western institutions, the Yugoslav case confirmed their worst fears.

Conflicts in the East are most likely to occur due to the absence of strong moorings within western institutions, as well as the lack of solid state structures combined with economic and political reform. The former factor may be crucial for the countries of central and western Europe, whereas the latter factor may be more important for several former Soviet republics, such as Belarus, Ukraine and countries in central Asia. In many former communist countries state structures are often weak and borders are in question. Institutions like the CSCE are involved in negotiating settlements in several of these regions of tension. NATO has also established a platform which incorporates all central and eastern European countries as well as the countries of the FSU (see below). However, institutions are very loosely structured and they have evidently not been capable of checking military conflicts among several Soviet successor states.

This fragmentation scenario foresees little good for peace and cooperation in Europe, and it does not allot an important stabilizing role to international institutions. What is more, it expects even relatively strong organizations such as the EU and NATO to be weakened by intensified security dilemmas.

An 'international society' on a regional level?

The question arises whether neo-realist pessimism is justified, and whether the cement of western institutions will not ensure continued cooperation among the countries of western Europe. To rephrase this question, one could ask whether what Hedley Bull has called 'an international society' has not developed in western Europe, albeit on a regional level. Such an 'international society' has been defined as 'a group of states, conscious of certain common interests and common values . . . [that] conceive themselves to be bound by a common set of rules in their relations with one another, and share in the working of common institutions.'[20] Bull's Grotian view of world politics (which assumes 'sociability' among states), is based on the postulate that states stick to the rules because of mutual fears of unrestricted violence and of violations of their sovereignty, as well as because of a rational calculation that peaceful and cooperative behaviour will produce mutual benefits.

On a rhetorical level most west European politicians have committed themselves to a variable extent to the goal of further

European integration on economic and monetary issues as well as on foreign and security policy. Some may prefer to work through west European institutions like the EU and the WEU, others may favour NATO, the CSCE or the United Nations. But there still exists agreement within this policy-making elite that a renationalization of western Europe's economic and political structure would be counterproductive: no west European statesman will argue that his country is capable of solving major international problems without cooperation within established international institutions. Of course, national interests of major west European states differ, as do national traditions and identities. One could also argue that the degree of enthusiasm for an institution is closely linked to the degree to which a state can exercise influence within it.[21] These differences make cooperation difficult and may result in institutions vying for power and prestige amongst each other.

It is important to stress, however, that the limitations to further integration can not be found only at the level of political elites. One could argue that the principal focus of Europe's new insecurity may not be on the state or international institution as such, but rather on society. Barry Buzan has recently maintained that the European integration process may be undermined because societies in western, central and eastern Europe may find themselves under threat from its consequences.[22] In the western part of Europe, French farmers may feel that their way of life is threatened by the EU's change in agricultural policy; in Great Britain and Denmark, people may seriously question the loss of sovereignty and national identity involved in constructing an EU which will increasingly acquire a state-like character. Domestic constraints and domestic opposition may therefore hinder internationally negotiated agreements of cooperation and integration, resulting in so-called 'involuntary defection' of some states.[23] Since the EU still suffers from a 'democratic deficit', and since policy-making in Brussels is seen as complex and opaque, west European citizens may put a halt to further European integration.

The novel role of international institutions

Now that bipolarity has given way to a considerably looser international structure, international institutions are looked upon to play a more important and active role in European politics, as well as in the world at large. Although many institutions now face more difficult tasks, it must be acknowledged that post-Cold War cooperation between the United States and Russia has done much to provide many institutions with increased political support. For example, the United Nations now has the opportunity to develop into a collective security organization with its own global 'police force' to defend the principles of its charter. One of the problems, however, is that these rising expectations have generally not been paralleled by a similar strengthening of the capacities of these institutions.

Consensus has gradually been built that the 'new Europe' will be based on many institutions, of which the EU and NATO are likely to become the main pillars. The WEU, as the organization responsible for defence within the EU, is to function as the bridge between both organizations. Over time, WEU may develop into a fully fledged European defence organization taking responsibility for handling some problems Europeans can no longer expect the United States to solve for them (either directly or working through NATO). Institutions like the United Nations, the CSCE and the Council of Europe will, of course, remain essential frameworks for preserving international peace and security, managing essential European and global problems, and – perhaps most importantly – for developing a regional society based on law which can be monitored and enforced.

Enlarging west European institutions

One of the main tests for western institutions is how to respond to post-Cold War challenges, of which the challenge of enlargement is becoming increasingly important. Western institutions are now called upon to 'project security eastward', or to engage in 'security and stability transfer' in the same direction.

The Council of Europe was the first western institution to offer central and eastern European countries full membership. After free parliamentary elections were held, most central and eastern European countries became members: Romania joined the Council in October 1993; Albania, Belarus, Croatia, Latvia, Moldova, Russia and Ukraine were still on the waiting list in early 1994. Although the Council of Europe does not provide security guarantees or economic aid, membership is considered important since it is seen as one of the prerequisites of EU membership. But although membership of the Council of Europe is an important recognition of the achievements of these countries in the field of human rights and parliamentary democracy, it only means a first, rather tentative step towards further integration into western structures.

As a Europe-wide framework for securing peace and stability the CSCE has gained new impetus from the enthusiastic support of most central and east European politicians. Despite its obvious drawbacks (like its unwieldiness, and the difficulty of reaching consensus – or consensus minus one – among more than 50 participating states), the CSCE continues to perform its important function as platform, forum and meeting place. It also provides an 'early-warning' system for interstate and intrastate conflicts: the High Commissioner on National Minorities has been appointed to provide an early warning, and where appropriate early action, in regard to tensions involving national minority issues which could develop into conflicts within the CSCE area, affecting peace and stability. Several new bodies have been established to deal with conflict prevention, free elections and arms reductions.[24]

But it is the EU and NATO to which EFTAns and countries in central and eastern Europe and the FSU are looking as the main providers of economic prosperity, stability and military security. Although the Council of Europe and the CSCE are functional and necessary, they fall short of providing the sturdy economic and security moorings which these countries require. Member states of the EU, NATO and the WEU are now all seriously considering strengthening their relationship with the East (as well as with northern Europe). In 1991–2, the EC signed association agreements with all central and east European countries and initialled a partnership agreement with Russia (a similar accord with Ukraine is under negotiation). The association agreements are now considered a first step towards full membership, although Brussels has long been hesitant to commit itself to such an enlargement eastward.[25]

NATO reacted to the collapse of the Warsaw Pact by creating the North Atlantic Cooperation Council (NACC) in November 1991. NACC holds annual meetings at the ministerial level and includes its former adversaries in working groups on a wide range of issues, including defence conversion. NACC membership does not entail security guarantees and since all republics of the FSU have been included, it is too much of a motley crew to provide the central and east European countries with the level of reassurance they consider necessary. WEU created a Forum of Consultation (FoC) in June 1992 (during its summit at Petersberg, near Bonn), which includes Bulgaria, the Czech Republic, Hungary, Poland, Romania, Slovakia and the three Baltic countries. Like NACC, the FoC was set up to strengthen existing relations by restructuring the dialogue, consultations and cooperation between WEU and the East. In the case of WEU, the FoC is considerably less diverse and may therefore be a useful vehicle to enable these countries to acquaint themselves with the future security and defence policy of the EU and to find new opportunities for cooperation. The Western European Union will absorb Greece as a new full member; Iceland, Norway and Turkey are now 'associate members'; Ireland and Denmark have become 'observers'.

Regional cooperation in central and eastern Europe

The low institutional density in central and eastern Europe stands in sharp contrast to western Europe's elaborate institutional complex. West European governments operate in dense policy spaces where almost every major decision affects other countries; this is certainly not yet the case in the former communist East. But the return to democracy and market economics in these countries has resulted in an extended but constant process of institutionalization.

The process of regional cooperation in central and eastern Europe has been slow. At first regional cooperation was considered an unattractive alternative to far-going integration within western structures. Enthusiastic cooperation among former Soviet satellite states was expected to delay EC membership, and reform-minded countries like Poland and Hungary were initially wary that close links with other countries would diminish their chances of 'joining Europe'. Unpleasant experiences with economic and political cooperation during the communist era did little to stimulate further teamwork. Nevertheless, central and east European countries have taken steps towards further cooperation, one of the main reasons being that it soon became clear that western institutions were not ready to accept new members from the East. Some loosely knit coalitions have been formed, such as the Visegrad group, which was established in early 1991, and involves the Czech Republic, Hungary, Poland and Slovakia. Numerous ministerial-level meetings have been held, and a Council of Ambassadors has been set up to assure coordination. A system of defence coordination has also been established. One of the main goals of the Visegrad Four is to encourage economic and political reform and to ensure speedy and full integration within the EU.

Other regional initiatives include the Council of Baltic Sea States, set up in March 1992, which serves as a platform for cooperation on a wide range of issues which are of interest to the states around the Baltic Sea. It has no elaborate structure, but will organize periodic ministerial meetings as well as several official committees. The so-called Central European Initiative (CEI), initiated by Italy, encompasses the countries of Central Europe and the Balkans. It has no political aspirations but focuses on transport and communications projects. In the FSU Russia set up the Commonwealth of Independent States (CIS) directly after the breakdown of the Soviet Union. It now incorporates most Soviet successor states (with the exception of the Baltic republics; Azerbaijian has joined in September 1993, and Georgia agreed to join one month later). Moscow considered the CIS as a framework for economic, political and military integration which could eventually develop into a Union with Russia at the helm. Russia signed a CIS Treaty on collective security with Armenia, Kazakhstan, Kyrgyzstan, Tajikistan and Uzbekistan at the Tashkent summit in May 1992. As is the case with most CIS agreements, the Tashkent Treaty has not yet been ratified, let alone implemented.

Whatever their legal status, these arrangements do not form an alternative to joining the EU, WEU and NATO. Although western institutions have a mixed record of post-Cold War efficacy, for central and east European countries (as well as for the Baltic republics and Ukraine), the appeal of these institutions has hardly diminished. On the contrary, they may have drawn the lesson that only full membership of the EU, WEU and NATO will provide them with sufficient economic and security support to counteract centrifugal forces.

Wider but weaker? Dilemmas of enlargement

Enlargement is now high on the agendas of the EU, WEU and NATO. At the Copenhagen summit of the EC Council in June 1993, the Twelve agreed that the 'associated countries in central and eastern Europe that so desire shall become members of the European Union'. However, they added a number of caveats. Quite understandably, Brussels demands that these countries 'assume the obligations of membership by satisfying the economic and political conditions required.' But the European Council also stated that, when considering enlargement, the 'Union's capacity to absorb new members, while maintaining the momentum of European integration, is also an important consideration in the general interests of both the

Union and the candidate countries.'[26] The Council has thereby indicated that it does not want to slow down the integration process among the Twelve by opening its gates towards the East; the EU does not want to become wider but weaker.

The debate about the enlargement of western institutions will again emphasize the diverging views on European cooperation and integration among EU member states. Most states cherish their own European visions, and support economic, political and/or security integration for a wide variety of reasons. Great Britain's Prime Minister, John Major, recently remarked that '[i]t is for nations to build Europe, not for Europe to attempt to supersede nations. I want to see the Community become a wide union, embracing the whole of democratic Europe, in a single market and with common security arrangements firmly linked to NATO.'[27] Germany, by contrast, cherishes a more far-reaching integrationist vision on Europe, which has recently been set out in an internal policy paper by Germany's ruling Christian Democratic party. The paper argues that 'it is essential, despite the problems that have recently beset the EMS, that the goal of monetary union and the timetable proposed be adhered to . . . The expansion of the Community . . . must not be allowed to weaken the degree of integration already achieved by the present core, on the contrary this must be strengthened. Otherwise the European Union will not be able to help solve the increasingly life-threatening crises of the nations that make it up . . . For that reason, institutional reform of the Community must be undertaken in parallel to the membership negotiations currently in hand with the EFTA countries.'[28] Far-reaching German proposals to reform the EU's institutions in order to maintain efficient decision-making in a Union of 16 or more members were placed before the Twelve.[29] The WEU declared that there will be a parallel development in economic and security relations of the European Union and the WEU with third countries. This may imply that the WEU will invite those European countries which have concluded association agreements with the European Union to participate in the activities of WEU and to be involved in its missions.[30] Hence, enlargement of the Twelve towards the East is bound to lead to an extension of WEU, which will provide these countries with the security guarantees they are craving.

For NATO, strengthening relations with the East is considered to be an almost existentialist matter. Some have called upon NATO to get involved in conflicts outside the NATO area ('out of area, or out of business', as this was dubbed). They made the case for including the countries of central and eastern Europe, giving preference to the Visegrad Four for geopolitical reasons. Since Russian President Boris Yeltsin expressed his understanding of Poland's wish to join NATO, this option became a topic of fierce debate. But Yeltsin's *volte-face* on central and east European membership of NATO only complicated the arguments. Manfred Wörner, NATO's secretary-general, argued that '[t]he time has come to open a more concrete perspective to those countries of central and eastern Europe which want to join NATO and which we may consider eligible for future membership.' During a meeting of NATO Defence Ministers in Travemunde, in late October 1993, there was wide support for an American proposal (agreed by NATO in January 1994) providing a so-called 'partnership for peace' to all NACC members, which would not encompass security guarantees, but would include the possibility of close consultations in times of crisis.[31] This was generally seen as a compromise to assuage the fears of central and east European countries without, however, antagonizing Russia.

It is clear, however, that these enlargements will run up against several major difficulties. Apart from the economic and financial costs of incorporating new members, enlargement also raises the question whether these institutions can maintain their cohesion and effectiveness. In 1991, Helen Wallace raised two relevant questions which are applicable to extending NATO as well as the EU. First, whether existing procedures can be used in a more elastic manner so as to meet the economic and political needs of new members; second, whether there was not a case for a radical overhaul of the individual institutional organs, the relationship between them, as well as a redefinition of the levels and scope of governance?[32] These questions are relevant since most international institutions have been set up during the Cold War, under circumstances which are radically different from the present ones. Although the enlargement of the EU, NATO and WEU towards the East is still undecided, the impact of such a step on the nature and character of these institutions, as well as on European stability in general, must be seriously considered. Since enlargement of institutions is likely to necessitate significant reforms in decision-making procedures as well as radical changes in policies (e.g. to the EC's Common Agricultural Policy, NATO force structures, nuclear strategies, joint military activities), one could argue that this requires almost as much effort as establishing institutions from scratch. With Cold War security parameters no longer applying, the process of enlargement is therefore bound to be both arduous and protracted.

Prospects for discord and cooperation in the new Europe

There are reasons to assume that the threat of a fragmented Europe will be sufficient for most west European states to go ahead with the integration process, or at least not to allow its disintegration. Fear of fragmentation has always been a major force in the integration process. The EU's competition policy, for example, puts limits on the protectionist measures member states may introduce; but similar restraints do not yet exist in foreign and security policy. A lack of political will combined with a limited commitment to federalist solutions, may make a genuine *west European* foreign and security policy something for the end of the decade. Whether this concern for disintegration will be as powerful a force for cooperation as the threat of Soviet domination was during the Cold War, remains a moot point. But the past few years have indicated that west European states have been careful to refrain from fractious unilateralism, which indicates that in times of rapid and unanticipated change, governments are inclined to make use of available institutions rather than to go it alone or try to redesign these institutions.[33]

For the near future, it is both unlikely that western Europe will take great steps towards the European Union planned at Maastricht, and that cooperation in this part of the continent will break down altogether. The west European institutional complex will probably prove sturdy enough to maintain at least a minimum level of cooperation, although the new pressures emerging from enlargement will cause new tensions among member states.

Notes

1. Joseph de Maistre, 'Considerations on France', in *The Works of Joseph de Maistre*, New York: Schocken Books, 1971, p. 61.
2. See E.H. Carr, *The Twenty Years' Crisis, 1919–1939. An Introduction to the Study of International Relations*, New York: Harper Torchbooks, 1964; Hans J. Morgenthau, *Politics Among Nations. The Struggle for Power and Peace*, 6th edn, New York, Knopf, 1985; Raymond Aron, *Peace and War. A Theory of International Relations*, Malabar, Florida: Robert E. Krieger Publ. Co, 1966.
3. Kenneth N. Waltz, *Man, the State, and War. A Theoretical Analysis*, New York: Columbia University Press, 1959, and Waltz, *Theory of International Politics*, Reading, Mass.: Addison-Wesley, 1979.
4. See, for example, Immanuel Wallerstein, *The Capitalist World System*,

Cambridge: Cambridge University Press, 1979; and Ernst B. Haas, *Beyond the Nation-State. Functionalism and International Organization*, Stanford: Stanford University Press, 1964.

5. See Graham T. Allison, *Essence of Decision. Explaining the Cuban Missile Crisis*, Boston: Little, Brown, 1971; and Robert Jervis, *Perception and Misperception in International Politics*, Princeton: Princeton University Press, 1976.

6. Quoted in Joseph M. Grieco, *Cooperation Among Nations. Europe, America, and Non-Tariff Barriers to Trade*, Ithaca and London: Cornell University Press, 1990, p. 6.

7. Stephen D. Krasner (ed.), *International Regimes*, Ithaca and London: Cornell University Press, 1983.

8. See, for the main argument: Robert O. Keohane, *After Hegemony. Cooperation and Discord in the World Political Economy*, Princeton: Princeton University Press, 1984.

9. Keohane, *After Hegemony*, p. 79.

10. See Keohane, *International Institutions and State Power. Essays in International Relations Theory*, Boulder: Westview Press, 1989; and Keohane, *After Hegemony*, part 4.

11. Arthur A. Stein, *Why Nations Cooperate. Circumstance and Choice in International Relations*, Ithaca and London: Cornell University Press, 1990, p. 52.

12. See for an analogous definition of 'security complex': Barry Buzan, *People, States and Fear. An Agenda for International Security Studies in the Post-Cold War Era*, New York: Harvester Wheatsheaf, 1991, Chapter 5.

13. Van der Beugel, *From Marshall Aid to Atlantic Partnership. European Integration as a Concern of American Foreign Policy*, Amsterdam: Elsevier Publishing Company, 1966, p. 215.

14. See Kenneth N. Waltz, 'The Stability of a Bipolar World', in *Dædalus*, vol. 93, Summer 1964; Aron, *Peace and War*, pp. 125–49; and Glenn H. Snyder and Paul Diesing, *Conflicts Among Nations. Bargaining, Decision Making and System Structure in International Crises*, Princeton: Princeton University Press, 1977, especially Chapter 6.

15. John J. Mearsheimer, 'Back to the Future. Instability in Europe After the Cold War', in *International Security*, vol. 15, no. 1, Summer 1990.

16. Whereas bipolarity by definition is characterized as a system wherein two Great Powers dominate, multipolarity is generally defined as a system with five or more Great Powers. See Peter van Ham, 'The European Community After Hegemony: The Future of European Integration in a Multipolar World', in *International Relations*, vol. 11, no. 5, August 1993.

17. See Waltz, *Theory of International Politics*, pp. 170–71.

18. See Hedley Bull, *The Anarchical Society. A Study of Order in World Politics*, Houndmills, Macmillan, 1977, Chapter 9.

19. Quoted in Jonathan Eyal, *Europe and Yugoslavia. Lessons From a Failure*, London: Royal United Services Institute for Defence Studies, Whitehall Paper, February 1993, p. 25.

20. See Bull, *The Anarchical Society*, p. 13, and Hedley Bull and Adam Watson, (eds), *The Expansion of International Society*, Oxford: Clarendon Press, 1984.

21. See Louise Richardson, 'British State Strategies after the Cold War', in Robert O. Keohane, Joseph S. Nye and Stanley Hoffmann (eds), *After the Cold War. International Institutions and State Strategies in Europe, 1989–1991*, Cambridge, Mass.: Harvard University Press, 1993, p. 169.

22. Barry Buzan, 'Introduction: The Changing Security Agenda in Europe', in Ole Wæver, Barry Buzan, Morten Kelstrup and Pierre Lemaitre, *Identity, Migration and the New Security Agenda in Europe*, London: Pinter Publishers, 1993.

23. See on this topic Robert D. Putnam, 'Diplomacy and Domestic Politics. The Logic of Two-Level Games', in *International Organization*, vol. 42, Summer 1988.

24. CSCE Secretariat in Prague, the Centre for Conflict Prevention in Vienna, and the Office of Free Elections in Warsaw. A CSCE Forum for Security Cooperation will be involved in animating arms reductions and limitations, confidence and security-building measures, and the development of security structures.

25. See Peter van Ham, *The EC, Eastern Europe and European Unity. Discord, Collaboration and Integration Since 1947*, London: Pinter Publishers, 1993, Chapters 9 and 10.

26. See European Council of Copenhagen, 21–22 June 1993, 'Conclusions of the Presidency', in *Europe Documents*, no. 1844/45, p. 5.

27. 'Major on Europe', in *The Economist*, 25 September 1993, p. 29.

28. See *Financial Times*, 27 September 1993.

29. This is likely to include more majority decision-making (which might be with a so-called 'double majority,' of both a majority of member states and a majority of their populations). *Financial Times*, 25 August 1993.

30. See the Luxemburg Declaration of the WEU Council, 22 November 1993.

31. *Atlantic News*, 27 October 1993.

32. Helen Wallace, 'The Europe that Came in From the Cold', in *International Affairs*, vol. 67, no. 4, October 1991, p. 661.

33. See Robert O. Keohane and Stanley Hoffmann, 'Conclusions: Structure, Strategy, and Institutional Roles', in Keohane, Nye and Hoffmann (eds), *After the Cold War*, p. 382.

12

The Impact of German Unification on the New European Order

Emil J. Kirchner

Introduction

The end of the Cold War has drastically changed the status of Germany, making it freer, more independent, larger in area and population, and potentially stronger, both economically and politically. This has led to expectations in other countries that Germany, while maintaining its main principles of foreign policy, will take on greater responsibilities in international affairs and channel these responsibilities predominantly through international institutions. How is Germany responding to this newly found freedom and responsibility, and how are its changed status and policies affecting other countries and European integration? Answers to these questions necessitate a number of different analyses. Firstly, there are the intentions or declarations provided by the German government as to how it sees its role both in Europe and internationally. Secondly, there are German foreign policy actions with regard to events such as the Gulf conflict, the war in the former Yugoslavia, and the Maastricht Treaty. Thirdly, there are direct and indirect consequences associated with German unification. Direct consequences relate to the upheavals caused by domestic German adjustment to the ERM and to the interest rate policies of other European countries. The indirect ones can be seen in terms of rising anxieties in neighbouring countries over, for example, potential German dominance. Attention must therefore be paid to the linkage between Economic and Monetary Union and Political Union. Besides attempting to provide an analysis along these three dimensions, this chapter will explore how internal and external constraints operate in the formulation of German foreign policy.

German unification: fears and expectations

German unification was not received with universal approbation. Changes in Germany's status, size and power potential were greeted with anxiety, and, in part, with apprehension by European countries. Past behaviour, the temptation to seek power and the changing climate in East-West relations were seen as dangerous by-products of German unification. These reactions coincided with what is perceived in the post-1989 period as a declining emphasis on the territorial and military aspect of security and a rise in importance of economic, environmental, human rights and migration issues for security – areas in which the FRG has traditionally been strong.

It is one thing, however, to associate Germany (like Japan) with heavily commercial perspectives towards foreign policy, and to see it as strongly positioned to dominate an international system in which economic strength and technological powers are the most important measures of influence.[1] It is quite another to speak of German aspirations to power or hegemonic tendencies.[2] Both external and internal constraints militate against such tendencies. A brief look at these constraints is in order.

The fashionable view of economic primacy in international relations assumes politico-military stability, within and outside Europe. This is called into question by instability in central and eastern Europe, the Middle East and elsewhere. In the future, as Richard Burt points out, the challenge facing a newly ascendant Germany could well become formidable. Working with its European partners, the United States and Japan, Germany may have to protect its global economic interests against a proliferating number of political and military threats.[3] Hence, Germany's role will, in part, depend on the stability and prosperity of the international system.

Domestically, Germany will be preoccupied with the immense task of bonding what was the GDR to the Federal Republic. The economic cost of German unification and the problems of bringing the two halves of Germany into a cohesive social and political entity may effectively brake German foreign policy initiatives. While the miscalculations in economic costs are becoming increasingly apparent, and their repercussions are painfully felt, not only in Germany but elsewhere in Europe in terms of interest rate policies and levels of economic performance, the problem of integration, which has received less attention, might turn out to have the greatest impact on German foreign-policy making. Whereas in 1972 Willy Brandt, in the then divided Germany, coined the phrase of 'one German nation and two German states', an appropriate reference might now be 'one German state and two German nations'. Together with the economic difficulties, this problem of identity is likely to affect, if it has not done so already, expectations other countries have about Germany, either in terms of the arrangement for collective security, the 'partners in leadership' formula, or the drive for European integration.

Economic factors and clashing identities are strong influences in their own right on foreign policy action. What reinforces the impact of these factors is the existence of a huge number of political asylum-seekers, migrants and resettled ethnic Germans who live in Germany. The 6.5 million foreigners living in Germany comprise 8 per cent of the total population, competing for jobs and social services. Superimposed on this is the legacy of the past and a psychology based more on pacifism, self-restraint, internationalism, and European unification than on military interventions, self-assertiveness, nationalism, and national identity. The strength of this legacy and psychology is, however, unevenly spread and held mostly by the 'forty-five plus' generation and has most resonance with SPD, FDP and Green party activists. As a consequence, it has proved very difficult for the German government to make constitutional changes on two of the most crucial issues which affect internal and external German policy: political asylum, and 'out of NATO area' military and humanitarian interventions. While a solution to the former was eventually achieved in the summer of 1993, the latter was still unresolved by late 1993.

The prevailing economic and social difficulties are linked, on the one hand, to a growing uncertainty within the German population and among German policy-makers, and on the other, to a diminished level of consensus between the public and policy-makers, and among the policy-makers themselves.

To appreciate the gap which exists between, on the one hand, German leadership intentions and outside expectations about Germany's international role, and on the other, Germany's domestic constraints, a closer examination is required of how Germany has matched words with deeds in foreign policy.

German foreign policy: the view from the outside

It would be too strong to portray the behaviour of German foreign policy-makers as 'don't judge us by what we say but by what we do'. Such a characterization would certainly misrepresent the genuine intentions and strenuous attempts by the German leadership to match objectives with actions. Yet, to the outside, much of what Germany has either done or failed to do, both domestically and internationally, appears in this way. Part of the reason for this is that Germany's leading role in European trade, monetary affairs, and European institutions/regimes is associated with corresponding expectations. Criticisms are levelled against Germany's economic, monetary and immigration policies, its role within the EC, NATO and the UN, its relationship with central and eastern European states, and its 'partner-in-leadership' responsibilities. Does this imply that the German leadership has been too idealistic, optimistic or naive about what it can and cannot deliver? Has it simply underestimated the problem of unification and the rigidities of attitudes and lifestyles associated with a 'civilian power' syndrome? Or is it confronted with expectations it cannot fulfil, e.g. expectations which go beyond its means? There might even be a question whether some of the expectations held concerning Germany could be better or more appropriately fulfilled by other western states or by the EC as a whole.

What then, have been German actions, or inactions, and how have they been perceived by the outside world? Firstly, we have to acknowledge the decision by the German government to reduce the Bundeswehr from around 540,000 to 370,000 in accordance with the Two Plus Four Treaty. This reduction is in line with military cutbacks elsewhere in NATO. Germany has also reaffirmed its pledge not to manufacture, possess or use nuclear forces. These decisions satisfied a considerable section of German society and helped to allay fears about German power politics held in other European countries. However, John Mearsheimer, the neo-realist thinker, in a somewhat extreme view, questioned the validity of this decision, arguing that Germany should have nuclear weapons in order to contribute effectively to the stability and security of Europe.[4]

Secondly, the Gulf crisis, following right on the heels of German unification, exposed the major dilemma of the German political inability to engage in 'out-of-area' military conflicts. While unable to send any forces or military equipment to the area, Germany tried to save face through large financial contributions, by deploying soldiers and military equipment to Turkey (which as a NATO member could be assisted in its defence against any Iraqi attack), and by providing humanitarian assistance, e.g. hospital ships near the zone of conflict. What exacerbated outside criticisms of German cowardice and lack of responsibility was that Iraqi Scud missiles had been modified with the help of German technicians to extend their range and as a result could hit targets in Israel. This was acutely embarrassing for Germany and revived a sense of guilt, which in turn dampened the influence of pacifist thinking on German foreign policy-making.

Thirdly, while Germany stood out by inaction over the Gulf conflict, it sought, in part, to compensate with a more animated policy in former Yugoslavia. In part, this policy also reflected a deeply held conviction over the right to self-determination, analogous to: 'what was good for us must be good for others'. A more vociferous engagement over the former Yugoslavia derived from the large number of Croatian migrant workers in Germany and the sympathies they provoked, particularly within the Catholic Church. There is also a link between Croats and the Catholic Church in Bavaria, which may have fed through into the demands of the CSU within the governing coalition for recognition of Croatia as an independent republic. The fact that the Croatians and Slovenians had been allies, while the Serbs had been enemies, in the Second World War, might also have played a role in German pressures for recognition of both Slovenia and Croatia. Yet this decision was in contravention of the Helsinki security dialogue and earlier German declarations that existing borders in Europe should only be changed by peaceful means. It wholly undermined the initial peace mission process of the then EC negotiator, Lord Carrington, whose remit had been to keep Yugoslavia intact, and forced some EC partners into a decision they were extremely unhappy about. German insistence and threats of unilateral recognition were thus met with a collective EC reply, partly to safeguard the fragile arrangement found just a few months previously under the December 1991 Maastricht treaty, for collective action in the foreign policy and security field. This did not stop France from making veiled accusations that Germany was encouraging the breakup of eastern Europe into small states which would then be economically dependent on Germany.

Fourthly, the massive German aid programme to central and eastern Europe since 1989, exceeding £30 billion, or more than half the West's total,[5] aroused suspicion, with accusations that it was motivated more by hegemonic ambitions than by altruistic principles; that Germany sought the creation of satellites rather than fostering economic recovery, democratization, and political stability in these countries, or laying the foundation for eventual EC membership.[6]

Fifthly, Germany has undertaken limited, though significant, UN humanitarian and peace-keeping missions. For example, Germany participated in the 'Safe Havens' operation in Northern Iraq, provided soldiers to the UN in Cambodia, helped in food and medical airlifts to Sarajevo, contributed both to the monitoring of UN sanctions against Serbia and of the 'no-fly zone', helped in the food airlift to Somalia, and sent military personnel there.[7] But none of these actions have taken German soldiers into combat missions. Moreover, these missions could only be carried out after intervention by the German Supreme Court, which resulted, uncharacteristically for a German governing coalition, in one partner, the FDP, accusing another, the CDU, of pursuing policies which violated constitutional principles with regard to 'out-of-area' engagements.

Sixthly, the decision by Chancellor Kohl to exchange the Ostmark with the Westmark on a one-to-one basis became an important contributing factor to the major disruptions in the ERM, forcing out a number of countries in September 1992 and resulting in a widening of the exchange-rate bands in 1993. To finance unification, large-scale borrowing and publicly financed projects had taken place which fuelled domestic inflation in Germany and which could only be controlled by an increase in interest rates. Given the anchor role held by the DM within the ERM, this forced other members to keep their interest rates higher than domestic conditions required, and therefore delayed a much needed economic recovery. When the tension came to breaking point, it occurred with much acrimony; Britain accused Germany of 'selfishness and uncommunitarian behaviour'. Undoubtedly, this acrimony strengthened the 'Euro-sceptics' in other EC countries, burdened the Maastricht ratification process, soured relations generally among EC members, and jeopardized the timetable agreed at Maastricht for the establishment of EMU and a single currency.

After this consideration of views from the outside, a brief treatment of how Germany sees or defends its own actions is in order. This will concentrate on German actions with regard to the EC and out-of-area military engagements.

German foreign policy: the view from the inside

Four official German views can be identified with regard to the link between German interest rates, ERM disruptions and interest-rate policies elsewhere in the EC. These either place the blame on prevailing ERM rigidities and EC partners, or stress the temporary and benign nature of ERM adjustments.

The first official view was provided by Helmut Schlesinger, former president of the Bundesbank, in his farewell address.[8] In it, Mr Schlesinger protests against the conventional wisdom that economic pressures resulting from unification caused high interest rates which were then transmitted throughout Europe. He singles out the inadequacy of ERM realignments as the main cause for transmitting high interest rates, and not the actions of the Bundesbank.

The second view, advocated by the chairman of Dresdener Bank, acknowledges that Germany maintained high interest rates to the detriment of its Community partners, but argues that redeveloping the five new Länder required additional capital which could only be attracted through high interest rates.[9] Had other EC countries or the EC itself helped to provide capital for the process of east German absorption then the fall-out in terms of higher interest rates would not have occurred to the extent it has. This view criticizes the EC for treating the integration of the former GDR as a purely German problem and cites an inconsistency when compared with Mediterranean policy. (It should be pointed out, however, that the EC decided in the autumn of 1993 to grant 'poor region' status to the five new Länder, which will make them eligible for priority funding from the structural funds.)

Another dimension to the argument over EC help was added when the Bundesbank, in November 1993, called for lower German payments to the European Union, arguing that the current high net level of contributions was no longer justified and indicating that although Germany has slipped to sixth place in the EU prosperity table as a result of unification, it remained by far the largest contributor to EU coffers.

A third official view is put forward by Mr Waigel, the German Minister of Finance, which seeks to put the ERM debate into a wider economic context as well as in a longer time frame.[10] He points out that German unification initially generated a surge of growth in the other EC countries amounting to 1 per cent of their GNP in 1990/91. He goes on to argue that unlike Belgium, Italy, Sweden and the UK which have run high deficits for a decade or more, Germany will bring down the fiscal deficits within a clear time frame and therefore return within the next few years to a policy of fiscal rectitude and monetary stability. In the meantime, according to Waigel, by phasing-in higher taxes and other fiscal charges, Germany has avoided shifting the burden onto its EC partners.

Fourthly, Mr Haller, secretary at the German finance ministry, noted that all the EC member states which kept their currencies close together within the broad band ERM after 2 August 1993 had proved justified in resisting calls for rapid interest-rate cuts.[11] To him this indicated that those countries were determined to pursue a sensible financial and monetary policy, even without the narrow exchange-rate band.

All these responses signal a more self-confident but also more introspective Germany; a country less prepared to pursue European integration at any cost, or to act as an unlimited paymaster. It may also indicate that EC membership has become a sensible option rather than the imperative it was in the past. Given the tremendous task of completing German unification, such a development is not surprising. One might even add that this task has made the Germans declare explicitly that they have 'interests' after all in EC bargaining.

Regained sovereignty and a change in East-West relations has meant a re-examination and redefinition of the role of the Bundeswehr. While there are deep divisions between political parties and even among the governing coalition, the Federal Ministry of Defence's planning is preparing for a restructuring of the Bundeswehr to enable it to undertake new military missions in the future. This development, in itself, has resulted in its own political controversy and created new tensions in civil-military relations.[12] Thomas-Durell Young deems the current security debate to be at least equal in importance to the one surrounding the creation of the Bundeswehr in 1955.[13] He suggests that

> . . . what Bonn must eventually come to terms with is the need to 'reinvent' the Bundeswehr. . . . Germany no longer needs a Federal Armed Forces for the sole purpose of deterrence. . . . What it needs is a war-fighting force, with the capability of deploying outside the Central Region. This transfiguration requires a completely different internal political foundation . . . the international political implications of such a sea-change are not inconsequential.[14]

Such a desired or required change would not be an easy undertaking in any country, given economic constraints and an evolving international situation, but it proves particularly difficult in the German case. As Stephen Szabo points out: 'It is difficult to think of another country in which domestic and foreign policy have been so closely intertwined as in Germany. Foreign policy is often the extension of domestic politics by other means, but the reverse is also often the case'.[15]

Domestic constraints

For much of the postwar period, the Federal Republic could pride itself on having had a widespread consensus for its policies. This situation has changed after 1989 with both public opinion and key institutions within Germany either opposing or not supporting government policies on a number of key issues, hence contributing to the growing level of uncertainty among policy-makers.

In many ways one can speak of the conduct of two debates within Germany: firstly the official discourse; and secondly the public discourse. This split affects all the major issues such as ERM, a single currency, EC federalism, and 'out-of-area' engagement of the Bundeswehr. Despite the genuine commitment of the German leadership to European integration, German politicians can no longer rely on a strong public consensus that the Community is the best way for Germany to defend its interests. This is particularly noticeable on the issue of a single currency to which two-thirds of the population is opposed.[16] To most Germans, the DM has taken on a symbolic importance which is associated with postwar economic success.

There is also a feeling among the German public that Germany has more important domestic priorities than EU integration. There is increasing resistance, particularly from the five new Länder, to subsidizing the poorer EU members. This is coupled with resentment of having to bear the sole burden of absorbing the GDR, of also providing the lion's share of aid to central and eastern Europe, and of accepting a disproportionate number of refugees from central and eastern Europe – admitting, for example, around 300,000 from wars in the former Yugoslavia. These sentiments will have repercussions on the willingness of German policy-makers to act as the 'milch cow' for further EU integration.

The second important issue where the official debate is different from that of the public is with regard to 'out-of-area' interventions. Here a contrary picture emerges to that on EU integration. In public opinion polls the number of Germans supporting German participation in peace-keeping or peace-making operations, e.g. in Bosnia, has been rising constantly.[17] In contrast the major political parties remain at odds over how to amend the Constitution with regard to these interventions, and what the outcome should be.

These popular reactions are largely motivated by prevailing economic difficulties and problems of national identity. Unification has placed the political system under strain, as has been demonstrated most visibly by the political gridlock over the large number of economic and political refugees which have flowed into the country, totalling 436,000 in 1992. Until mid-1993, the political class, and particularly the left-wing segment of the SPD, struggled with a twofold problem. On the one hand, they were searching for a way of preserving a liberal conception of the Federal Republic, a view motivated by memories of the Nazi era. On the other, they were confronting the necessity of handling a political problem which arose directly out of Germany's new position, and which threatened the stability of Germany, particularly the five new Länder. Connected with indecision in the political class is a fundamental uncertainty about German national identity. West Germany has developed since its inception in 1949 into a successful, stable, federal system based on a high degree of consensus on the goals of democracy, economic development, and west European integration. The experience of the Nazi era, the division of the nation, and the provisional status of the Federal Republic, which was recognized in the Basic Law, all combined to prevent the use of the past as a reference point for the construction of the concept of national identity. In certain respects, European integration substituted for a national impulse, and economic growth provided the instrumental justification for the Federal Republic. The unification of Germany, the integration of 16 million more citizens with a distinct historical experience, the exposure of the country to the historical zone of *Mitteleuropa*, and uncertainty over the progress of European unity, have created the necessity at least to re-evaluate or, one could argue, to actually establish a national identity. The problem is further compounded by widespread perceptions that Germany still has to justify its national identity or to apologize for it.[18]

Hence, while the country is undergoing a process of identity formation, the challenge is whether or not this identity will be only a reflexive response to volatile change, or one formed from a stable self-concept, through which Germany can help to shape its external environment as a major international actor.[19]

All these instances, it can be argued, are part of a trend in which public opinion has emerged as an indirect policy actor, whereas previously it played merely a supportive role.[20] Yet, it is not only public opinion which is affecting consensus and uncertainty among policy-makers. For some time observers have noted the impact of domestic structures on foreign policy-making, and this has increased in the post-1989 period. Fragmentation in decision-making at the institutional level goes to the heart of the federal system, governing coalitions and party alliances. Although there have always been tensions between the Bundesbank and the federal government over interest rate and fiscal policies, up until 1989 they did not challenge the otherwise prevailing consensus over economic and monetary policies. But both the conversion of the Ostmark to the Westmark and the timescale and conditions advocated by the federal government for EMU left the Bundesbank strongly opposed. Similarly, both the Länder[21] and the Constitutional Court (over the transfer of sovereignty) and the German Parliament (over EMU development) extracted substantial concessions from the federal government in the ratification of the Maastricht Treaty. These developments undermine policy coherence, add to the uncertainties of German policy-makers, and may make it difficult for Germany either to honour its obligations entered into under the Maastricht Treaty, or to engage in the establishment of a federal Europe. The explicit disagreement expressed, in the autumn of 1993, by the leader of the CSU, the Bavarian sister party of the CDU, over the aims of a federal Europe further undermined consensus. Already, in the spring of 1993, in an unprecedented move, the FDP, the junior partner in the governing coalition, had taken the CDU/CSU to the Constitutional Court over the issue of 'out-of-area' military engagements. Clearly there is a limit to the extent to which German leaders can pass the buck to the Constitutional Court in Karlsruhe for every major problem they encounter.

Impact on other countries

Given these domestic constraints, what impact is German policy, or the absence thereof, going to have on other countries and in what areas will this manifest itself?

Germany is seen as an important international actor, especially in economic and political terms, but Germany's role is also seen as uncertain or incompletely formed. This is in part due to the fluidity of current international politics, including those within Europe; but Germany causes anxiety abroad because it is perceived to be unsure about its own direction. Daniel Vernet has described the perception of Germany as 'Ihre Kraft macht Angst, aber ihr Wille zur Machtlosigkeit verwirrt; ihr kommerzieller Aktivismus beunruhigt genauso wie ihre politische Vorsicht'.[22] There is also a danger, as

Brigitte Seebacher-Brandt suggests, of uncertainty changing into aggression at any time.[23]

These domestic circumstances, as well as the opportunity and challenges which international cooperation entails, pose some fundamental problems for Germany. Three aspects will be of particular concern to German foreign policy-makers in the future.

The 'out-of-area' problem

Can domestic political obstacles to 'out-of-area' involvement in Germany be overcome, and if not, what other forms of contribution can Germany make to European security? In this context, there is also the question of whether Germany can fulfil the 'co-leadership' role of the western world in the manner which the United States apparently envisages.

It is difficult to imagine a Germany standing on the sidelines of conflicts in central and east European (CEE) countries and elsewhere in the world. As the *Economist* points out 'because of its weight and where it stands, Germany cannot be a Switzerland – an introverted hedgehog in a turbulent world, quietly getting fatter.'[24] Germany's considerable commercial and security interests necessitate an active external role. It is important to Germany to help stabilize CEE states, industrially, democratically and politically. Germany also requires measures on the issue of immigration, either in the form of a common EC immigration policy or through bilateral arrangements, like the 'good neighbour' treaties with Poland, the Czech Republic and the Slovak Republic. While many of the aforementioned aspects seem to evoke a continuation of Germany's cheque-book diplomacy and 'civilian power' mentality, military commitments cannot be excluded. To meet its defence obligations to NATO and WEU partners in the new European security environment, or for that matter if it wants to match its aspirations for a seat on the UN Security Council with effective help in peace-making/keeping missions, Germany will have to significantly improve its national military command and operational capabilities.[25] It is here that public opinion and the SPD opposition are major impediments. What might help to overcome this opposition would be for the German government to demonstrate that it has no intention of creating a defence capability in support of national external policies, but rather to integrate external objectives into international organizations and efforts to maintain stability and predictability in Europe and elsewhere.[26]

Policy towards international institutions

Can the German position of pursuing multiple policy options or institutional channels (NATO, EC, CSCE, Franco-German) – the 'as well as' position – be maintained, and if so, under what conditions? If abandoned, what would be the implications for relations necessary with major partners such as the United States, France, the United Kingdom, the EU and Russia?

Germany wants to secure a continued, though reduced, American commitment in Europe (possibly as a dual insurance against uncertainties with regard to the establishment of a new European security order and against the emergence of neo-isolationism by America). This clashes with French interests for an independent and confederal Europe freed from the postwar constraints imposed on European states by the United States and the ex-Soviet Union. It also leaves open the question of how NATO can be extended into eastern Europe beyond the existing North Atlantic Cooperation Council (NACC) and the 'partnership for peace' formula, and how it can be effectively used in crisis management situations in that region. Volker Rühe, the German Defence Minister, is particularly keen for NATO to admit Poland, Hungary and the Czech Republic. He insists that 'If we do not export stability, we will import instability'.[27]

The collorary to Atlantic ties would be upgrading the Eurocorps and a strengthening of the WEU. Such a move is likely to be perceived as challenging both NATO and the American commitment to Europe. The United States wants any European units to be 'separable but not separate' in the Alliance's force structure so that NATO is not undermined.[28] It might also enlarge rather than narrow the link between EC member states and WEU member states.[29] Finally, it remains to be seen to what extent the existing Eurocorps can draw France closer to NATO and whether WEU can become a more effective – and equal – European pillar within NATO.

Previous German efforts to make the CSCE a core institution in the construction of a new European security order, while finding Russian support, have not only been checked by the apparent inadequacies of the CSCE itself with regard to the crisis in former Yugoslavia, but have also received a cool reception from the United States, the United Kingdom and France.

In keeping with West Germany's history and basic constitutional aim of subordinating national interests to international institutions, Genscher saw the strengthening of the CSCE as a way to allay fears of German security and economic domination of central and eastern

Europe and of a new German *Sonderweg*.[30] The CSCE has not so far proved to have the political will behind it to act as an effective guarantor of economic, political and military stability in the wider Europe, but there remains the possibility of its importance growing in the future. In this context, it might be interesting to consider Kissinger's assertion that 'the plethora of institutions (EC, CSCE, WEU, NATO and UN) contribute[s] to rising nationalism'.[31] In his opinion they provide a menu for any country to choose whatever instruments most favour its immediate national goals on any given issue – as happened in the case of Yugoslavia. While, for the time being, it remains unclear whether Germany can continue to attribute equal weight to such organisations as NATO, WEU or the UN, there is also some uncertainty over the extent to which Germany intends to commit itself towards EU integration in the future.

Reconciling unification with European integration

Has the massive task of unification shifted German attention and resources inward, i.e. has integrating Germany become a more pressing goal than integrating the Community? Rather than accelerating European unity (as some observers thought it would[32]), will German unification delay it? Short-term implications need to be separated from medium- to long-term ones. In the short term, adjustment to German unification will affect the EC regional aid programme, development within the ERM, the economic convergence criteria, and possibly the time plan for establishing a single currency and EMU. The latter is particularly placed in jeopardy with the ruling of the German Constitutional Court in October 1993 which seemed to call into question the EMU's original 'irreversibility', requiring further confirmation along the way by either the German parliament or the European Parliament.

In the medium to long term, Germany is likely to gain in strength economically (with expanding trade in central and eastern Europe acting as a major stimulant). The EC, especially when enlarged, will remain Germany's largest trading partner with over 70 per cent of Germany's exports going to EC and EFTA countries, which guarantee every fourth job and represent an important basis for Germany's GDP.[33] There is still sufficient commitment from the Kohl generation who see themselves as 'good Europeans'.[34] Bonn is likely to continue to press for a wider, stronger and more open EU. A deepening of integration is deemed the main priority and seen as a precondition for pan-European growth and thus for a peaceful Europe. Helmut Kohl, and those close to his outlook, might also seek to guard against temptations that if the DM is left to itself and if German industry becomes stronger, Germany might become too powerful by the end of the 1990s and hence might lose the political will to forgo monetary sovereignty in the process of establishing a single currency and a European Central Bank. With ratification of the Maastricht Treaty being finally completed in October 1993, the German government was considering plans as to how best to strengthen EC institutions and decision-making.[35] These included proposals for more majority voting within the Council of Ministers, further competencies for the Commission, greater powers for the European Parliament, a strengthening of the role of the presidency of the EC, and new prescriptions for the application of Article 236. Implementing these proposals will not only require consent from other EU partners, some of which, like the United Kingdom and Denmark, strongly resent a loss of national sovereignty; it may also encounter resistance from ambivalent domestic constituencies in the public, Bundesbank, Bundestag, Länder and political parties. In short, it may be difficult for Germany to balance domestic priorities with European and global responsibilities. This might also limit the degree to which sovereignty will be forgone. Intergovernmentalism rather than strengthening of federalism therefore looks the most likely background against which further EU developments will take place.[36]

In such a future Germany will continue to engage in a substantial pooling of national sovereignty across the spectrum of EU policies; a fact, as Anderson and Goodman point out, that is difficult to reconcile with alleged hegemonic tendencies.[37] This might also help to allay French fears. As Stanley Hoffmann points out: 'The formal anxiety about being governed from Brussels barely conceals a real anguish about being dictated to by Bonn, entrapped in a Community that would be an extension of German might rather than, as was hoped originally, French power.'[38] Already, as Hoffmann suggests, there is a fear that 'the Community begins to resemble much more the German model of Federalism and social market economics than the French model of the unitary and regulatory state.'[39] For the time being Germany seems prepared to work in tandem with France on the construction of European integration. This was evident once again in November 1993 when both countries jointly presented the broad outlines of plans to bring their economies together as prescribed by the Maastricht Treaty for EMU by the end of the decade. A similar development can be observed in the foreign policy and security field through, for example, the establishment of the Eurocorps, the development of 'joint actions' with the CFSP, and the initiative for a Europe-wide security conference.

What is questionable, however, is whether France shares the same degree of commitment both to supranational goals and to the transfer of sovereignty to EU central institutions. Germany has accepted that national solutions are not really possible anymore and, in any case, run counter to EU cooperation. This realization has yet to occur to the same extent in France and Britain.

Given the relatively brief period since German unification and the extreme fluidity in international relations, especially with regard to central and eastern Europe, it is not surprising that no clear German line exists as to what role it intends to play in the new European order. Uncertainty about Germany's role (within and outside Germany) will thus prevail for some time to come. Germany will veer between two courses: on the one hand, it will attempt to become a 'normal' national actor and take on more international responsibility (especially as a donor of aid and mediator of conflicts in central and eastern Europe); and on the other hand, it will continue to be characterized for some time to come either as cowardly, indecisive, aggressive or dominant. However, there are indications that Germany will continue with many of its pre-1989 foreign policy goals, based on the 'civilian power' concept and on multilateralism. Moreover, unless other major European actors, such as Britain or France, insist on narrow nationalism or for that matter provoke Germany to act similarly, there does not seem to be any danger of a nationalist revival in Germany. Rather, while Germany may be the first among equals in the new Europe, there is a predisposition to create a European Germany rather than a German Europe.[40]

Conclusion

No security structure serving the needs of Europe appears conceivable without Germany, and as the economic motor of European integration, Germany appears well placed to become one of the main architects of European unity in whatever form it takes. However, unification and the regaining of full sovereignty have placed new international responsibilities on Germany, to which it finds adjustment difficult. There is a gap between what might be expected of Germany, given its geographic position in Europe, its economic strength, and the changed geopolitical context, and the reality of what the memories of the National Socialist era and then 40 years of peaceful Federal Republic development, under the overarching western security and economic system, have left as a legacy for Germany's perception of its place in the world.

It is therefore not inappropriate to counsel caution about Germany's ability to take a more activist role in foreign and security policy. On the other hand, this seems to point to a more nationally oriented Germany in which its national interest will surface more strongly in EU decision-making than before. This might also suggest an alteration in the balance of power among the Twelve. While such a development might not result in destabilizing Europe, Mrs Thatcher might have been correct to suggest that a united Europe would increase and not limit the influence of a united Germany.[41]

Germany will continue to exercise its power resources most effectively in and through international institutions. These power resources are primarily economic in nature. Militarily, 'out-of-area' forces would only be acceptable to German and foreign publics if mobilized within a combined military or peace-keeping operation of the United Nations, NATO, or the WEU. A constitutional change to facilitate military action outside the NATO area would probably be contingent on such assurances in any case. It is possible that in the future the WEU will develop into a 'European pillar' of NATO, or perhaps, further into the future, into a separate European military and security organization. In such a case German military participation would also be facilitated.

The political and economic stability in central and eastern Europe will remain a major preoccupation of German foreign policy. However, as Germany becomes more involved in affairs relating to both eastern and western Europe, it seems to have learned that it can play neither a bridging nor a pivotal role between East and West.[42] The new Germany is likely to be more willing to assume the responsibilities of leadership which its new weight implies. Yet this weight should not be exaggerated. It will be an economic power of the first rank but a political power of only medium rank because it will not possess nuclear weapons nor the conventional capabilities to act independently outside of Europe. It will, therefore, project its influence in non-military ways and through its role within the EU. Only if the progress towards the building of a new Europe fails, or is deemed too costly, will Germany be faced with any realistic national option.[43]

More than any other world power, Germany operates in a thick web of interdependent relationships. Its status as the world's largest trading partner and its partial subordination to the EU point to only the most obvious of these.[44] Germany will continue to carve a distinct role for itself in world affairs (a role which also aims at integrating Germany into Europe as an equal state), but it will be a role informed by the benefits of almost 50 years of multilateralism and collective action.

Acknowledgment

I would like to thank Charlie Jeffrey, Hugh Miall and James Sperling for their comments on an earlier version of this chapter. I would also like to acknowledge the financial support of the Nuffield Foundation.

Notes

1. Fritz Stern has suggested that in the future, the industrialized world could be organized into three economies or camps: one in a dollar zone led by the United States; the second in a Japanese-dominated yen zone; and the third in a German Deutschmark zone. Hence, he argues, Germany will become one of the world power centres. Fritz Stern, 'A New Beginning in Germany', *The Washington Post*, 29 July 1990, p. C7.
2. The argument about German hegemonic tendencies is made by Markovits and Reich. However, they see it more as a voluntary subordination on the part of central and eastern European states. Andrei Markovits and Simon Reich, 'Should Europe Fear the Germans?', *German Politics and Society*, issue 23, pp. 1–20. For an alternative view, which makes the distinction between influence and hegemony, see Jeffrey J. Anderson and John B. Goodman, 'Mars or Minerva? A United Germany in a Post-Cold War Europe', in Robert O. Keohane, Joseph S. Nye and Stanley Hoffmann (eds), *After the Cold War: International Institutions and State Strategies in Europe, 1989–1991*, Harvard University Press, 1993, pp. 23–62.
3. See Richard Burt, 'Germany and World Politics', in Shahram Chubin (ed.), *Germany and the Middle East: Patterns and Prospects*, London, 1992, pp. 11–24.
4. See John Mearsheimer, 'Back to the Future: Instability in Europe After the Cold War', *International Security*, Summer 1990, pp. 5–57.
5. This includes commitments to Russia. See *The Economist*, 20 November, 1993, p. 23.
6. See A. Markovits and S. Reich, *op. cit.*
7. See Karl-Heinz Kamp, 'The German Bundeswehr in out-of-area operations: to engage or not to engage?', *The World Today*, Aug., Sept. 1993, pp. 165–8.

8. Mr Schlesinger, quoted in *The Independent*, 29.9.1993.
9. Mr Sarrazin, Chairman of Dresdener Bank, quoted in *The Financial Times*, 15.9.1993.
10. Theo Waigel, 'Unified Germany no drag on Europe', *The Financial Times*, 11.10.1993.
11. Quoted in *The Financial Times*, 6.10.1993.
12. For further details see Thomas-Durell Young, *The 'Normalization' of the Federal Republic of Germany's Defence Structures*, Strategic Studies Institute, US Army War College, September 1992; see also his paper *Germany's Defense Guidelines and the Centralization of Operational Control*, Strategic Studies Institute/RIIA, forthcoming 1994.
13. Thomas-Durell Young, *Normalization*, *op. cit.*
14. Ibid.
15. Stephen Szabo, 'German Society and Foreign Policy', in Shahram Chubin (ed.), *Germany and the Middle East: Patterns and Prospects*, London, 1992, pp. 93–112.
16. See *The Economist* of 25.9.1993.
17. Karl-Heinz Kamp, *op. cit.*
18. See Brigitte Seebacher-Brandt, 'Deutschland: Vier Jahre Danach', *Magazine of Die Zeit*, 24.9.1993.
19. For further details on how the process of establishing or redefining a national identity has resulted in considerable uncertainty over domestic and foreign policy action, see Gregor Schollgen, *Angst vor der Macht: Die Deutschen und ihre Aussenpolitik*, Ullstein Verlag, Berlin, 1993.
20. I am indebted to Charlie Jeffrey for this point.
21. For further details see Barbara Lippert, Rosalind Stevens-Ströhmann, Grit Viertel, Stephen Woolcock and Dirk Günther, *German Unification and EC Integration*, RIIA/Pinter, London, 1993.
22. 'Its power creates fear but its determination not to use it confuses people; its commercial activity is as unsettling as its political cautiousness.'
23. Brigitte Seebacher-Brandt, *op. cit.*
24. *The Economist*, 25.9.1993.
25. Thomas-Durell Young, *'Normalization'*, *op. cit.*
26. Ibid., p. 28.
27. Volker Rühe, quoted by James Jackson, 'Trying to Enlist in NATO', *Time*, November 8, 1993, pp. 50–51.
28. See *The Independent* 18.10.1993.
29. The Petersberg Declaration of the WEU raised the threshold for accession to WEU, e.g. to accept the 1987 WEU Platform which includes a strong affirmation of nuclear deterrence. This may pose problems for countries such as Austria, Switzerland and Sweden.
30. Hans-Dietrich Genscher, 'German Responsibility for a Peaceful Order in Europe', in A. Rotfield and W. Stutzle (eds), *Germany and Europe in Transition*, Oxford University Press, 1991, pp. 20–29.
31. Henry Kissinger, 'The Atlantic Alliance Needs Renewal in a Changing World', *International Herald Tribune*, 3.3.1992, p. 5.

32. R. Stuth, 'Germany's New Role in a Changing Europe', *Aussenpolitik*, vol. 43, no. 1, 1992, p. 29.
33. Helmut Kohl, 'European Union – A Challenge of our Times', *German Comments*, October 1993, pp. 4–10.
34. Ibid., p. 6.
35. Karl Lamers, 'Germany's Responsibilities and Interests in the Field of Foreign Policy', a paper presented to the conference of the Executive Committee of the CDU/CSU parliamentary party in the Bundestag, held in Berlin on 23–24 August 1993. Translated and distributed by the Konrad Adenauer Foundation, London Office, 27. 9. 1993.
36. See Emil J. Kirchner, *Decision-Making in the European Community: The Council Presidency and European Integration*, Manchester University Press, 1992.
37. Jeffrey Anderson and John Goodman, 'Mars or Minerva?' *op. cit.*, p. 62.
38. Stanley Hoffmann, 'Thought on the French Nation Today', *Daedalus*, vol. 122, no. 3, Summer 1993, p. 75.
39. Ibid.
40. Stephen Szabo, *op. cit.* p. 106.
41. See Steve Crawshaw, 'Sturm and Drang over Thatcher memoirs', *The Independent*, 14.10.1993.
42. See Michael Sturmer, 'Historical perspectives to the Cold War's fault lines, *Frankfurter Allgemeine Zeitung*, 3.3.1992, reprinted in *The German Tribune*, 13.3.1992.
43. See Stephen Szabo, *op. cit.*, p. 107.
44. Germany's exports account for 38 per cent of its GDP; the EC purchases 77 per cent of total German exports.

Part III
International Implications

13

Redefining Europe: Implications for International Relations

Robert O. Keohane

International relations during the first two post-Cold War years, between the collapse of the Berlin Wall in November 1989 and the failed Soviet coup of August 1991, could be described in terms of the responses of states to a sudden transformation of world politics. The end of the Cold War was defined by the collapse of Soviet political control and the withdrawal of effective Soviet military forces from central Europe. It led quickly to the reunification of Germany, and the implications of this for the future European order became the principal focus of attention. State strategies quickly shifted in response to changes in the relative capabilities of major states.[1]

Although change had been precipitated largely by economic, social and political pressures within the Soviet Union, and by the Soviet leadership itself, initial reactions to it by the West were guided by state elites; and although change was sudden, it took place peacefully in a spirit of optimism, even euphoria. Even observers who discounted the rhetoric of a 'New World Order' were impressed by the adaptability of the West and of its major institutions – NATO and the European Community. Indeed, members of the Community reacted to the end of the Cold War by accelerating their drive towards 'European Union,' culminating in the Maastricht Treaty of December 1991.

The two years since Maastricht have challenged both the previous belief that the victorious western powers retained control over events, and the earlier optimism. Previous chapters in this volume describe the series of unanticipated and disturbing events that have shaken Europe's confidence: the collapse of the Soviet Union and the subsequent military conflicts along its southern and eastern borders, from Moldavia to the Caucasus to central Asia; increasingly severe political conflict in Russia itself, including the military attack on the parliament building in October 1993; difficulties with German unification and their implications for other countries; narrow ratification of Maastricht and monetary crises in Europe; and the undeterred and uncontrolled war in the former Yugoslavia. These events could not be described in terms of state strategies, since they were not the result of calculated state action but of miscalculation (as in the economics of German unification and monetary issues in Europe), internal political struggles (as in Russia), ambitious political leaders taking advantage of ethnocentrism and nationalism (as in the former Yugoslavia), or popular reaction against elite decisions (as in the Danish defeat of the Maastricht Treaty in June 1992 and its narrow approval by the French electorate later that year). Indeed, the ineffectiveness of western state responses to unanticipated challenges has revealed weaknesses in international institutions, including the European Community, which despite the Maastricht Treaty has been unable to implement either a coherent monetary system or a common foreign and security policy.

The most basic question for international relations raised by these disturbing events concerns how state interests are being redefined, since the likelihood of conflict and the potential for cooperation will be fundamentally shaped by these interests – as defined by those in power. These interests are not fixed by geography but vary, in response both to internal politics and the incentives provided by the nature of world politics. In 1990–91, Germany's policies were a major source of concern; but Germany has a well-functioning democracy and a unified Germany is a satisfied power. A secure Europe with strong international institutions and current national boundaries would be entirely satisfactory to Germans. As Jeffrey Anderson and John Goodman argue, 'Germany has every reason to remain firmly ensconced in its institutional web.'[2] Russia, however, is less likely to be satisfied: most of its formerly subservient European republics are now hostile (the Baltic states and Ukraine), quarrelling with each other (Armenia and Azerbaijan), or engaged in civil war (Georgia); and 25 million Russians now live outside of Russia's borders, under the rule of governments often inclined to discriminate against them.[3] Hence, as a number of the contributors to this volume have pointed out, Russian politics, determining how Russian leaders define their interests, are likely to be the key to stability or instability in Europe during the coming decades. Such policies can be affected at the margin by the West, but it should not be expected that western actions will be decisive in determining the nature of political change in a country as large as Russia.[4]

Even if the great powers' definitions of their interests leave room for mutually beneficial cooperation, there is no guarantee that such cooperation will actually occur. Cooperation depends not only on compatible interests but on information about each others' policies, sufficiently low costs of negotiating and enforcing agreements, and the ability to make credible commitments – all of which require international institutions.[5] During the Cold War, western Europe and the North Atlantic area had such institutions, notably the European Community and NATO. The key question now at the international level is whether existing institutions can be adapted quickly enough to adjust to major changes in the actors, in their perceptions of their interests, and in their relative power.

In my view, answers to these questions will be different in western Europe and the former Soviet Union. Western Europe remains stable and democratic, part of a pluralistic security community as described by Karl Deutsch.[6] Conflicts occurring within it do not involve threats of military force. But neither common interests nor effective international institutions link the countries of the former Soviet Union. As Joseph Nye and I wrote earlier:

powerful self-reinforcing dynamics are likely to operate in both the western 'zone of peace' and the zone of conflict to the east; and it will be impossible to characterize world politics as a whole either as a jungle of unrelenting conflict or as a reflection of patterns of complex interdependence and institutionalized cooperation.[7]

We can describe recent events in Europe, at least superficially, but we cannot explain them. Explanation requires both rich description, of complex social movements and hidden actions of governments, and coherent theory. Consider, for instance, the concept of nationalism. Karl Deutsch characterized a nation as 'a group of persons united by a common error about their ancestry and a common dislike of their neighbors,' and assessed it as an aspect of social mobilization, resulting from modernization and urbanization.[8] But neither Deutsch's conceptualization of nationalism nor subsequent work on this subject provide a tight explanatory theory to explain when national sentiment will lead to aggression against disliked neighbours. In his introductory essay to this volume, Hugh Miall points out that 'strong national identities and weak states combine with economic insecurity to make a dangerous cocktail;'[9] but we have no theory to tell us when that (Molotov) cocktail will explode. Subsequent sections of this essay will not attempt explanation, but seek to achieve more modest objectives: to put recent events in Europe into a broad historical context, and then to ask two questions: (1) what does the ongoing revision of Europe suggest about enduring realities ('old truths') of international relations; and (2) what crucial questions does it raise about the current situation and the choices that we face?

Pressures on Europe from changes in world politics

Many of the most important international political changes in Europe since 1815 can be seen as results of the ends of wars – as in 1815, 1918–19, and 1945. Wars have typically been followed immediately by radical political changes in defeated countries (France in 1815; Russia beginning in 1917; Germany and Austria in 1918–19; Italy after 1943; and Germany in 1945). For their part, winning states have sooner or later often become over-optimistic about their ability to reshape the politics of other states – one thinks of the Holy Alliance in the years before 1848; British, French and American intervention in Russia in 1919–20; and imposition of Soviet rule in eastern Europe after 1945. Finally, it is a cliché that victorious wartime alliances typically collapse shortly after the conflict is over.

Another major source of political change in modern Europe has been the collapse of an empire that dominated part of the continent, as in the slow decline of the Ottoman Empire during the second half of the nineteenth century and in the years prior to 1914. The decline of Ottoman power stimulated nationalist movements in the Balkans, precipitating civil and international wars. Although we do not have a good explanation of nationalism, it does seem to occur where social mobilization is occurring but civil society is weak: national identification under these circumstances becomes a means of self-identity. Furthermore, when political leaders have seized on national differences to generate support for their ambitions a self-sustaining dynamic seems to take over, as in the former Yugoslavia: identifying with an ethnic group seeking to gain national status becomes a primitive form of protection against other people who are likely to identify you in national terms whether you like it or not. In such a society, cosmopolitan individuals without ethnic identities are in danger of becoming victims of nationalist forces.

One way of viewing Europe since 1989 is that political change is resulting from the *conjuncture* of these two changes: the end of a 'war' (the Cold War) and the collapse of the Soviet empire. In this light, it is not surprising that radical social and political change has occurred in the former Soviet Union, nor that fervent nationalism has appeared within countries formerly under domination from Moscow. Ends of world wars and collapses of empires do not lend themselves to smooth management, even by victorious states.

Old truths reinforced by the experience of 1991–3

From the standpoint of international relations theory, the experience of 1991–3 reinforces some conventional generalizations about world politics. These generalizations are not very helpful as predictors of events, they only warn against naive arguments that the nature of international relations has been fundamentally transformed. Three generalizations seem worth briefly stating.

1. In the absence of stabilizing institutions, conflict is endemic in world politics.

Realists from Thucydides onward have emphasized that changes in power relations and associated uncertainty and fear lead to war: 'the growth in the power of Athens, and the alarm which this inspired in Lacedaemon, made war inevitable.'[10] Events in the former Yugoslavia and the former Soviet Union since 1991 have borne out realist pessimism about peace suddenly breaking out in Europe after the Cold War.[11] However, the unconditional statement that 'anarchy' in world politics necessarily leads to power maximization and war does not explain variation among time periods or regions: in particular, it does not account for the peacefulness of western Europe since 1945, and its continuation as a security community despite the end of the Soviet threat. Such a view fails adequately to take into account variations in the compatibility of state interests, or the impact on mutual confidence that international institutions can exert. The inability of international institutions to enforce order is obvious; but the real functions of such institutions are more modest – to provide information and help to make commitments credible. Realists and institutionalists agree that without stabilizing institutions conflict is endemic in world politics, but not about its causal implications: strict realists see institutions as so weak that they cannot moderate anarchy, while institutionalists view them as sometimes, but not always, capable of exerting significant effects.

2. The nature of international relations depends on politics within societies.

This would be a difficult proposition to deny: the impacts on war of revolution (as in the wars between 1793 and 1815), authoritarian politics and nationalist mythmaking (as in the First World War), and of totalitarianism (as in the Second World War and the Cold War) have been well documented. Whether stable democracies are necessarily peaceful is currently hotly disputed, although the recent foreign policy of democratic Serbia should give pause to those who are enthusiastic about the view that democracies are pacific by nature. In any case, democratization can hardly be taken for granted: it is difficult to attain, particularly on the first try, and depends on conditions that are not necessarily present in much of the former Soviet Union.[12] In Deutsch's terms, democracy could be seen as depending in part on political integration: the identification of people with their state, and their resulting active consent to, and support of, state action.[13] Such consent and identification cannot be taken for granted: most non-Russians in the Soviet Union, for instance, never seem to have identified with the Soviet state.

Unfortunately, the generalization that the nature of international relations depends on domestic politics begs the central question for international relations theory and foreign policy: given the crucial importance of politics within societies, what impact can other states' policies, and international institutions, have on such politics? Mearsheimer was right to point out in 1990 that Soviet control over eastern Europe decisively prevented war in the region; but we have no theory that predicts the impact of lesser degrees of outside influence. Economic sanctions and threats of bombing have not deterred the Serbs; but democrats in Hungary, Poland and the Czech Republic have certainly been encouraged by Western support.

3. Collective security continues to be unattainable.

In his classic analysis of collective security, Inis L. Claude pointed out the stark difference between it and balance of power politics:

> By assumption (under collective security), peace and security are indivisible; the initiation of war anywhere is a challenge to the interests of all states, because it undermines the general order

which is central to the security of every state. The balance of power concept, on the other hand, leaves much more latitude for the *ad hoc* calculation of what the national interest requires in particular circumstances.[14]

The policies of western European states and the United States with respect to Serb and Croat attacks on Bosnia demonstrate that what Claude labels balance of power politics continues to prevail over the calculations demanded by collective security. Britain, France, Germany and the United States all made *ad hoc* calculations of the national interest; furthermore, they assumed (correctly, so far) that peace is divisible rather than indivisible – that continued warfare in Bosnia would not lead to a European war as a result of intervention, such as occurred in 1914. Whatever the role played by international institutions in maintaining order, it will not be that of enforcing the peace according to the abstract requirements of Wilsonian collective security – which, like Christianity according to Voltaire, has never been tried.

Questions and choices

Structure and interests

As suggested at the outset, the most important question for the future of Europe is whether the structural changes that have taken place – in actors, interests and power – have remained within a range that provides sufficient space for cooperation. That is, are there potential mutual gains from negotiated agreements, given the interests of the actors as they define them? It seems clear that within the European Union and NATO, and in the broader economic society defined by GATT, the answer to that question is yes. Cooperation persists in the European Union, even if at a lower level than some participants desired, and across the Atlantic. Since cooperation is always closely associated with conflict, and emerges only from tough bargaining, we should not be misled by the lack of harmony to discount its persistence in the West.

On the other hand, in Bosnia, Croatia, Georgia, and between Armenia and Azerbaijan, interests are so sharply in conflict that only force seems able to settle issues. The potential for armed conflict between Russia and some of its neighbors, over territory (as with the Ukraine) or the treatment of Russian nationals outside of Russia,

seems substantial – and will depend both on actions by its neighbours and the evolution of Russian domestic politics.

In between – both geographically and in terms of their prospects –
lie the former Soviet satellites of eastern Europe. As discussed in this
volume, there seem to be reasons for optimism about the Czech
Republic, Hungary and Poland – less so for Slovakia, Bulgaria and
Romania. From one standpoint, the breakup of Czechoslovakia
should be taken as a positive sign of successful adaptation, since it
was peaceful.[15] At any rate, eastern Europe seems to be an area in
which Western support, economic and perhaps in terms of security
guarantees, could be decisive in creating or maintaining democratic
politics – as many contributors to this volume argue.

Institutional adaptation

Given a set of interests, the key question, raised at the beginning of
this essay, is whether existing institutions can be adapted quickly
enough to adjust to major changes in structure of European politics.[16]
It seems to me that the answer depends on the institution. The CSCE
has, it seems to me, been a failure, and is likely to continue to be
ineffective. In my view, the difficulty with CSCE does not result, as
Trevor Taylor claims in his chapter (p. 175), from the fact that it
represents ' the idealist tradition' in international relations. After all, it
was established during the 1970s as part of a Cold War compromise
by statesmen who were anything but idealists. The difficulty of the
CSCE is that its structure, which was useful to the western powers
when human rights issues could be used against the Soviet Union,
cannot readily be adapted to provide security, support for democratic
infrastructure, or economic aid – the purposes for which the West
needs international institutions now in eastern Europe.

The European Single Market, however, continues to be implemented; far from being concerned about collapse, NATO is discussing
possible expansion; and the GATT negotiations reached agreement –
albeit, limited agreement that fell short of the original objectives of
the Uruguay Round – in December 1993. All of these institutions
seem to have weathered the first four years since the end of the Cold
War. However, as Helen Wallace points out, the European Union is
unlikely to advance much further until it has acquired a clearer role.
The European Community had first grown as a way of reinforcing
and extending state powers, then opportunistically became a vehicle
for deregulation and competition with the Single European Act of

1985. Before 1989 it was reinforced by Cold War politics; afterwards, the push toward Maastricht was fueled by concern to lock Germany into a strong Community. The messages sent by these various initiatives, their institutional implications, and their potential constituencies, were somewhat contradictory and certainly confusing; and the 'democratic deficit', and lack of citizen involvement, precluded active popular support for and identification with Europe. Common interests will keep Europe together as a Single Market; but effective realization of the Maastricht goals of European Union will require, as Wallace says, a new consensus on Europe's mission.

In the broader trade area, GATT may be 'dead', as Lester Thurow famously proclaimed some years ago, but like the phoenix it has only died in order to be reborn (subject to ratification by key members) as a multilateral trade organization, with broader powers and stronger dispute settlement procedures. Adaptation has indeed occurred, responding to the reality of non-tariff barriers and the connections between trade and industrial policy. Much more adaptation will be needed in the future; in particular, trade policy will have to take account explicitly of the value of environmental protection, which has become politically significant in many democracies.

Finally, NATO has been given new life by the uncertainty, turmoil, and conflict so evident in Yugoslavia and the former Soviet Union. Insecurity is good for alliances. Institutional adaptation is difficult, although (as the EC and GATT have shown), it can take place. From an institution's standpoint, it is easier when events outside its control make it seem necessary again.

Policy choices

Although the most important issues concern Russian domestic politics, the West can only have a marginal impact on them, as the events of 1991–3 indicate. Indeed, the impact of economic reform on politics may be negative. If, as Vincent Cable (p. 92) suggests, the economic lesson of experience is that 'radicalism pays,' the political lesson, overlooked by economists, may be that 'radicalism leads to a reaction toward socialism or fascism'. To their cost and ours, most contemporary economists learn little history, ignore political science, and ignore earlier economists who had a stronger sense of history and politics. From Adam Smith to Joseph Schumpeter and Jacob Viner, economists had a clear understanding of the dependence of

market economies on social, political and legal institutions that were
not created by capitalism. They would not have been surprised that
'getting the prices right' has been only a necessary, not a sufficient,
condition for workable capitalism in the former socialist countries.
Karl Polanyi taught that 'the human economy is embedded and
enmeshed in institutions, economic and non-economic. The inclusion
of the non-economic is vital. For religion or government may be as
important for the structure and functioning of the economy as
monetary institutions or the availability of tools and machines
themselves.'[17] And although his anthropomorphic view of 'society'
seems oddly archaic, Polanyi's words about early nineteenth-century
capitalism in Britain, written during the Second World War, remain
relevant to Russia today:

> Our thesis is that the idea of a self-adjusting market economy
> implied a stark utopia. Such an institution could not exist for any
> length of time without annihilating the human and natural
> substance of society; it would have physically destroyed man and
> transformed his surroundings into a wilderness. Inevitably society
> took measures to protect itself, but whatever measures it took
> impaired the self-regulation of the market, disorganized industrial
> life, and thus endangered society in yet another way.[18]

However, even if western policies can only have marginal effects on
internal politics in Russia, the stakes are so high that we should
attempt to exert positive effects – sensitively, with politics as well as
economics firmly in mind. In eastern Europe our actions are likely to
have greater impact, and it is particularly incumbent on the European
Community to open its markets and in other ways actively to
encourage east European democracy.

With respect to the scenarios outlined by the editor in his introduction, I would submit that the re-emergence of security concerns in
the former Soviet Union, and the conflict in the former Yugoslavia,
make both fortress Europe and fragmented western Europe very
unlikely scenarios. The end of Cold War has not liberated Europe,
after all, from dependence on United States security protection; nor
has it provided incentives for the members of the European
Community to engage in security competition with one another. My
own view is that even without a security threat from the East, Europe
would neither have become a fortress (since trade with North
America and Japan is so vital to it, and investment in those areas
crucial to the future of big European companies) or fragmented (since

the economic and security interests in staying together are so great, and since European institutions enable those interests to be realized). However, even apart from those incentives, the turmoil in the East seems to preclude the fortress Europe scenario and the prospect of fragmentation in western Europe itself.

The key issues, still unresolved, involve how creative and supportive Europe (and other advanced democracies, including Japan as well as the United States) can be in encouraging moderate politics in Russia and eastern Europe, and in adapting international institutions to new situations. Democracy in Russia is neither likely nor necessary for Western interests; but moderation is. How fortunate the next generation would be if Russia, during the next 30 years, could have a government as stable and progressive as Mexico's during the last three decades! But Mexico has hardly been an effective democracy. If the West can help to build an institutional infrastructure in Russia that will promote social order, economic development, and gradual democratization – and if it can adapt its international institutions to new challenges – it will have good reason to be proud.

Notes

1. For such a description of this 21-month period, see Robert O. Keohane, Joseph S. Nye, and Stanley Hoffmann (eds), *After the Cold War: International Institutions and State Strategies in Europe, 1989–1991*, Cambridge: Harvard University Press, 1993.
2. Jeffrey J. Anderson and John B. Goodman, 'Mars or Minerva? A United Germany in a Post-Cold War Europe,' in Keohane, *et al.*, *After the Cold War, op. cit.*, p. 61.
3. Hugh Miall, *Shaping the New Europe*, London: Pinter Publishers for the Royal Institute of International Affairs, 1993, p. 78.
4. The long history of futile Western attempts to restructure Chinese political life does not provide grounds for optimism; nor does the record of the International Monetary Fund in restructuring the political economies of countries in Africa, Asia and Latin America during the last 30 years.
5. Robert O. Keohane, *After Hegemony: Cooperation and Discord in the World Political Economy*, Princeton: Princeton University Press, 1984, chs 5–7.
6. Karl W. Deutsch, *et al.*, *Political Community in the North Atlantic Area*, Princeton, N.J.: Princeton University Press, 1957.
7. Robert O. Keohane and Joseph S. Nye, 'Introduction', in Keohane, *et al.*, *After the Cold War, op. cit.*, p. 6.
8. Karl W. Deutsch, *Nationalism and Its Alternatives*, New York: Alfred A. Knopf, 1969. The quotation is on p. 3.

9. Chapter 1, p. 8.

10. Thucydides, *The Peloponnesian War*, Book I (paragraph 24), New York: Modern Library, 1982, T.E. Wick (ed.), p. 14.

11. John Mearsheimer, 'Back to the Future: Instability in Europe after the Cold War', *International Security*, vol. 15, no. 1, Summer, 1990, pp. 5–56.

12. For a stimulating analysis, see Samuel P. Huntington, *The Third Wave: Democratization in the Late Twentieth Century*, Norman: University of Oklahoma Press, 1991.

13. Karl W. Deutsch, *Nationalism and its Alternatives* (cited, above), p. 29. See also Deutsch, *Nationalism and Social Communication*, Cambridge: MIT Press, 1953; and Deutsch, *Political Community in the North Atlantic Area* (*op. cit.*).

14. Inis L. Claude, *Power and International Relations*, New York: Random House, 1962, p. 146.

15. How often has secession or division of a country been peaceful in the modern world? Belgium left Holland in 1830 but under French pressure; Norway became independent from Sweden in 1905. Civil war, however, has been more common as a response to secession.

16. In his valuable contribution, Peter van Ham (Chapter 11) raises this issue under the heading of two questions: 1) are institutions 'sturdy enough to survive the centrifugal forces which characterize post-Cold War dynamics?' and 2) are they 'still relevant to solving the main economic, political and security problems of Europe as a whole?'

17. Karl Polanyi, 'The Economy as Instituted Process', p. 250, in Karl Polanyi, Conrad M. Arensberg and Harry W. Pearson (eds), *Trade and Market in the Early Empires* (New York: Free Press, 1957; reprinted by Henry Regnery Company, Chicago, 1971), pp. 243–69.

18. Karl Polanyi, *The Great Transformation: The Political and Economic Origins of our Time* [copyright 1944], Boston: Beacon Press, 1957, p. 3.

14

The Middle East and Europe: the Post-Cold War Climate

Hussein J. Agha

It is obviously misleading to talk about either the Middle East or Europe as well-defined, separate, homogeneous entities. Perceptions of each by the other are more varied than even the number of states and communities that make up the two regions. Lazy attempts to aggregate the constituents of the two regions are not only intellectually unsound, but are also conducive to profound simplifications and misunderstandings of the parameters that govern the relations between the countries of the two regions. A side-effect of this aggregation is the adoption of its ensuing constructs by the elite of analysts and policy-makers on both sides to provide the tools of analysis by which they consider the relations between the two regions. Such mental constructs tend to develop a reality and a logic of their own that goes a long way in governing the understanding and the action of each party towards the other.

Europe and the Middle East work as distinct entities in the context of historical analysis and for the purpose of geography books where the world is divided into five continents. In our post-modern age, and approaching the millennium, it is evident that, for instance, Sicily has more in common with Lebanon than it has with Estonia, Greece more in common with Egypt than with Denmark, Spain more in common with Morocco than with Poland, and Albania more in common with Yemen than with the UK.

From a Middle Eastern point of view the Middle East is divided into the following regions:

(a) the Maghreb, which is referred to usually as North Africa in the West, but which is very much part of the collective consciousness of the Arab Middle East and certainly part of its historical past;

(b)   the Valley of the Nile, which comprises Egypt and Sudan (and
      to some extent Eritrea and Somalia);
(c)   the Mashrek, or the Fertile Crescent;
(d)   the Arabian Peninsula and the Gulf;
(e)   the non-Arab Middle East, comprising Iran and Turkey, and
      sometimes, but to a much lesser extent, Afghanistan and
      Pakistan.

What most unites this area is the Islamic religion and the history of
the Islamic Empire. Each of these regions, however, has its own set of
cultural identities, political idiosyncrasies, economic specificities,
perceptions, aspirations and concerns. Each of them is in the nature of
an informal little European Union, or a southern Scandinavia.

It is difficult to lump these regions together for any meaningful
purpose, especially with the apparent dissolution of the problem of
Palestine. This is not to deny that they may share from time to time
certain concerns – security and otherwise – or might find some value
in cooperation in some fields, but so do Korea and Japan or any two
countries that are in the vicinity of each other. The sad experience of
the Arab League is a powerful demonstration of the limits of
cooperation among the majority of these countries; while the ferocity
of the two Gulf wars and the civil war in Lebanon further
demonstrate the depth of indigenous conflicts in the area and the
total breakdown of peaceful mechanisms to deal with them.

With the defeat of Arabism, both ideologically and militarily in its
confrontation with Zionism and Israel on the one hand, and
politically and economically in its inability to build a legitimate state
and a viable economy on the other hand, the one salient reality that
brings the different regions in the area together is political Islam.
This, perhaps more than any other characteristic, makes it possible
to address the area as a separate unit. What political Islam is
effectively saying is that the 75 years or so of secular nationalism
has been an aberration in the history of the area that has been
Islamic for well over a millennium. It does not matter whether some
of these Muslim empires were decadent, or did not really practise
true Islam. What matters is that they were Islamic and the identity
of the society and its values were indigenous Islam rather than
imported western, in this case European secularism. In this context
a secular national state is the continuation of the rule of the western
powers by other than direct physical means and thus is not genuine
and true independence. Devoid of its religious content, Islam, in its
pure political guise, becomes a movement for independence. Therein

lies its political antipathy to the West, rather than in a clash of religious beliefs between a Judaeo-Christian outlook and a Muslim one.

But even here political Islam is not a uniform phenomenon in the Middle East. The circumstances to which it is a response are not the same in the different regions of the area and it does not always have the same characteristics. In Algeria political Islam has to do mostly with the incomplete independence from France; in Egypt with the nature of the state and its alliances; in Lebanon with the Israeli occupation of the south of the country; in Palestine with dispossession. In Turkey it is a late reaction to the forced secularism of Ataturk; in Saudi Arabia it is a demonstration against the excesses of the regime; in Iraq it is a struggle against a tyrannical dictatorship; in Sudan it is a response to decades of ineffective and corrupt regimes; in Jordan it is more concerned with political participation; while in Iran it is a social and revolutionary experiment.

While in essence political Islam is an assertion of a separate identity, a call for cultural independence, and a reaction to certain political, economic and social conditions, it is evident that it is not entirely the same thing, serving the same purpose for all its practitioners. Here again, even in the most unifying case, the diversity of considerations makes it difficult to develop a meaningful common analysis and understanding of the area as a whole, rendering attempts at formulating common policies futile.

In the collective consciousness of Middle Eastern countries Europe means western Europe. Eastern Europe and all the western CIS states are not yet considered to be part of Europe. Russia is certainly perceived as being more eastern and thus Asian than western and European. Scandinavia is, with Iceland, a separate zone altogether. Of course atlases in the Middle East have the same frontiers for Europe as those in the West, but Europe as a political, social, economic and cultural entity is perceived to include only western Europe. There are a number of reasons for this:

(a) historical – it is the part of Europe that was closely involved in the Middle East politically and economically;

(b) political – it was the part of Europe, along with the United States, that constituted the West in the Cold War era;

(c) economic – it is the affluent part of Europe which Middle Eastern countries trade with and look up to;

(d) cultural – it is the part of Europe that has influenced current Arab and Middle Eastern culture most;

(e) ideological – democracy, free market economy, modern political
     institutions and so forth are very much associated with the
     western part of Europe; and
(f) institutional – reasons that are to do with the emergence of the
     Single Market and the European Union.

As for Russia, the western CIS states and eastern Europe, the
perception in the Middle East is of a situation that could both provide
new opportunities and give rise to new concerns. It is an area that is
in a state of flux, where stability has not yet been established. As a
whole the region is regarded as underdeveloped, and although some
trade existed before the fall of the Soviet Empire (apart from arms
sales) it was not substantial or important. The area's most important
contribution was the provision of political cover for Middle Eastern
causes where the West was not forthcoming in its support – such as
the Arab-Israeli conflict – and as an arms supplier for countries in the
region that could not procure weapons from the West (Egypt's 1955
arms deal with the Czech government, the first with an eastern-bloc
country in the area, came after its efforts to secure weapons from the
West were frustrated by Western support for Israel and antipathy
towards Nasser). Both these roles were perceived, in most cases, as
being second best in the absence of Western support. The alliance
between the Soviet world and its friends in the area was mostly a
case of *faute de mieux*. While depending on Soviet and east European
weapons, those Middle Eastern states that received them were only
too aware of their shortcomings and were enthralled by Western
technology and in awe of Western political and military might. This
was not helped by the reluctance of the Soviet bloc to supply state-of-
the-art weapons or the kind of uncritical political support its friends
desired and perceived the West to be providing for their enemies. The
demise of the Soviet Empire inevitably led to a reconsideration and
redefinition of the positions and attitudes of those countries in the
area which had depended on it. This quickly increased the influence
of the West in the area and its ability to shape events.

In the present situation of the former Soviet Union, the opening
up of eastern-bloc markets for foreign investment and trade may
provide new economic opportunities for Middle Eastern investors.
The relatively low prices of east European and Russian products is,
however, often offset by the quality of the goods; moreover,
political instability could inhibit the flow of capital to these
countries. The availability of some Russian and east European
products in the international markets – such as food products and

some petrochemicals – could also increase the competition facing Middle Easterners in these markets.

The breakdown of Russian oil production has helped Gulf oil retain a certain level of prices in the international market, albeit weak. The possible rejuvenation of this source of oil and gas could go a long way towards destabilizing oil markets, to the disadvantage of the Gulf producers – Russia was, until the collapse of the Soviet Union, the world's largest oil producer. The decline in Russian oil production also led to some Middle Eastern producers stepping in and filling the gap, and in the process making political capital. The supply of energy often opens the doors for economic and political cooperation of a higher level. When Russia reduced its delivery of fuel oil to the Ukraine, enforcing a fiftyfold rise on the price and transportation of natural gas, Kiev rushed to consolidate its relations with Iran for the sake of its energy needs. This produced a letter of understanding on mutual cooperation in the political, cultural, oil, trading and banking sectors, and the formation of a joint political/economic committee. A joint venture for the construction of a gas trunk-line transporting Iran's gas to Europe via Ukraine has been finalized. Through this project Ukraine will obtain a secure source of energy, a portion of the profit from the joint investment and a transit benefit charge. The competition between the former Soviet republics and also between east European countries for economic relations with other countries also helps – Ukraine, for example, is concerned by the aid policies of western countries whose focus and priority in the former Soviet bloc is Russia. Consequently, Ukrainian leaders have sought other sources of assistance and support to improve their country's economic situation – in this case Iran, whose leadership has warned the former Soviet republics to avoid dependence on the West.

Another source of concern for the region arising from the political changes still unfolding in the former Soviet bloc is the possibility of the emergence of leaders who may enter into disruptive alliances with some of the states in the area. Zhirinovsky's emergence as a popular figure in Russia and his friendship with Saddam Hussein are a cause of concern for anti-Saddam regimes. A potential alliance between the two could be very disruptive to the fragile balance of power in the region. The possibility of 'irresponsible' arms sales by ex-Soviet republics could further upset the balance of power, especially if sales of weapons of mass destruction were involved. Such possibilities are not considered far-fetched from a regional perspective and are alarming. The mere possibility of changes in Russia that may reintroduce it to the region in a variation of its old capacity will upset the present calculations of the states in the region, with both friends and foes of the old Soviet Union contributing further to the uncertainty and instability of the Middle East.

On the other hand, the possibility of alliances between some countries of the region and a combination of east European, ex-Soviet republics and Russia might emerge at some point in the future to check the influence of an increasingly powerful western Europe. Such an alliance could also emerge as a response to potential alliances between other countries in the region, say Turkey and the Central Asian republics. In this context there are four factors whose interplay will determine to some extent the shape and nature of future alliances:

- Russia with its size and vast resources will at some stage recover from its post-communist decline and will again look south for friends.
- Eastern Europe and the Baltic republics jointly or separately may decide that their well-being, development and aspirations are not irrevocably linked to western Europe.
- The Middle East, partially or in blocs, might not be convinced of the economic and political benefits of a close relationship with western Europe.
- Western Europe or the EU might restrict its interest in the Middle East region to its immediate southern flank (North Africa) for the sake of concentrating on markets further east, in the Indian subcontinent and the Far East.

Further south in the Balkans the fate of the former Yugoslavia is of profound significance for both the people and the states of the Middle East. This operates on many levels, all of which are a cause of concern for the region. The actual disintegration of a modern state into its national constituents rings alarm bells in the Middle East where most states have substantial minorities belonging to different ethnic, confessional and sometimes national groups, whose allegiance to the state is not strong at the best of times. Such groups might be emboldened by the experience of the former Yugoslavia and might decide to take their fate into their own hands and commence a secessionist process. The example of Yugoslavia is more pertinent to their case than that of the ex-Soviet Union, where the national differences are so vast and the repressive apparatus of the state was so powerful that it was always assumed that, with the collapse of the central state and its extensions, the different republics would find their own way. Also, in the ex-Soviet Union the whole disintegration took place relatively smoothly, implying an ultimate acceptance of the process by Moscow. The Kurds in Iran, Iraq and Turkey; the Arabs, Turkmans, Azeris and Balushis in Iran; the Shia in Iraq and eastern Saudi Arabia; the Maronites and Druzes in Lebanon; the Alawites in Syria; the Palestinians in Jordan and Israel; the Copts in Egypt; the Christians in southern Sudan; and the Berbers of North Africa are all communities in the region that either have suffered discrimination, or have long held aspirations for self-determination. It is significant that some of these groups already have a secessionist agenda that has historical roots, while others are already actively involved in attempting to implement it.

Such a fragmentation of the Middle East is a nightmare for the states in the region. But one should not forget that most of these states are recent constructs that have been put together almost gratuitously, from the local point of view, by the European colonial powers in the aftermath of the First World War, and as such have not acquired the kind of legitimacy that provides states with longevity. It is also worth remembering that for a period of four hundred years preceding the formation of these states, these communities co-existed in a form of semi-autonomy within the wider Ottoman Empire.

What is perceived as the persecution and massacre of the Muslims of Bosnia reaffirms the people of the region's worst suspicions about European motives and attitudes towards the Muslim world. The relative ease by which Christian Slovenia and Croatia became independent states supported by Europe, in comparison with Bosnia, fuels the fears of the people of the region and its states. The European role in this conflict is particularly abhorrent for Middle Easterners when even the United States is critical of European complacency and its blocking of a more vigorous and robust international intervention on the side of the Bosnian Muslims. The people of the region believe that Europe is afraid of a Muslim state in its midst – albeit a Slav one – and is therefore allowing the gradual annihilation of its inhabitants. Coupled with the perception of the way Muslim communities are treated in the rest of Europe: Turks in Germany, North Africans in France, Muslims from India and Pakistan in Britain, etc., most Middle Easterners believe that Europe, for all its rhetoric about tolerance and human rights, harbours hostile intentions towards Muslims. The common perception in the region is that Europe is only interested in the resources and the markets of the area and bears no respect for its beliefs and traditions. While eager to promote its own brand of government to the countries of the regions, it has no tolerance for their own aspirations nor appreciation of their rights. Such feelings, which have historical roots from the Crusades to the colonialist era, are not conducive to a harmonious relationship between the two regions. They also play into the hands of Islamic revivalists who are promptly reassured of the validity of their position and outlook.

Events in Bosnia also demonstrate the impotence of the countries of the region to provide any meaningful support to their Muslim brethren in an area so close to them. With the exception of minor breaches of the arms embargo and the dispatch of symbolic numbers of fighters, Muslim states of the region can only participate in the international relief effort alongside the rest of the world. This inability to act deepens the feelings of frustration which could paradoxically increase the hostility of the general public towards their own governments who will be blamed for inaction, thus further contributing to instability.

Another aspect of the Bosnian crisis is the possibility of outbursts against Christian minorities in the region. If the situation is perceived of as being one where Moslems are persecuted directly and unfairly by Christians, while Christendom at large is watching passively, then Muslim hotheads in the region may use this to attack their own Christian communities whether they are the Copts in Egypt, or foreign Christians in Algeria. This will further exacerbate the inter-communal tensions in the area and make the resolution of chronic intercommunal strife, such as in Lebanon, that much more difficult.

A major worry in the region is the possibility of the Bosnian crisis spilling over into Macedonia and Kosovo and consequently bringing in Albania, Greece and Turkey. Turkey's involvement will directly involve the region and further activate both Arab states and Iran. This could set the scene for a confrontation between Europe and the Middle East of proportions that have not been experienced since the days of the Ottoman Empire.

How does the Middle East view the rest of Europe, or the EU? While it is true that when referring to Europe the region has the western part in mind, it is also true that the temptation to treat each country separately is quite evident and pronounced. To put it simply and clearly: when dealing with the region the different countries that constitute the Union behave as separate entities with their own often conflicting interests and national priorities. Relations are on a bilateral basis and any multilateral effort to deal collectively is more often than not either symbolic or of such an inane nature that collective positions are easily reached. It is fair to say that the kind of competition that exists within the community in dealings with the region is often more savage than that which exists between any member of the EU and an external country: Britain is more concerned if it loses an arms deal to France than if it loses the same deal to the United States. From a Middle Eastern perspective and for Middle Eastern purposes the European Union is made up of the following clusters:

- Countries that have been on good terms with the region in recent times and are the most immediate neighbours: Greece, Italy, Spain and Portugal. These countries of the south share a certain affinity with the region and sometimes certain habits and customs, but they are not considered political heavyweights, for they often defer to their more weighty political partners.
- Countries that have no political history in the region and are junior members in terms of influence and political clout: the Netherlands, Belgium, Luxembourg, Denmark and Ireland. These countries of the north have, on the whole, only an economic interest in the region. In political matters they apply international norms of civilized behaviour and liberal conduct, or else defer to their senior partners' experience and wisdom.
- France, which has been involved in the area as a colonial power and in recent wars – Suez in 1956 and the Gulf war. France is considered the country most understanding of Middle Eastern positions and concerns, especially Arab ones. It always distinguishes itself from the rest of the Western Alliance by taking independent positions (e.g. over the Gulf war) that cannot necessarily be implemented. It has invested this political capital to secure a large number of economic projects. But it is, on the whole, considered mercenary and is not trusted.
- Germany is the country for business *par excellence*. It has been politically castrated, but is perceived to be in the process of emerging as a political force. It is considered to be the fairest country in dealing with the region's concerns; this could be partly because it is not expected to play an active political role on behalf of its friends. Germany is highly respected for the quality of its goods and the reliability of its business practices.
- Britain, for almost all countries of the region, is the single country in Europe that is most associated with the Middle East. It has a chequered history in the area involving colonialism, the Balfour Declaration, Suez, South Yemen, and the Gulf war, to mention a few landmarks. It is considered now to be a country in decline, but there is still deep affection for it. It is considered the toughest among European countries and is the most respected, but feelings

towards it have become ambivalent especially since it chose to closely associate itself with US policies in the region.

With the demise of the Soviet Union and the end of the Cold War and East/West rivalry, the major global ideological confrontation of the post-War world has been put to rest. The decline and dissolution of political rivalry brought to the surface the more insidious economic rivalry. In the past the Western Alliance and Japan often had to close ranks in their dealings with the Middle East for fear of the common threat of communism and Soviet power. There were differences of nuance in the relations of the different countries of the Alliance with the Middle East, but the common vision that unified them was paramount. With the death of this vision the different countries of western Europe are more concerned with their distinct and separate economic interests than before. It is likely that their economic rivalries will be exacerbated now that the common enemy has been defeated.

The collapse of the USSR and the impact of the second Gulf war ended any semblance of a substantive unified European approach to the Middle East. In the absence of substantial policy initiatives from the EU, relations between European countries and the Middle East will be determined by the ability of each country's economy to fend for itself.

The one area where the EU acts as a unit is that of aid. The objective of EU grants and loans (4.5 bn Ecus Mediterranean aid package for 1992–6) is the promotion of 'regional cooperation'. Most of the money, however, will fund projects of direct interest to Europe like the 500m Ecus earmarked for cleaning up the Mediterranean and the gas pipeline planned to go under the Gibraltar Straits in the second half of the 1990s. But clearly throwing money at Middle Eastern countries is not sufficient to create stable economies and societies. The strings attached to these funds are usually more concerned with placating human rights concerns in the West and in the European Parliament than with the creation of representative and accountable regimes and structurally sound economies in the region. An effective mechanism to introduce some seriousness into conditionality has yet to be formed.

The political context of Europe's relations with the Middle East has been evolving over the past 50 years. Having been associated with governance and the modern traditions of statehood, and thus playing the role of a model to look up to, Europe witnessed over the years the erosion of its political influence in the region. From the position of being the main and dominant foreign power in the area, and the instigator or arbiter of political change, Europe finds itself half-a-century later with little to show for its historical preponderance. This is due partly to the real decline of Europe's global power with the dissolution of its various empires, partly to the rise of the United States as a substitute global power, and partly to an inability to formulate relevant policies that take into account the gap between the realities of the past and those of the present. If the 1956 Suez war demonstrated the limits of Europe's power in the modern world, its effective absence from the Madrid Peace Conference and the ensuing peace process showed its inability to construct policies commensurate with its historic, geopolitical and economic weight.

Over the past 20 years, the European position on the Arab-Israeli conflict, on both popular and state levels, shifted from total support for Israel to more understanding of the Arab side. Europe's position was somewhere between the close alliance of the United States with Israel and the Soviet Union's support for the Arabs. Theoretically, such a profile could provide its holder with an opportunity to play the role of an honest and fair broker between the two sides. But in practice Europe resorted to the politics of vocal but empty gestures. This culminated in the Venice Declaration of 1980 where the EEC recognized the right of Palestinians to self determination and a role for the Palestine Liberation Organization in negotiating this right. One way of judging this declaration is to see it as a courageous recognition by Europe of the realities of the Middle East. Another is to treat it as a supreme act of political folly that succeeded in effectively cutting out Europe from the very peace process it was hoping to generate. On an intellectual level the first judgment is sound. But in politics and history the second is more relevant. The effect of the Venice Declaration was to alienate Israel, which from then on lost its political trust in Europe. From Israel's point of view, Europe sold out to the Arabs and their oil weapon. On the Arab side, the Declaration did not succeed in 'moderating' sufficiently the Arab position to make a peace process possible. While dissatisfied with the extent of European support, the Arab world developed a false sense of what it was possible to achieve: this managed to postpone the Arabs' moment of truth for another decade.

The net result of the Venice Declaration was that Israel vetoed, until recently, any meaningful European participation in the Middle East peace process and the Arab world perceived a gap between what Europe declares and what it can do, which further eroded European influence.

Another demonstration of the failure of European policies to deal with strategic Middle Eastern issues was their dealings with Saddam's Iraq. By pampering the regime and tolerating its excessive indulgences the Europeans indirectly contributed to its Kuwait adventure. While the United States could correct its past mistakes with the regime by the sheer power and weight of its military might during the Gulf war, the Europeans' misconceptions, misunderstandings and errors were ultimately not redressed. From the Arab viewpoint the Europeans built up Saddam and then betrayed him in the best traditions of their colonialist past.

Although it has failed to end the war in Bosnia, western policy has brought about an important shift in the relationship the United States has with its key allies in western Europe. For the first time since the Second World War, Europeans have asserted primacy over the United States in handling a key regional conflict. The United States will continue to lead its allies in the construction of a new relationship with Russia and the containment of any resurgent imperialism by the world's second nuclear power, but all other disputes are extraneous. The refusal of two successive US administrations to commit ground troops to Bosnia reflects a US retreat from active leadership in Europe. There is a growing American reticence to become involved in any conflict not directly affecting its national interests. After the debacles involving US forces in Somalia and Haiti, the attitude of the US administration towards Bosnia is very indicative. Its reluctance to send ground troops undermined its leverage with the Europeans. In the end the United States allowed the Europeans to block an American plan to arm Bosnia's Muslims, and it has twice gone along with European-backed peace-plans that it initially opposed. The days when Europe has to deal directly with its Middle Eastern backyard without the leadership or shadow of the United States may not be far away.

15

Implications for Japan and the Asia-Pacific Region

Haruhisa George Takeuchi

Japan and Europe: in retrospect[1]

The relationship between Japan and Western Europe during the Cold War era has been described as the weakest link in the triangular relationship between Japan, Europe and the United States. The United States was the dominant force in the 'West'[2] and both Japan and Europe placed major emphasis on maintaining and strengthening their respective relations with the United States. Only the United States, as both an Atlantic and a Pacific power, was in a position to play the leading role in its relations, which encompass both Europe and the Asia-Pacific. The very existence of the Soviet Union guaranteed the consistency of American foreign policy towards the Atlantic and the Pacific during the Cold War era.

Although European civilization had been the major source of influence during the process of modernization in Japan following the Meiji Restoration of 1868, the American presence in every aspect of national life became predominant after the Second World War. From the Japanese perspective, the relationship with the United States has been the most important pillar of its foreign policy. Successive statements by the government of Japan declared that the relationship with the United States was 'the cornerstone of the Japanese foreign policy'[3] and that the Japan-US security pact was the foundation of relations between the two countries.

In the 1950s and 1960s, Europe was not viewed by Japanese policy-makers as a vital foreign policy concern, although it retained a positive image in the mind of many Japanese as the cradle of the democratic tradition and a cultural inspiration. At first the European integration process failed to attract much attention in Japan, partly because Japan did not see a vital interest at stake in Europe, but also because the process itself was so complex and at times confusing. Viewed from a region where fledging countries were still in the process of nation- and state-building, the very notion of creating an entity which goes beyond and above existing nation-states was not easily understood. Europe reciprocated with an even greater lack of genuine interest towards Japan. In terms of foreign policy towards Asia, China, as a nuclear power and one of the leading countries of the non-aligned movement, attracted more attention.

In the 1970s, the attention Europe and Japan paid to each other began to grow. The Europeans noticed the rapid economic growth of Japan, while Japan recognized the progress in the formation of the Common Market as well as the enlargement of the European communities in 1973.[4] The economic relationship between the two entities intensified in the 1980s; it was marked by the trade disputes as well as increased Japanese investment in Europe. Through the late 1970s and 1980s, both Europe and Japan emerged as major actors in the management of the international economic system. They were actively engaged in such frameworks as the G7 process and the Tokyo Round and Uruguay Round negotiations of GATT.

The relationship between Japan and Europe, however, remained dominated by trade and economic issues.[5] With rare exceptions, there has been little meaningful political and security dialogue between Japan and Europe. Although Japan was an original member of the G7 process, no country participating in the Guadeloupe Summit in 1979 seemed to have contemplated including Japan in the meeting.

One exception to this pattern occurred in 1983 when the head of states and governments of the G7 in Williamsburg declared that the 'security of our countries is indivisible and must be approached on a global basis'.[6] The statement was the product of the age of Pershing II and the SS-20s, when, from the Japanese perspective, it was feared that the withdrawal of SS-20s from the European theatre under the INF Treaty would result in their re-deployment in the Asian theatre. This was also a period when the United States perceived a direct threat in the Asia-Pacific theatre from the Soviet deployment of SLBMs in the Sea of Okhotsk. The statement was also significant in the sense that, through the G7 process, Japan had emerged from its traditional reticence and approved an international document about a strategic matter.[7] Yet, even after the 1983 Williamsburg Statement, the dialogue on security and political issues between Europe and Japan remained low-key.

The end of the Cold War and its impact on the Asia-Pacific region

The Cold War period in the Asia-Pacific was marked by at least two major hot conflicts (namely the Korean war and Vietnam war), numerous civil wars and insurgencies, and by genocide in Cambodia. The region has also seen rapid economic growth in Japan, South Korea, the 'dragons' of southeast Asia, and most recently China.

Many countries in the region gained independence after the Second World War and are in the process of nation-building. Regime legitimacy in these countries is often based on nationalistic aspirations. Even today, the region remains politically and culturally fragmented. While it is true that many Pacific nations have grown economically, national interests remain diverse. The Asia-Pacific remains a region where there is a high degree of dependence among nations, but still little sense of affinity.

The strategic structure in the region during the Cold War period was not symmetrical, as was the case in the European theatre where the NATO bloc confronted the Warsaw Pact countries. In the Asia-Pacific, the United States adopted a forward deployment strategy and maintained a military presence in the region through a series of bilateral pacts with regional countries. The Soviet Union continued to build up its military capability in its Far East region, while China, another regional nuclear power, remained non-allied and played an independent role. The tension between the Soviet Union and China along its long border marked their relations for years.

The end of the Cold War has been felt in the Asia-Pacific region, though not as dramatically as in Europe. The political climate has improved, through such moves as the normalization of the Sino-Soviet relationship, and the establishment of diplomatic relations between the Soviet Union and the Republic of Korea, as well as between the Republic of Korea and China.

There are, however, still sources of military tension in the region. The situation in the Korean peninsula and, in particular, the possibility of North Korea acquiring a nuclear capability continue to be matters of serious concern. Territorial disputes in the South China Sea are a potential source of conflict which could involve several countries in the region. China continues to modernize its forces, increasing its defence budget by more than 10 per cent annually. The region is a rich market for conventional arms sales now that the countries in the region are financially capable of making substantial purchases.

Regional cooperation in the Asia-Pacific began to take shape gradually in the 1970s, initially in the economic field and particularly through the ASEAN process.[8] The emphasis on economic cooperation reflected the fact that the main interest of the countries in the region was economic development and this was the only practical field in which to cooperate in this otherwise diverse region. There was, however, no grand design comparable to that of Jean Monnet whose vision was to 'lay the foundation of an ever closer union' among the European nations. Even after the first summit meeting of the Asia Pacific Economic Cooperation (APEC) in November 1993, the Asia-Pacific region is still far from seriously exploring the notion of 'community' or 'union' in the European sense of term.

There is, however, a slowly growing recognition among the countries in the Asia-Pacific region that, besides economic cooperation, there should be more political and security dialogue among themselves. The economic development and relative political stability among countries in the region have enabled them to look beyond their national concerns and consider wider problems such as political stability and security of the region as a whole. Bilateral and sub-regional dialogues on these matters are slowly emerging at both the governmental and non-governmental levels. The first meeting of the Asian Regional Forum was scheduled for July 1994 to exchange views on political and security matters in the Asia-Pacific.[9] The first summit meeting of APEC also had political ramifications, in that for the first time almost all the leaders of the Asia Pacific joined in a multilateral conference on the region and posed for a *'photo de famille'*.

Although these trends will gradually intensify in the years to come, it is difficult to conceive of a forum similar to CSCE or EU in the Asia-Pacific in the foreseeable future. Even after the end of the Cold War, in view of the present geopolitical situation, the future form that dialogue and cooperation takes will inevitably reflect the diversity of the region.[10]

There is general agreement among the countries in the Asia-Pacific region that the presence of the United States and its active involvement in regional security, political and economic matters will be crucial for stability and prosperity. The relationship between Japan and the United States will be one of the important factors which will determine the prospects of future cooperation in the region. On the economic front, the relationship between the two heavyweights was strained throughout the 1980s. The end of the Cold War ushered in a period of 'soul-searching' in both the United States and Japan, which has created new elements of uncertainty and risk in the relationship between the two countries. It will be a challenging and, at times, painful process through which the two countries will probably reach a mutual recognition that they have to live with the reality of interdependence which already exists across the Pacific today. The end of the Cold War has also affected the domestic political landscape of Japan, which used to be dominated by the confrontation between the 'conservatives' and the 'left'. After having the same party in power for nearly four decades, the general election of 1993 not only saw a change of government, but also started a broader process of transformation of the political landscape of Japan, the end result of which is difficult to predict.

Challenges for Japan

Japanese society is facing a series of new challenges as it approaches the twenty-first century.[11] The population is quickly ageing, with the percentage over 65 years of age expected to jump from 12 per cent to more than 25 per cent by 2025. What kind of political and social impact will this have on Japanese society? How will Japan finance substantial increases in its social welfare costs?

Economic systems and practices which proved effective in the past four decades now need substantial reforms and structural adjustments. Will Japan be able to maintain its economic vitality and cope with the economic dynamism of the Asia-Pacific region? How will consumers assert their interests more effectively in shaping economic policy decisions?

The debate on the future political role of Japan in the international arena could be divisive in the domestic political context. What kind of a nation does Japan want to be? How will Japan involve itself in international security issues? What would it mean for Japan to become a permanent member of the Security Council of the United Nations?

The ability of Japanese democracy to rise to these challenges will affect the making of Japanese foreign policy in the twenty-first century.

Cooperation between Japan, Europe and the US in the approach to the twenty-first century

After the euphoria of the end of the Cold War, the West is going through a painful period of readjustment.[12] Domestic economic and social difficulties severely constrain the ability of the industrialized democracies to act on the international scene. The mind-set of contraction is evident with states preoccupied by immediate local issues and reluctant to take on global commitments.

A zero-sum mentality in international affairs is on the rise. With the collapse of the Soviet bloc, the West has lost one of the major forces for cohesion. Economic disputes are coming to the fore, now that direct military threats on a global scale seem remote.

The need for cooperation between Europe, the United States and Japan is crucial, however, because the challenges of the post-Cold War era are increasingly global. In the international security field, the world is still searching for frameworks to cope with various 'risks' to international security. The importance of the United Nations in the context is self-evident, since it is the only body of a global character in the international community which can give legal and moral authority to actions related to the maintenance of international peace and security. As its recent experience in regional conflicts acutely demonstrates, however, it is unrealistic to expect the UN to be omnipresent and always effective. With the disappearance of bipolarity, the proliferation of nuclear weapons and international transfers of conventional weapons risk getting out of control. Russia and the former communist countries are still struggling with their economic, social and political reform, the fate of which continues to be a matter of major concern for the security of the world.

In the economic field, the need for financial and economic resources is greater than ever. Many countries of the Third World are still struggling to achieve economic 'take off', while the former communist countries are in the process of transforming their economy into a market economy. The international community must ensure sustained economic growth so as to provide much needed resources, by coordinating economic and aid policies, as well as by strengthening the multilateral free-trading system. The role of the industrialized democracies is vital since they represent more than 60 per cent of the total GNP of the world. Their economic difficulties, however, offer fertile terrain for protectionism and exclusive regionalism. Finally, issues such as the environment, drug trafficking and refugees need a global approach because of their very nature.

In each of these instances institutional frameworks, if not perfect, are basically already in place. It still remains to be seen if the international community, and especially the industrialized democracies, have the will to effectively mobilize such frameworks as the UN, the G7 process and other regional and sub-regional organizations and devise a collective approach which reflects the particularity of each problem.

Against this background and in view of the move toward integration in Europe, Japan and Europe have been working to lay the foundation for a relationship which is not limited to economic and trade issues and which opens new perspectives for joining forces in the management of the international system.[13]

Prime Minister Kaifu's visit to Europe in 1990 was an early expression of Japan's intention to involve itself more actively in European affairs after the end of the Cold War by supporting moves towards democracy in east European countries.[14] Japan subsequently joined the European Bank of Reconstruction and Development as the second largest financial contributor. Japan is also participating in the G24 process and extending technical and financial assistance to the east European countries. Japan has become involved in the discussions of the CSCE since July 1992. The 'Joint Declaration on Relations between the European Community and Its Member States and Japan in the Hague' was issued in July 1991 with the aim of establishing a framework for a more extensive relationship between the EC and Japan.[15]

As the trend toward regional cooperation develops, it is important for Europe, Japan and the United States to ensure that the EU, NAFTA and APEC remain open and consistent with the multilateral free trading system. As the Asia-Pacific becomes one of the most dynamic regions in the world, Europe has a new opportunity to participate in the economic and political life of the region. In Japan, Europe will find a partner which is committed to maintaining the open nature of the Asia-Pacific. Through such cooperation, Europe can also demonstrate to the countries in the Asia-Pacific that it too is committed to an integrated Europe which is open to the Asia-Pacific.

The actual process for such cooperation will often be clumsy, time-consuming and chaotic. As Europe and Japan gain relatively heavier weight in the triangular relationship, the decision-making process in the triad inevitably becomes more complex. The three pillars will also remain strong economic competitors against each other. Economic interdependence will not be an automatic guarantee against the possibility of a destructive spiral in the relationships within the triad, which cannot be ruled out. Managing a relationship which is both cooperative and competitive will remain a challenging task. The relationship between Europe and Japan will continue to be the most difficult of the three. Despite recent efforts to enlarge the scope of the relationship, policy-makers in both Europe and Japan must often first convince themselves and then persuade their publics that there are more than trade and economic issues between Europe and Japan and that they can be genuine partners in world affairs.

In the final analysis, Europe, the United States and Japan share common values, without which cooperation would be reduced to a series of *ad hoc* business arrangements which would be quickly abandoned once their purpose was served. Europe, the United States and Japan have already repeatedly stated that they share the common values of human dignity, freedom and democracy. They still need a renewed political will to substantiate their stated commitment in concrete actions.

Equally important is the public education which will open the minds of generations to come to the fact that physical distance does not necessarily separate people and that people thousands of miles away can still have values in common and share a common enterprise.

The extent to which Japan, Europe and the United States achieve success in this endeavour will be one of the important factors which will define the nature and shape of systemic change in international relations for years to come.

Notes

1. This short chapter deals with the relationship between Japan and Europe in general. Since European countries today are diverse in every aspect, the bilateral relationships between Japan and each individual country in Europe vary considerably and would merit a separate discussion.
2. In Europe, the notion of the 'West' implies the west European and North American countries, and does not necessarily include a country like Japan. In Japan, the 'West' usually means the family of democratic nations to which Japan believes it belongs. For the purpose of this article, the Japanese sense of the term will apply.
3. See the policy speech to the National Diet of Prime Minister Kiichi Miyazawa of 8 November 1991 as well as the policy speech to the National Diet of Prime Minister Morihiro Hosokawa of 23 August 1993. Despite the change of government, there seems to be continuity in Japan's general policy direction toward the United States.
4. The Office of the European Communities in Tokyo was opened in 1974. The Japanese Mission to the European Communities was opened in 1979, before which the Embassy of Japan in Belgium represented the Government of Japan to the EC.

5. The polls also show that the general public in Europe continues to associate the word 'Japan' with economic activities. See the *Japan Times*, 4 June 1973 and 3 July 1993.
6. The Williamsburg Statement, 29 May 1983.
7. As recently as 1981 the Prime Minister of Japan and his Foreign Minister openly disagreed on whether the word 'Japan-US alliance' which appeared in the Japan-US joint communiqué had a military connotation or not. The row ended with the resignation of the Foreign Minister.
8. The Association of South East Asian Nations (ASEAN) was formed in 1967. The member states at present are Brunei, Indonesia, Malaysia, Singapore, Thailand and the Philippines. For a historical review of ASEAN, see Tatsumi Okabe (ed.), 'Twenty Years of ASEAN – Its Survival and Development', Japan Institute of International Affairs, 1988.
9. The participating states will be the ASEAN countries, Japan, United States, Republic of Korea, Canada, Australia, New Zealand, European Union, China, Russia, Vietnam, Laos and Papua New Guinea.
10. For the position of the Government of Japan toward APEC, see the statement by Foreign Minister Tsutomu Hata at the fifth APEC Ministerial Conference in Seattle, 18 November 1993. For the evolution of the position of the Japanese Government concerning political and security dialogue in the Asia-Pacific region, see the statement by Foreign Minister Taro Nakayama to the General Session of the ASEAN Post Ministerial Conference (Kuala Lumpur, July 1991) and also the policy speech by Prime Minister Kiichi Miyazawa in Bangkok in January 1993. See also, 'Japan and the Asia-Pacific Region in the 21st Century– Promotion of Openness and Respect for Plurality', 25 December 1992, Report of the Round Table on Japan and the Asia-Pacific Region in the twenty-first century, presented to Prime Minister Kiichi Miyazawa.
11. See, 'Looking for new directions', *Japan Review of International Affairs*, vol. 6, no. 3, Fall 1992.
12. See, Hugh Miall, *Shaping the New Europe*, London: RIIA/Pinter, 1993.
13. In his first policy speech to the National Diet on 23 August 1993, Prime Minister Hosokawa expressed his hope 'to build even closer cooperative relations with the countries of Europe as they move toward integration and play an increasingly important role in the international community.'
14. For a general policy statement, see speech by Toshiki Kaifu of 9 January 1990 in Berlin. See also, Juliet Berenyi, 'The present and envisaged role of Japan in eastern Europe with special regard to the emerging multipolar world', JIIA fellowship paper 1993/no. 4.
15. For a detailed discussion on the Japan-EC relationship, see Brian Bridges, *EC-Japanese Relations: In Search of a Partnership*, London: RIIA, 1992; Kaoru Ishikawa, 'Japan and Europe: Handle with Care', *Japan Echo*, vol. XVIII, no. 4, winter 1991, pp. 70–75. See also, 'The New Era – The Japanese Perspective', keynote address by Hisashi Owada at the RIIA/Japan Foundation Conference 'Britain and Japan – The New Era', January 1994.

16

Conclusion: Towards a Redefinition of European Order

James Mayall and Hugh Miall

The redefinition of the European order is certainly not complete – indeed, the phase of deconstruction has probably not yet ended. Three central questions, which recur throughout this book, remain to be resolved. First, what will be the relationship between the nation-states of western Europe after the end of the Cold War, and will west European integration continue in its present form? Second, is it feasible for the west European integration process to be extended to east central Europe and to other countries of northern and southeastern Europe? Third, what will be the relationship between the countries of the former Soviet Union and the other parts of Europe?

Another preliminary question underlies these: in what sense are we to understand 'Europe' nowadays? For much of the Cold War, western Europe appropriated the word, identifying it with west European institutions (the Council of Europe, the European Community). Significantly, the Soviet-dominated institutions (WTO, COMECON) failed to lay claim to the title. It is obviously an over-simplification to identify even western Europe with the member states of the EU, although the tendency to do so in east central Europe and outside Europe appears to be strong. Even among EU members, rhetorical support for European construction often conceals considerable disagreement about the nature of the Europe that is being constructed. Typically member states look to a Europe in their own image: Germany to a federal Europe; France to a Europe with a strong executive based on French forms; the UK to a free-trading group of sovereign states. Many west Europeans associate Europe with western values, emphasizing not only liberal democracy but also universal values going back to the Enlightenment, which transcend the parochialism and nationalism of particular peoples and states. Yet nationalism and xenophobia have at least as strong a claim to represent European traditions. Against the European values of diversity, tolerance, openness, human rights and pluralism can be placed the no less European experience of colonialism, genocide, and total war. In the post-Cold War context, redefining Europe is a struggle over what European civilization is to mean both in its aspirations and in its political practice.

There is also the question of redefining relationships with the rest of the world. Part of the problem here lies in the compatibility of two contrasting conceptions of international society, both of European origin. At least with regard to its legal structure and underlying intellectual assumptions, international society is derived from the peace treaties which brought an end to the European wars of religion. The system which emerged was anti-ideological in a profound sense: it sought to ban wars over religion but to legitimize them for reasons of state. In the twentieth century there have been attempts to de-legitimize war as an act of policy and to qualify the sovereignty of states by inserting in the UN Charter the concept of inalienable human rights including the right of all peoples to self-determination. But Article 2(7) which prohibits interference in the domestic affairs of other states, remains the essential prerequisite for international cooperation at the global level, except in the most extreme circumstances. In this sense, international society remains a society of states not peoples.

The Cold War had the effect – paradoxically in view of the fact that it was in the main an ideological conflict – of upholding the traditional conception of international society and limiting any legal relaxation of sovereign rights. The principle of self-determination in particular was equated with decolonization. Secession was proscribed, and not only democratic but also tyrannical governments were protected by Article 2(7). Within western Europe, the Cold War also conveniently established the boundaries within which a series of experiments could be conducted in the construction of a denser and socially more inclusive conception of international society. The members of the European Union, the Council of Europe and signatories of the European Convention on Human Rights have not abandoned the traditional understanding of international society – indeed judging by British and French resistance to the reform of the Security Council, they remain deeply attached to it – but they have gone further towards the creation of an international civil society, even towards the alliance of civil republics which Kant envisaged in *Perpetual Peace* (1795), than elsewhere in the world.

Political and ideological orders are not proof against structural changes to their authority; but as long as they remain in place they do constrain the way in which these challenges manifest themselves. The end of the Cold War swept away these conserving constraints for both the wider international society and the nascent European civil society. The challenges in Europe, as elsewhere, came from two directions, above and below the state. The globalization of capital markets, technologies and communications, diminish the ability of even the strongest and best-administered states to deliver what their governments promised. By the same token, it increased the import-ance, widely recognized in theory, less frequently acted on in practice, of international governance. Globalization also provided the setting for the challenge from below – to the legitimacy of the state from ethnic and/or religious minorities. With the collapse of the Soviet empire on the one hand, and the debate about the principles of subsidiarity within the European Union on the other, such groups were now able to reopen the question of the right of self-determination.

Theoreticians disagree about how to represent these changes in their conceptualizations of international relations at both regional and global levels. Neo-realists and structural realists emphasize that the international system remains an anarchy in which the state is still the locus of power and decision. They expect the greater fluidity and multipolarity which followed the Cold War to give rise to increased conflict. Neo-liberal institutionalists argue that given reasonably compatible interests, institutions can sustain cooperation and limit conflict (Chapters 11 and 13). Liberal pluralists emphasize the importance of other transactions, including transnational ones, and emphasize the role of societies as well as states.

While these debates will not be easily resolved, it is possible to make a number of observations about the changing character of international society in Europe. In the western part of Europe, two trends have been important, although both are somewhat fitful and haphazard. One is a process of internationalization of policy making, driven by the need for states to coordinate policy action in order to be effective: this is linked to the development of relatively consensual decision-making practices and shared interests, which still appear strong enough to override conflicts. A second is the growing importance of the regions, the Länder and sub-national governance in a number of west European countries. In eastern Europe, in contrast, the period since 1989 has seen the formation of a new state system, which is much more a classical anarchy, in which bilateral diplomacy prevails and conflicts of interest appear stronger than shared

Table 16.1   Relationships between international institutions, states and societies in Europe

	Western	East central	Eastern
International institutions	1	2	3
States	4	5	6
Societies	7	8	9
Examples of interactions: 1 to 4: EU-state relationships 1 to 5: partnerships for peace, Europe agreements etc. 1 to 7: the Danish referendum 2 to 5: regional cooperation (Visegrad, Black Sea Cooperation Council) 3 to 6: CIS 4 to 5, 4 to 6, 5 to 6: bilateral relations between states 4 to 7, 5 to 8, and 6 to 9: civil society, domestic polities; state-minority relationships 7 to 8, 7 to 9, 8 to 9: transnational connections; for example, city twinning, media links, contacts between non-governmental organizations.			

interests. As in western Europe, internal regionalism has been a prominent feature, but in the east, it is often linked with minority fears and demands for independence and self-government.

Here the point we wish to stress is that the European order consists of several layers: the layer of societies (in which one might include societies' self-identification as nations), the layer of states, and the layer of international institutions and regimes. The European space is more or less densely interconnected at all these levels. Western Europe has the densest pattern of state-society relationships (civil society) and state-international institution relationships (supranational and multilateral intergovernmental bargaining). East central Europe has somewhat less well developed but nevertheless important state-society relationships and rather weak ties with international institutions. Further east and in the Balkans, the atomized post-communist societies for the most part lack developed institutions of civil society and have a less dense pattern of state-society relations and much weaker connections with international institutions[1].

These three levels and their interaction between East and West form a matrix (see Table 16.1) within which we can analyse the European order.

It was characteristic of the Cold War that the relationships within this table were separated most strongly from left to right. In the post-Cold War period in which internal conflicts dominate attention, the bottom two rows are in play. The top two rows represent the minimalist conception of international society viewed as little more than a framework of coexistence between sovereign states. In *The Anarchical Society*,[2] Hedley Bull's account of international order, he contemplates the possibility of a gradual transformation of inter-national society in ways which would break the jurisdictional monopoly of the sovereign state. The new order – he called it the new medievalism to conjure up the idea of overlapping authorities – would amount to an international civil society thus engaging the bottom row of Table 16.1. Were it to come about it would help to resolve two major problems that have emerged in post-Cold War Europe. In the west the supporters of an ethnic revival are generally in favour of a strong federal European Union because they scent that it is impossible to opt out of the interdependent world economy. At the same time, they are strongly in favour of increased political autonomy in cultural and educational matters and local government. In the east, many of the new nationalists are similarly committed to the open market economy, although even on the most optimistic assumptions their prospects of early entry into the European Union are slim. If eastern Europe is not to fracture further, during the interim, some way has to be found of confronting minority fears, possibly by the further development of the principles and procedures of the Council of Europe and the CSCE. The only practical way that a new European order can be built is by gradually opening up societies to democratic scrutiny while accepting that uniformity of practice and institutional membership is a long way off. Just how difficult it will be to create a multi-layered European society of this kind will be clear if we consider in more detail the challenges which it faces.

Challenges facing the European order

Economic universalism, political parochialism

Globalization is a source of rapid and cascading change for all societies. In western Europe, the challenge has been felt at the level of economic activity, political order and national identity. Market liberalization (see Chapter 6) has opened western Europe irreversibly to the international economy, while in central and eastern Europe marketization has become embedded even in economies with large remaining state sectors. Although important economic barriers remain, there is a sense in which it is possible to see the emergence of a wider European economy, more or less open to trade, capital flows and cross-investment. While the economic driving forces increasingly operate at a European as well as a national level, politically western and eastern Europe continue to operate mainly at a parochial, national level. As a result national economies continue to be buffeted by external events and cannot readily resist external pressures, nor control the movement of capital, production facilities or even people.

Greater international economic competition affects societies in ways which states cannot wholly protect against. New economic sectors are developing and traditional ones declining at an exceptionally rapid pace. Unskilled industrial workers are exposed to competition from workers in the Third World, and industrial employment generally may be on a similar downward trend to that completed earlier in agriculture.[3] In order to remain competitive, and under the pressure of high structural unemployment, western societies have attempted to reduce expenditure on their welfare regimes; in eastern Europe, the collapse of old industry has undermined welfare provision. As George Kolankiewicz shows (Chapter 9), the consequence has been the growth of an underclass in western and eastern Europe, directly threatening the welfare of those who fall into it, and indirectly posing a potential threat to social stability. Similar external forces have put under pressure the Scandinavian welfare model and the German social market economy. Migration is another powerful pressure, strongly felt especially in Germany and also in southern Europe.

As Helen Wallace observes (Chapter 2), the political response to these external challenges has been a defensive and parochial one. She links the state's withdrawal from public provision on a national scale to the failure of the EC to go beyond the Single Market by stimulating a new phase of modernization and to provide public goods for societies. In other words, the link between international institutions and society (Table 16.1) is not working well enough in western Europe.

The end of the Cold War has also threatened to undermine at least the external underpinning for the close relationships between west European states. The setbacks to efforts to consolidate the EC by establishing monetary and political union leave the EC member states in an unstable state, with the disagreement over ultimate objectives for the Union as strong as ever.[4] There have been ominous developments which might suggest that European integration, having clearly stalled, may go into reverse: recriminations following the breakdown of the EMS, French and British threats to revive an 'empty chair' policy, German demands for a budget rebate, disagreements between large and small states over institutional reform, and emergent clashes over enlargement policy towards central and eastern Europe. Against these developments, however, must be set the ability of the EC member states to find agreements to maintain momentum at the Edinburgh and Copenhagen summits, to ratify the Treaty on European Union and to reach a compromise over GATT. If one accepts the neo-liberal institutionalist arguments (Chapter 11), the 'public goods' that the European Union continue to provide are probably sufficient to make the 'fragmentation' scenario unlikely unless member states take an exceptionally short-term view of their own interests. Nevertheless, it is clear that the European Union needs to find a redefinition of its goals simply in order to establish consensus among its present members on the way forward, let alone if it is to meet wider aspirations for a pan-European role.

A leaderless Europe in a turbulent world

To some extent, the difficulties of sustaining the cohesion of international institutions and close international cooperation in western Europe reflect the broader dissensus on the international stage. The relative economic decline of the United States compared with its Japanese and EC partners weakened US leadership in monetary and broader economic management of the world economy. The end of the Cold War has also raised question marks over whether US leadership will be preserved in security affairs. In a third emergent domain of international politics, the management of global environmental change, the US role has more often been to delay than to initiate coordinated international policies.

As Haruhisa Takeuchi writes (Chapter 15), a more even distribution of power in the triad has made it more unstable. The last minute success of the Uruguay Round suggests that common interests can still preserve the international economy from a self-destructive slide into competitive protectionism; but this did not preclude the development of subsequent trade disputes between the new 'blocs' of the world trading system. The negotiations also demonstrated that it was difficult for the EU to be much less protectionist than its most protectionist member. On the security front, the United States remains pre-eminent in the military domain. But the long-term future for NATO remains uncertain, despite its shift towards a more 'political' role, and the new emphasis on crisis management and peace-keeping in 'out-of-area' operations. The decision of the NATO summit in January 1994 to establish 'combined joint task forces' meant a further shifting of weight within the Atlantic Alliance towards the European pillar. But the United States still played a crucial role in European security, for example in the nuclear relationship with Russia (and Ukraine), in arms control, as a partner in air and sea operations, as a security guarantor, and even as a factor in securing borders in the Balkans.

The European Union, despite agreements at Maastricht, seemed likely to take over the former role of Germany, as a large civilian power practising cheque-book diplomacy, and carrying on *Ostpolitik* at an EU level. The uneasiness of Germany about returning to a 'normal' military role (Chapter 12) made a strong defence identity for the European Union appear a somewhat remote prospect.

Even the Common Foreign and Security Policy remained more impressive on paper than in fact. Although there is a strong tendency among non-Europeans (see Chapters 13, 14 and 15) as well as among some Europeans[5] to see the European Union as a major actor on the world stage, the divisions among European Union members over foreign policies have remained serious. What has been significant about the CFSP and its predecessor, EPC, has not been so much the emergence of powerful common stands, but the willingness of west European states to consult each other and coordinate their foreign policy-making.

The European difficulty in reaching powerful common policies reflects, in part, its lack of leadership – another quality shared with the wider world. Germany is the country most fitted by its size, wealth and centrality to play a leadership role, but it is disinclined to do so, in part because of its current internal preoccupations, in part because of its history. However, a Europe without leadership is also a Europe without hegemony. So far the European role is one of bargaining, log-rolling, agenda-setting, and using economic rather than military power to shape the context of international relations. This may not always make for comprehensible or noble politics, but at least it constitutes a non-bellicose contribution to international politics.

The post-communist condition

If Western Europe has become less of an island of stability, and less a single actor than some hoped, the difficulties of the post-communist societies of eastern Europe are much more grave.

Forty years of communist domination has left the east European societies in many ways poorly equipped to meet the challenges of the new Europe. In their atomized and fragmented societies people lost respect for law and institutions, and elites are unused to compromise and pluralism. They face the triple challenge of nation-building, economic transformation and democratization without the opportunity that west European societies had gradually to adjust to each other and to economic integration and globalization. They are having to absorb external and internal economic shocks, a drastic drop in personal security, a changing structure of elites and a new party system which has not yet had time to put down social roots (see Chapters 3, 8 and 9). On top of this the legitimation of the national state is widely contested in societies with substantial national minorities.

The response to these common difficulties has been highly diverse, and this has contributed to the 'regionalization' of Europe. Countries with relatively well-established civil societies, or with a prewar democratic tradition to draw on, have been able to adjust most successfully; there have been, as Judy Batt points out (Chapter 3), virtuous as well as vicious circles. However the low turn-out of the electorate in elections in 1992, followed by the success of authoritarian parties in some countries in 1993, illustrates the difficulties of democratic consolidation. George Schöpflin's analysis (Chapter 8) suggests these are deep-rooted. In particular, a kind of nationalism has become powerfully established that is deeply inimical to west European civic values. Although eastern Europe has adapted itself quickly to the outer forms of market economies and constitutional democracy, the extent to which they have taken root is both variable and uncertain (Chapter 7).

Throughout the continent, the term 'Europe' is politically loaded. At first both the aspirations of the post-1989 elites and the conditions stated by the west European governments for a 'return to Europe' emphasized liberal democracy, European unity, and a sense of universal values. In time it became apparent that those who voiced this cluster of aspirations were not always in a majority. Other traditions emphasized national rather than European orientations, collectivism rather than individualism, social defence rather than market reform. Nevertheless, in central and eastern Europe, even those who appealed to nationalist traditions still sought entry into NATO and the EU; and opinion polls taken in 1992 suggested strong popular support for integrating with (western) European institutions.[6]

This suggests that simple absorption into a western version of Europe would not necessarily be the answer, although there was a demand for using western institutions as the basis for a wider international order. The disintegration of Comecon, the Warsaw Treaty Organization and the Soviet Union left the region bereft of significant international institutions, and the new instruments of regional cooperation, such as the Visegrad group, were not a comparable substitute. The European order was certainly even less defined in central and eastern Europe than in the west. Not only had the alignments imposed by the Cold War disappeared; the post-Versailles settlement was being revised in the Balkans (Chapter 4) while the disintegration of the Soviet Union left behind states without well-defined borders or national composition. The reappearance in political discourse of such ancient cleavages as the division between the western and eastern Roman Empire, and those between Muslim, Orthodox and Catholic Europes, is an indication of how thoroughly the old order has been shaken.

New patterns of conflict

If in western Europe the difficulty in constructing a post-Cold War order lay mainly in the relationships between states and international institutions, in the Balkans and the former Soviet Union, the relationships between states and society, and between states, were the crucial problems. The attempt to consolidate political communities in states with large national minorities has proven difficult, and conflicts or potential conflicts over secessionist and irredentist claims are serious. The war in the former Yugoslavia has shown, at one extreme, where the logic of fragmentation can lead when such attempts break down. The sensitivity of the issue of Russians outside Russia is another warning indicator. The armed conflicts over ethnic/national issues in the former Soviet Union are a sign of the centrifugal turbulence throughout the former Soviet space. Leaving these conflicts to brew by themselves is a course with clear dangers, especially given the possibilities of spill-over into interstate conflict.

Perhaps even more serious than these ethnic conflicts, however, is the danger of a new pattern of polarization developing in the international relations of Europe. The controversies over NATO enlargement and the Russian claim to a security role in the space of the former Soviet Union clearly indicate the possibility that Europe may enter a new period of division. The rise of Zhirinovsky and the setbacks for westernizing reformers in Russia opened spectres of a new confrontation between states adhering to 'liberal democracy and market reform' and those which might be tempted to resort to exclusive nationalism, the defence of state industries and eventually militarism as a means of mobilizing social support: the mixture pioneered by Slobodan Milosevic. A more cautious view of Russian developments, however, would argue that mainstream Russian elites are pursuing a mainstream 'Eurasianist' policy, emphasizing Russian national interests as a regional power, which, although they might be formulated in neo-imperialist terms, are not intrinsically incompatible with western (or even east European) interests.[7]

Redefining Europe: the need for a new response

This is a formidable group of challenges, and the analyses in this book suggest how strong are the forces driving European societies in parochial, nationalistic and in some cases authoritarian directions. It is clear that active policies are needed in response. A policy of 'wait and see', or drift, would risk allowing the situation in the wider Europe to deteriorate into a new confrontation, to which the accumulating pressures of economic insecurity, social conflict and ethnic tensions could provide the spark. Reformulating tried and tested policies from the past may also be dangerous. If states return to asserting national interests through nationally based security policies, the risk of a return to fragmentation that Mearsheimer warned of is serious. In eastern Europe the old Balkan nationalisms and dreams of the old Russian empire may be consoling in unfamiliar times but they do not point forward to a realistic future for these societies, which, no less than west European ones, have to cope with an open world economy and instantaneous global communications. As regards western Europe, Maastricht-style efforts to find solid ground by consolidating west European integration, without an effective response to eastern Europe, seem unlikely to succeed. Western Europe cannot insulate itself from the consequences of the central and east European transition going seriously wrong, nor from the need to adjust the balances between member states (and between states and Community institutions) to the new circumstances.

Before sketching a framework for policy responses, three preliminary remarks are in order. First, the *political* order in Europe must be one which represents two cardinal features of the current situation: on the one hand, the strength and importance of local and national identities and political communities, and on the other, the importance of interdependence. Political arrangements must therefore be worked out at multiple levels, with arrangements for societies to consult and adjust to one another balanced by respect for the integrity of regional and national communities, who rightly wish to take their own decisions. Secondly, the *security* order must be one which reflects the three levels outlined in this chapter (international, national and societal security). Towards the end of the Cold War many people accepted the insight that, in an interdependent age, we live in an age of *common security* (or common insecurity). The end of the Cold War has made this no less true. A security order which operates only at the level of *national* security would be a recipe for fragmentation. Equally a system of security at the international level with only western membership would not offer full security either for eastern nor ultimately for western Europe if eastern Europe remains fragmented. Moreover, the dimension of *societal security* is becoming increasingly important.[8] Societies have to feel secure, in the sense that people's needs for identity, cultural and social expression, physical security and economic needs are met. It is possible (especially in nationally divided states) that national security and societal security may conflict, but it is also possible for societies to foster 'common' societal security, through transnational and international measures – such as the 'Euro-regions' which facilitate contacts between peoples divided by interstate borders and the democracy-building efforts of the Council of Europe and the CSCE. If this wider perspective of security is accepted, it is evident that responses to security threats cannot be limited to military arrangements and must encompass economic and social stability. This certainly has implications for the direction of expenditures earmarked for security purposes.

Thirdly, the *economic order* is irreversibly interdependent, both across states, and with the political and security order. Given the regional disparities in Europe, it is inevitable that the European economy will be dominated for some time by a relatively rich north- and west-central 'core', with a poorer southern 'periphery' and a much poorer eastern periphery. Nevertheless, there is a strong case for promoting the development of the peripheries, which is in the general European economic interest (Chapter 6). Trade access, cohesion funds and regional funds are ways forward.

In all three respects, of course, European arrangements cannot be sealed off from wider international arrangements and an open Europe must take extra-European societies into account in its political, economic and security structures.

A 'wider Europe' programme should be seen as a balanced attempt to provide political order, security and economic stability at the three levels of international, national and societal interaction. The enlargement of the European Union would have a central role, although other pan-European institutions should also be strengthened. The European Union has already indicated that countries with European agreements can expect eventual accession, though probably not until after the year 2000. Before then, much can be done to help prepare them for accession and involve them in EU decision-making. It is in the interests of economic and political stability to promote freer trade access, west European investment and support (especially in training, banking reform, infrastructure) and possibly participation or associate membership in the Union's common foreign and security policy pillar.

Helen Wallace (Chapter 2) argues that widening – and a new commitment to modernization – could offer a new dynamic impulse for the European Union. Gordon Smith (Chapter 7) argues that there is little choice but to open the Union to new applicants, though he is sceptical about whether the EU can guarantee successful democratic transitions. Vincent Cable (Chapter 6) makes an economic case for Wider Europe. It is important here to be clear about the objectives: the main one would be to use European institutions, as after the Second World War, to consolidate habits of cooperation and to reduce the risks of conflict among European states. For the time being this should take priority over efforts to strengthen integration.

Nevertheless, widening may well involve adjustments to EU policy areas, and strengthening of its decision-making capabilities. The CAP, for example, may have to be reformed again to make widening to eastern Europe feasible: there are of course strong economic and environmental grounds for doing so in any case. Widening would probably make further calls on EU budgets. The difficult issues of institutional reform and democratic deficit will need to be tackled in a way which preserves effective decision-making, an effective say for smaller states, subsidiarity and popular legitimacy. In a wider Europe the regional dimension will be important too.

The implication of widening may be a certain slowing of deepening; certainly the EU that is actually developing, and the one which seems most compatible with a wider Europe, is one in which 'variable geometry' and multi-speed arrangements are developing in practice.[9]

Given the existing disagreements within the Union, however, it will probably be necessary to expand the Union in other directions too, in order to expand the 'public goods' available to make widening palatable. A stronger EU policy towards the Maghreb for example might be needed to reassure Spain and Portugal that the southern dimension was not being neglected. Even larger cohesion payments may become necessary. In policy terms, the case for a strengthening of 'social Europe', to offer a bigger stake to European citizens (in western and eastern Europe) is strongly made by George Kolankiewicz (Chapter 9).

With regard to the republics of the former Soviet Union, while accession of the Union is a remote prospect (except perhaps in the case of the Baltic States), the Union would do well to maintain its 'concentric circles' of trade and cooperation agreements with its neighbours. There is a strong case for triangular trade arrangements between EU members, east central Europeans and former Soviet republics.[10] The EU and other western institutions (together with the United States) have a role to play in moderating the conflicts among the latter – as they did in 1993 between Estonia and Russia. As Andrei Zagorski argues (Chapter 5), what Russia seeks is arrangements for consultation with western states and institutions – not necessarily membership.

Both the Council of Europe and the CSCE have importance because of their wide membership, and the contribution they can make to societal security, in the form of human and civil rights, minority protection, citizenship and democratization. Although the CSCE is sometimes derided as an unwieldy body, crippled by its consensus rules, it has in fact proved to be a flexible structure, in which *ad hoc* innovations, such as the Long Term Missions and the High Commissioner for National Minorities, have played a very useful role – and one which has opened the domestic affairs of states to wider scrutiny.[11] They are helping to develop a body of European law and standards, binding on all states, with international courts and conventions to hold governments accountable both to each other and to their citizens (though most European states including west European ones still have a long way to go in opening themselves to effective monitoring.)

Whether the CSCE can also become the basis for a stronger regime of collective security is, as Trevor Taylor suggests (Chapter 10), perhaps unlikely. The emphasis given to peace-keeping by both NATO and the CIS, and the possibilities for collaborating that this suggests, do however make it clear that a return to military confrontation is not inevitable. As frameworks for cooperation the NACC and Partnerships for Peace are useful beginnings.

Such institutional steps are important since they extend habits of multilateral diplomacy and would contribute to a wider 'Europeanization of elites', steps towards the type of transgovernmental cooperation which is already important in western Europe. However, measures directed only at the level of international institutions and interstate relations cannot deal comprehensively with the problems analysed in this volume, which also crucially involve the state-society dimension. These cannot be easily touched by intervention by outside states. Perhaps even more important than policies at the national and international level are the transnational contacts between societies – not only at the level of investments and trade, crucial as these are, but also through educational and cultural exchanges, training, links between towns, cooperation between political parties, media, and active citizens. If through such contacts a wider sense of European solidarity develops, the prospects for cooperation between states will be better. When Europeans encounter and engage with one another in these ways, they redefine Europe and open the potential of the future.

Notes

1. See George Schöpflin, *Politics in Eastern Europe*, Oxford: Blackwell, 1993, chapter 10.
2. Hedley Bull, *The Anarchical Society*, London: Macmillan, 1977
3. Richard Brown and DeAnne Julius, 'Is Manufacturing Still Special in the New World Order?', in Richard O'Brien (ed.), *Finance and the International Economy: 7*, AMEX Bank Review, Oxford: Oxford University Press, 1993.
4. Finn Laursen and Sophie Vanhoonacker (eds), *The intergovernmental conference on political union: institutional reforms, new policies and international identity of the European Community*, Maastricht: European Institute of Public Administration, 1992.
5. For example, Günter Burghardt, 'European Union – a global power in the making?' in Werner Weidenfeld and Josef Janning (eds), *Europe in Global Change*, Gütersloh: Bertelsmann Foundation Publishers, 1993.
6. Commission of the European Communities, *Central and East Eurobarometer*, no. 3, 1992.
7. See Neil Malcolm, 'The new Russian foreign policy' in *The World Today*, vol. 50, no. 2, February 1994, pp. 28–32.
8. Ole Waever, 'Societal Security', Paper presented to the Pan European Conference of the European Political Science Consortium, Heidelberg, 1992; see also Ole Waever *et al.*, *Identity, Migration and the New Security Agenda in Europe*, London: Pinter, 1993.

9. Sarah Collinson, Anna Michalski and Hugh Miall, *A Wider European Union? Cooperation and Integration in the New Europe*, Discussion Paper 48, London: Royal Institute of International Affairs, 1993.
10. Wolfgang H. Reinecke, *Building a New Europe: The Challenge of System Transformation and Systemic Reform*, Brookings Occasional Papers, Washington: Brookings Institution, 1992.
11. See Richard Dalton, 'The CSCE and Minorities' and Klaus Schumann, 'The role of the Council of Europe' in Hugh Miall (ed.), *Minority Rights in Europe*, London: RIIA/Pinter, 1994.

Index